JAHANGIR

Part of 'The Broadway Travellers', *a collection of significant travelogues and exploring, edited by* 'Edward Denison Ross' *and* 'Eileen Power'

JAHANGIR AND THE JESUITS

With an Account of
The Travels of Benedict Goes and The Mission to Pegu

From the Relations of
Father Fernão Guerreiro, *S.J.*

Translated by
C.H. Payne, *M.A.*

Low Price Publications
2015

First Published 1930
Reprinted in **LPP** 2015

ISBN 10: 81-7536-556-0
ISBN 13: 978-81-7536-556-8

Published by
Low Price Publications
A-6, 2nd Floor, Nimri Commercial Centre,
Ashok Vihar Phase 4, Delhi 110052 (INDIA)
tel.: +91-11-27302453 fax.: +91-11-47061936
url: www.LPPindia.com e-mail: info@LPPindia.com

Printed at
D.K. Fine Art Press Pvt. Ltd.
Delhi

PRINTED IN INDIA

THE BROADWAY TRAVELLERS

EDITED BY SIR E. DENISON ROSS
AND EILEEN POWER

JAHANGIR AND THE JESUITS

With an Account of

THE TRAVELS OF BENEDICT GOES

and

THE MISSION TO PEGU

From the RELATIONS of

Father FERNÃO GUERREIRO, S.J.

Translated by C. H. Payne, M.A.

Published by

GEORGE ROUTLEDGE & SONS, LTD.
BROADWAY HOUSE, CARTER LANE, LONDON

First published 1930

PRINTED IN GREAT BRITAIN BY
BILLING AND SONS LTD., GUILDFORD AND ESHER

CONTENTS

CONTENTS

CONTENTS

CHAPTER SIX

CHAPTER SEVEN

CHAPTER EIGHT

LIST OF MAPS

PREFACE

In an earlier volume of this series (*Akbar and the Jesuits*) I gave an account of the Jesuit Missions to the court of Akbar, translated from the *Histoire* of Father Pierre du Jarric. It was my intention to let the same author tell the story of the Jesuits at the court of Jahangir; but as the third Part of the *Histoire*, in which the period in question is dealt with, is based almost exclusively on the *Relations* of Father Fernão Guerreiro, it seemed better to translate the latter work, and thereby get a step nearer to the original letters. I made the choice with some regret; for though du Jarric did not hesitate to abridge his authorities, at times somewhat drastically, he is a more polished and, on the whole, a more engaging writer than Guerreiro.

Parts II and III contain Guerreiro's accounts of the travels of Benedict Goes, and of the Portuguese occupation of Pegu. All three Parts belong to the first decade of the seventeenth century, and each adds something of value to our knowledge of that period. As I have said elsewhere, the Jesuit Fathers did not profess to write history. But though their letters tell us little of the political happenings of the time, they light up the picture as a whole, and we see detail where before only outline was visible.

In the text I have allowed Guerreiro to have his own way with the spelling of proper names. In this respect he was nothing if not inconsistent; or perhaps he had a passion for variety. Father Ricci's name is spelt in four different ways in a single chapter.

The portrait of Jahangir, which forms the frontispiece, is from a miniature in the possession of the British Museum. The portrait, which is unsigned, was probably painted in the early part of the seventeenth century, and is a particularly fine example of the Mogul art of the period.

My grateful acknowledgments are due to Sir E. D. Maclagan for the help he has given me in the preparation of this volume, which owes much to his expert knowledge of the Mogul period and of the Jesuit writings. I am also indebted for valuable information and suggestions to Mr. J. P. Hardiman, formerly Commissioner of Tenasserim, who has been kind enough to read through the proofs of Part III. Of the numerous authorities quoted or referred to in the notes, I have specially to acknowledge the assistance I have received from the writings of the Rev. H. Hosten, S.J., and the works of Col. Sir Henry Yule. Lastly I have to express my gratitude to my wife, who has drawn the sketch maps for Parts II and III, and whose advice throughout has been of great value.

C. H. P.

INTRODUCTION

The *Relations* of Father Fernão Guerreiro, from which the three narratives in this volume have been taken, constitute a complete history of the missionary undertakings of the Society of Jesus in the East Indies, China, Japan, and Africa, during the first nine years of the seventeenth century. The work was compiled from the annual letters and reports sent to Europe from the various missionary centres. It was published in five Parts, or instalments, each covering a period of about two years, as follows:

Part I (1600–1601)	published at	Evora	by Manoel de Lyra	in 1603
„ II (1602–1603)	„	Lisbon	by Iorge Rodrigues	in 1605
„ III (1604–1605)	„	„	by Pedro Crasbeeck	in 1607
„ IV (1606–1607)	„	„	by „ „	in 1609
„ V (1607–1608)	„	„	by „ „	in 1611

The title of Part I is: *Relaçam annval das covsas qve fizeram os Padres da Companhia de IESVS na India, & Iapão nos annos de 600. & 601. & do precesso da conversão, & Christandade daquellas partes: tirada das cartas geraes qve de lâ vierão pello Padre Fernão Guerreiro da Campanha de IESVS.* The work, which has never been reprinted, is extremely scarce. All five Parts are in the library of the British Museum; but I know of no other complete set. A copy of Part V occasionally finds its way into the market; but the earlier volumes are to all intents and purposes unprocurable. A Spanish translation of Part I, by Father Antonio Colaço, was published at Valladolid in 1604, and in 1614 a translation into the same language of Part V, by Suarez de Figueroa, was published at Madrid. Figueroa's work appears hitherto to have escaped notice, due no doubt to the fact that he does not disclose the name of the author whose work he is translating. Its title is, *Historia y Anal Relaçion de las cosas que hizieron los Padres de la Compañia de Jesus, por las partes de Oriente y otras, en la propagaçion del Santo Evangelio, los años passados de* 1607 *y* 1608. It is a good translation, but is almost as scarce as the original work. The same remark applies to Father Colaço's Spanish version of Part I.

Of Guerreiro himself little is known. De Backer, in his *Bibliothèque des Ecrivains de la Compagnie de Jesus*, states that he was born at Almodovar in 1567, and that he died in 1617, having held many honourable posts. Father Pierre du Jarric, who had some correspondence with him in connection with the preparation of his *Histoire*, in which he made extensive use of the *Relations*, says, in the preface to his work, that he was at that time (i.e. about the year 1608) Superior of the House of Profes at Lisbon, and refers to him as a man " of ripe and solid judgment, and very learned in these histories, who every two years has collected, and compiled into a single volume, the letters from the Indies, to the great edification of those who desire to study the progress of the Christian faith in foreign lands."

INTRODUCTION

Owing to its inaccessibility Guerreiro's work has received little notice. The chief contribution to the subject is an account of the fifth Relation, written by the Rev. H. Hosten, S.J., whose researches have added so largely to our knowledge of the Jesuit publications. This account, which appeared in the *Journal of the Panjab Historical Society* for 1918, contains an abstract of the chapters relating to 'Mogor,' with translations of the more important passages, and many valuable notes. A translation by the same writer of a chapter relating to the mission to Pegu (see p. 265, note 5) appeared in the *Catholic Herald of India* (November 11th, 1908), and in 1926 an English version of the account of the revolt of Khusru, by I. A. d'Silva, was published in the *Journal of Indian History*. It is possible that other portions of the work have been translated, but the above are all that I have seen.

Jahangir and the Jesuits.

The passages which make up the text account are taken from Part IV (fols. 148*a*-151*b*) and Part V (fols. 6*a*-22*b*) of the *Relations*, Chapters I to IV being from the former, and Chapters V to IX from the latter. In these chapters (with the exception of the last, which is taken from another source) Guerreiro has reproduced the substance of three letters written by Father Jerome Xavier to the Provincial of Goa, and dated respectively September 25th, 1606, August 8th, 1607, and September 24th, 1608. The first two were written from Lahore, and the last from Agra. The portions relating to each letter are indicated in the notes.

INTRODUCTION

When Jahangir ascended the throne, Father Xavier had already been ten years at the Mogul court, whither he had been sent in 1595 as leader of the third Mission to the court of Akbar. The other original members of this Mission were Father Emanuel Pinheiro and Brother Benoist de Goes. In 1602 Brother Goes started on his travels to Cathay, and his place was taken by Father Francis Corsi; and the same year the Mission was further strengthened by the arrival from Goa of Father Anthony Machado. At the time of Akbar's death Fathers Xavier and Machado resided at Agra, and Pinheiro and Corsi at Lahore.

I have fortunately been able to consult the originals of Father Xavier's letters, which I came upon amongst the Marsden MSS. in the British Museum Library. I have, therefore, been able to amplify, and occasionally to elucidate, Guerreiro's narrative. As the letters have never been published, and because of the value and interest attaching to them as contemporary records, I have not hesitated to quote from them freely. The manuscripts are, considering their age, in a good state of preservation; but they are naturally time-worn, and have not altogether escaped the ravages of insects. Fortunately the damage is mostly to the margins of the pages; but here and there a word, or even a whole line of the text has been obliterated. The letters are closely written, and on both sides of the paper. As I found Xavier's writing very difficult to read, I cannot guarantee that my transcriptions are free from mistakes.

I have been unable to trace the original documents used by Guerreiro in Chapter IX, in which he gives an account of Jahangir's embassy to Goa. From certain statements contained in the last chapter (see note 20, p. 114) it is clear that the documents in question must have been written immediately after the negotiations at Goa had terminated. In all probability Guerreiro derived his information from a letter, or letters, written by Father Pinheiro, and forwarded with, or incorporated in, the Provincial's report for the year 1609.

As I endeavoured to show in my introduction to *Akbar and the Jesuits*, the Missions to the court of Akbar had both a religious and a political purpose, though some time elapsed before the latter became prominent. As religious enterprises they aimed at two things: the conversion of the Emperor, and the spread of Christianity in his dominions. So far as the first of these aims was concerned, the Missions were failures; for Akbar, despite his genuine admiration for the Founder and the teachings of the Christian religion, refused to be bound by its dogmas, and died in his own faith—whatever that may have been. As far as the second aim was concerned, a certain measure of success was achieved. The converts made each year were few in number, but they were carefully selected; and at the time our story opens a small but staunch Christian community had grown up both in Agra and in Lahore.

Apart from any political considerations, the existence of these Christian communities necessitated the continued residence of Fathers of the Society at the Mogul court. Moreover, strong hopes were entertained of the conversion of Jahangir, who, while his father was alive, had never lost an opportunity of ingratiating himself with the Fathers, and had frequently made public profession of his attachment to the faith they preached. Such hopes, however, were soon shown to be groundless. The Fathers had, in fact, been completely taken in by these early outbursts of religious zeal, the sincerity of which they apparently never doubted. But Jahangir, or Prince Salim, as he then was, had his own reasons for the attitude he assumed at this period. He knew that his succession to the throne was by no means a foregone conclusion; and he also knew that, in the event of his having to fight for his kingdom, the Portuguese had it in their power to render him very valuable assistance. In these circumstances, he was naturally anxious to stand well with the authorities at Goa. The attitude of the latter would be largely determined by the reports received from the Mission; and it was to make sure of being presented in a favourable light, that he cultivated the friendship of the Fathers, and posed as a prospective convert to Christianity.

Unlike his father, Jahangir had no feeling for religion. Though he was interested in, and took some pains to understand, the doctrines of Christianity and other faiths, he was in no real sense a seeker after the truth. The study of religious problems was with him nothing more than a hobby. It amused him to listen to disputes between his Mullas and the Fathers, just as it amused him to watch a fencing match or a cock-fight. When either side scored a point, he clapped his hands with delight, particularly if the point was scored against his Mullas, whose discomfiture always afforded him intense amusement. He frequently joined in these disputes; and as he usually took the side of the Fathers, and made no effort to conceal his contempt for his own faith, new hopes began to be entertained of his conversion. These were strengthened by the fondness and reverence he displayed for pictures of Christ and the Virgin and the Christian saints, of which he possessed a large number. But once more the Fathers were too sanguine. If Jahangir sided with them in their disputes, it was mainly for the pleasure of shocking his Mullas, and showing his own knowledge and skill in debate; while he prized the sacred pictures which the Fathers gave him, not, as they fondly imagined, out of veneration for the subjects represented, but because he had a passion for works of art and curios of all kinds, and especially for pictures, of which he was not only an enthusiastic collector, but a very competent judge. He respected Islam as little as, or even less than, Akbar; but though he, too, appears to have had a genuine admiration for Christianity, he was never, like his father, drawn towards it. Akbar felt the want of a religion; and Christianity made so strong an appeal to him that, if he could have accepted its dogmas, he would probably have been baptised. "Explain the Incarnation to me," he once said, "and I will become a Christian, though it cost me my kingdom." Jahangir would have subscribed to one set of doctrines as readily as to another; but he had very little use for any religion, and none at all for one that would not permit him as many wives as he wanted.

INTRODUCTION

Until the last two years of Akbar's reign, the political aspect of the Mission was very little in evidence; though we may suppose that, from the first, the Fathers had been expected to keep a watchful eye on what was going on around them, and to forward to Goa any information likely to be of value to the Portuguese authorities. But after the accession of Jahangir, the Mission began gradually to assume the character and functions of an embassy, and, *pari passu*, the cause of evangelisation lost ground. The Fathers, as we shall see, succeeded in outplaying the English traveller, Hawkins, and Guerreiro ends his narrative on a note of victory. But the knell of Portuguese supremacy in the East had already sounded. The employment of the Fathers as political agents, while it did much to impair their spiritual influence, did little to retard the impending ruin, the cause of which was not only the appearance on the scene of such powerful rivals as the English and the Dutch, but the fact that for years past Portugal had been unable to afford her eastern enterprises the support in men and money which they so urgently needed; for, since her union with Spain in 1580, Portugal had ceased to be mistress of her own resources; and the means which might have been expended in rendering her overseas possessions secure, were diverted into other channels. There was another circumstance which contributed to the completeness of the collapse. From the days of Vasco da Gama onwards, the Portuguese had never laid themselves out to win the affections of the eastern races with whom their commercial ventures brought them into contact. Their courage inspired respect wherever they went, and their skill in battle, by land or sea, led many to court their alliance. But they were proud and intolerant; and their general attitude towards Oriental peoples and Oriental beliefs and customs was one of arrogant contempt. Added to this, their control of the seas, which they exercised with relentless severity, was regarded with deep and widespread resentment. Thus the Portuguese were admired, feared, and hated. But they were feared and hated more than they were admired; and when their position was challenged, they found themselves without a friend in the East.

The Travels of Benedict Goes

Apart from a few brief references in the letters of Father Jerome Xavier, all that we know for certain of the journey of Benedict Goes to Cathay is contained in the writings of Father Matteo Ricci and Father Fernão Guerreiro. Father Pierre du Jarric has frequently been cited as an authority; but the account of Goes' travels contained in his *Histoire* is taken entirely from the *Relations* of Guerreiro, and has, therefore, no independent value. It is important only because of the extreme rarity of the latter work. We are, however, indebted to du Jarric for the preservation of a curious and interesting account, taken from a letter written by Father Xavier on the 26th July, 1598, of the circumstances which led to the dispatch of a Mission to Cathay. This occurs in Part II of the *Histoire*; and as it explains to some extent the strange beliefs regarding Cathay that were current in Brother Benedict's day, and enables us to understand the nature of the problems he was sent to investigate, I have incorporated its translation with the text, as an introductory chapter to Guerreiro's narrative.

Father Ricci's account of the Cathay Mission, derived from the fragments of Goes' diary, and the information supplied by his servant Isaac, has, until quite recently, been known only through the Latin version of Father Nicolas Trigault, which was first published in 1615, and of which we have an English translation in Sir Henry Yule's well-known work, *Cathay and the Way Thither* (IV., pp. 198-254). In 1911, however, Ricci's actual memoirs were published at Macerata, under the editorship of Father Tacchi Venturi, S.J., to whom we owe the discovery of the original manuscript. Father Venturi's work is entitled, *Opere Storriche del P. Matteo Ricci, S.J.* It consists of two volumes, the first (*Commentarj della Cina*) containing a general history of the Chinese Mission, and the second (*Le Lettere dalla Cina*), Father Ricci's letters. The account of the Mission to Cathay occurs in the *Commentarj* (pp. 526-558), and additional details are furnished by several of the letters in the second volume. The discovery and publication of Ricci's own work naturally displaces Trigault's Latin version, which, though in the main reliable, is very far from being a literal translation. M. Henri Cordier was fortunately able to make use of Father Venturi's two volumes in his revision of *Cathay and the Way Thither*; so that the account of Benedict Goes contained in that work still remains the most complete and authoritative that we possess.

Like Ricci's memoirs, the *Relations* of Guerreiro are still known, except to a very few, only through a translation, and that a very incomplete one. For though du Jarric drew the materials for the third part of his *Histoire* almost exclusively from the *Relations*, considerable portions of which he literally translated, there are many passages of the Portuguese work which he either abridged, or briefly summarised, or even omitted altogether. On the whole it may be said that du Jarric abridged wisely; but there are not a few instances, and this applies particularly to his account of the mission to Cathay, in which he has deprived his readers of matter that is both important and interesting.

Guerreiro's account of Goes' Mission is to be found in Part II (fols. 61*b*-65*a*), Part IV (fols. 162*a*-168*b*), and Part V (fols. 23-28) of his *Relations*. The first two instalments are of special value, being based on the letters which Goes sent back to India whilst on his way to, and during his sojourn at, Yarkand. They thus shed light where it is most needed; for Ricci, who never saw these letters, knew very little about the earlier stages of Goes' journey, of which his account is not only meagre, but manifestly inaccurate, or perhaps 'incorrect' would be the better word; for Ricci, no doubt, did the best he could with the scanty and fragmentary data he had to work upon. The chronological confusion which faces us in his account of the journey from Lahore to Yarkand suggests that the first part of Goes' diary reached him in a worse state of mutilation than the last part; while for filling up blanks in the record, the memory of the Armenian Isaac was doubtless of less and less assistance, the further it had to travel back. It must also be borne in mind that Goes did not keep a diary in order that someone else might describe his travels, but that he might describe them himself. And not only were his notes and figures intended for his own information only; they must often have been written under the most trying circumstances, when the cold alone was sufficient to make the act of writing almost a physical impossibility. It is not surprising, therefore, that Ricci found a difficulty in reconstructing his pilgrimage. His task would have been no easy one if Goes' diary had reached him intact.

After his departure from Yarkand, Goes sent no more letters to his friends in India, and from this point Guerreiro followed Father Ricci, reproducing even his blunders, though he contradicted his own narrative in doing so. He could not, of course, have seen Ricci's memoirs, since Part V of his *Relations* was published in 1611; it was, in fact, completed in 1610, as we know from the *licenças* for printing it, the first of which is dated "em Lisboa 23 de Dezembro 1610"; whereas Ricci did not complete the composition of his memoirs till March or April, 1610, and another five years elapsed before the publication of Trigault's Latin version gave them to the world. That being the case, it is, I think, evident that Guerreiro made use of the earlier account of Goes' travels, which we know that Ricci sent, at the end of 1607, to the Provincial of India, for transmission, *via* Portugal, to the General at Rome. This account Ricci refers to in two letters written from Peking in 1608 to the General of the Society, one dated March 8th, and the other August 22nd. In the latter he says: "Nel tempo che qui stette Isaac, con quello che ritrovai fra gli scritti del fratello Benedetto, aguitandomi di quello che Isaac aveva anco visto, feci una relatione di tutto il viaggio, arrivata, stata in Succeo e morte del detto fratello Benedetto e, di quello che poi successe al fratello Giovanni, e la mandai al p. provinciale dell' India, per portersi mandare a V.P. per via di Portogallo: e l' istesso feci al p. viceprovinciale del Giappone, pregandolo mandasse a V.P. per via della Nova Spagna. E se bene fu scritta in lingua portoghese, con tutto là la potranno voltare in italiano; e cosi non volsi tornarlo a ripetere in questa, per tenere per cosa certa che o per l' Oriente o per l' Occidente saprà V.P. tutto quello che sopra di ciò mi occorse scrivere" (*Op. Stor.*, II 356). Unfortunately no copy of this earlier narrative exists; but Guerreiro, by preserving the substance of it in this chapter, has to a large extent compensated us for the loss. It was evidently much less detailed than that which Ricci subsequently wrote; for of the journey from Yarkand to Su-chow Guerreiro gives us little more than the bare outline.

Even of the journey from Lahore to Yarkand the *Commentarj* contains numerous details which are not to be found in the *Relations*; for apart from the letters of Goes, Guerreiro can have had little information at his disposal. His account of the Mission to Cathay must, therefore, be regarded as a supplement, though a very valuable supplement, to Ricci's narrative. The notes to my translation are also intended to be of a purely supplementary character. The difficulties which beset the student of Goes' travels are legion; but they are for the most part exhaustively dealt with in the revised edition of Colonel Yule's work. Only in one or two instances are the conclusions there given affected by the evidence of Goes' letters. As those who desire to make a special study of the subject will necessarily take Yule's work as their chief guide, I have attempted to give only such additional explanations as Guerreiro's narrative seemed to me to call for. As Father Ricci's letters are almost unknown in this country, I hope the reader will regard the quotations I have made from them as an interesting feature of my notes. I shall not resent it if he regards them as the redeeming feature.

The Mission to Pegu

I have called this extract "The Mission to Pegu" because Guerreiro himself uses this expression. But the missionary element enters very little into the story, for which a more appropriate title would be "The Portuguese at Syriam," or perhaps "The Rise and Fall of Philip de Brito"; for de Brito has every claim to be regarded as the hero, or villain (according to the reader's choice) of the piece, since it was to him that the Portuguese owed their temporary possession of the Syriam fortress.

INTRODUCTION

Our chief authorities for the events of Philip de Brito's brief 'reign' at Syriam are the *Relations* of Guerreiro, the *Decada* of Antonio Bocarro, and Faria y Sousa's *Asia Portuguesa*. Of these the last named is the best known, and is the only one of the three that has been translated into English. The original work, in three volumes, was published at Lisbon between the years 1666 and 1675, and an English translation by Captain J. Stevens appeared in 1695. Bocarro's *Decada* (usually known as *Decada* 13) was completed in 1635; but it remained practically unknown until the year 1876, when it was printed for the first time by the Royal Academy of Sciences at Lisbon (*Collecção de Monumentos Ineditos*, Vol. VI).

The Portuguese occupation of Syriam covered a period of thirteen years, namely from 1600 to 1613. Unfortunately the *Relations* of Guerreiro take us down only to the year 1609. It has been necessary, therefore, to complete the story from another source, and this has been done by the addition of a chapter from the *Decada* of Bocarro. I have chosen Bocarro in preference to Faria y Sousa, partly because his work is still unknown in this country, and also because his account is more detailed and more authoritative than that contained in Faria y Sousa's later work. Antonio Bocarro was for some years (1631 to 1649) official historian at Goa, and Keeper of the Records (Guarda mór da Torre do Tombo da India). His *Decada* was intended as a continuation of the *Decadas da Asia*, written by his predecessor Diogo do Couto, which was itself a continuation of the *Decadas* of João de

Barros. The latter writer composed four *Decadas*, his account ending with the year 1539. Do Couto continued the history down to the end of the sixteenth century, his last volume being *Decada* 12. Bocarro's work has consequently been known as *Decada* 13, though the title he gave to it himself was *Decada primeira*. Its detailed character may be judged from the fact that it covers 756 quarto pages, while the period dealt with is only five years (1612-1617). Sr. de Lima Felner, the editor of the sixth volume of the *Documentos Ineditos*, refers to Bocarro as a highly conscientious writer, and a severe, though impartial judge of men and affairs: "Não occulta, levado por vão patriotismo, as ulceras que lavraram até á medula nos principaes personagens d'aquelle tempo, nem esconde o estado de decadencia a que havia chegado o nosso poderio e o nosso commercio, n'uma época em que a gente da India parecia haver completamente esquecido a sombra d'aquelles vultos gigantes que sobresaíam entre tantos heroes, como D. Francisco de Almeida e Affonso de Albuquerque."

Although at the commencement of the sixteenth century the power of Portugal was already on the wane, her maritime supremacy in the East had not yet been seriously threatened or shaken. Her eastern settlements were more numerous, and were scattered over a wider area, than ever before. The places occupied were in nearly all cases seaports, which served the double purpose of trading centres and naval bases; for she had, from the first, no desire to burden herself with extensive territorial possessions. The only '-territory' over which she sought to reign supreme, and through which a right of way was denied to all who refused to pay her price, was the sea. In fact, it may be said that Portugal's eastern possessions consisted of a large tract of sea with numerous settlements and fortresses on its boundaries. Of this watery realm, the city of Goa was the metropolis and the G.H.Q. of the administration. Outside India and the Bay of Bengal, the principal strongholds were Mozambique, Mombasa, Muscat, Ormuz, Colombo, Malaca, and Macao. It was the attempt to establish yet another 'frontier post,' or, as Guerreiro would have put it, 'to add another jewel to the crown of this realm,' that forms the subject of the present extract.

The fact that more than three hundred years ago one Philip de Brito built a fort on the Pegu river, held it for a dozen years, and then lost it, is not in itself of outstanding importance. Nevertheless, the attendant circumstances are worth our attention, because of the insight they afford into the maritime policy of the Portuguese at this period, the methods by which it was pursued, and the causes which contributed to its failure. The story of Philip de Brito's short-lived triumph and its tragic conclusion is the history in miniature of the rise and collapse of Portuguese power in the East.

PART I

JAHANGIR AND THE JESUITS

CHAPTER I

The Rebellion of the Prince against his Father, and the Consequences thereof[1]

EIGHT days after the death of King Aquebar,[2] the new King went to the palace to take possession of the realm. By his orders a daïs, very splendidly adorned, had been erected, and he came forth and took his seat thereon. The people brought gifts to him, and all shouted *Pad Iausalamat*, 'Hail King.'[3] Then he entered the fortress, which he made his royal abode.

All men hoped much from the new King, and especially the Fathers, who believed that his accession would lead many to embrace the Christian faith. For up to that time he had been looked upon almost as a Christian, and had been openly spoken of as such by his adherents. But these hopes were disappointed; for he had sworn an oath to the Moors to uphold the law of Mafamede [Muhammad], and being anxious at the commencement of his reign to secure their good will, he gave orders for the cleansing of the mosques, restored the fasts [*ramesas*][4] and prayers of the Moors, and took the name Nurdim mohamad Iahanuir,[5] which signifies, "The Splendour of the Law of Mafamede, Conqueror of the World." Of the Fathers he took no more notice than if he had never seen them before.[6]

Not long after the death of the old King, and the accession of the new, the Prince, the son of the latter, revolted against his father, just as the new King when Prince had himself revolted against his father Aquebar. On account of certain grievances and suspicions, the Prince, on the night of Saturday, the 15th of April,[7] left the fortress with a number of his friends and adherents, without letting it be known whither he was going. Those who accompanied him gave out that it was his purpose to visit the tomb of his grandfather, and with this excuse he was able to pass safely by the Merinho Mor[8] and all the King's guards. His followers now commenced to call him Soltam Ia,[9] that is, King Soltam, and they collected as many horses as they could find, and whatever else they needed for defending themselves.

On being informed of these things, the King, after listening to various counsels, determined to go himself in pursuit of his son, and as soon as day broke he set forth.[10] It happened that the Prince fell in with a great Captain[11] who was on his way to Lahor to see the King, and succeeded in persuading him to join his side. Soon afterwards, he met another Captain who had with him a hundred thousand rupees (equal to forty thousand *crusados*, more or less), which he was taking to the King. The Prince seized the money, and persuaded this Captain also to join him. He then made a liberal distribution of his plunder amongst his soldiers, the report of which, being noised abroad, soon brought twelve thousand more men to his side, so that by the time he reached Lahor (which is a hundred leagues from Agra whence he had fled) he was at the head of a considerable force.

But the people of Lahor, who had been informed of his flight, closed the gates of the city and refused him entrance. For eight days the Prince closely besieged the city; but he was unable to take it. On learning that his father was coming, and was already near at hand, he gave up the siege and turned to encounter his pursuers, hoping to prevent them from crossing the river. But he was too late; for already a portion of the King's army had made the passage; while to add to the difficulties of the unfortunate Prince, rain fell so violently that it rendered the bows of his men useless and their horses unmanageable. Nevertheless, putting all to the hazard, he threw himself upon the King's troops. During this onset many of those who had crossed the river were slain, and all this portion of the imperial army might have been put to flight, had not one of the King's Captains, seeing that the resistance of his men was weakening, made use of the following stratagem. Having disguised a number of foot-soldiers as messengers, he bade them go and mingle with the troops of the Prince, and spread the report that the King had crossed the river, and was rapidly approaching with a great army. As messenger followed messenger, each bringing the same news, all the Prince's soldiers believed it to be true. After a short while, the same Captain suddenly ordered trumpets to be sounded and drums to be beaten, as is always done when the King marches.[12]

The Prince was for continuing the attack, and had he done so he would have completely routed the troops on that side of the river, which might have caused those who were with the King to lose heart, and so his enterprise might have succeeded. But his followers, overcome by their dread of the King, whom they wrongly believed to be close at hand, lost heart and counselled instant flight; and when the Prince would not listen to their words, his General, seizing the bridle of his horse, forced him to turn back, telling him that he was going to his destruction. But this sealed the Prince's fate; for his troops, seeing that he had set his back to the enemy, straightway turned and fled in disorder. They were pursued by the King's troops, and many of them were slain.[13]

The King now crossed the river, while the Prince fled towards the Kingdom of Cabul, which also belonged to his father. Messengers had already been sent to every place where it was possible for the Prince to cross the intervening river, with orders that every passage was to be held against him; and by the time he reached one of these passages,[14] the King's message had already been received, and the Captain who governed in those parts was waiting to intercept him. He had given orders that all boats were to be removed except one, and that when the Price had embarked, the boatmen were, as if by mischance, to steer the boat on to a sandbank which was in the middle of the stream, and then, on the pretext of fetching others to their assistance, were to come and report to him. All this the boatmen did, whereon the Governor, entering another boat, made his way to the Prince, with whom were his General and one or two others.

The Governor treated him with due ceremony, and conducted him, all unsuspecting, to his fortress. As soon as he had his captives safely lodged, he excused himself on the ground that he was going to give orders for their refreshment, and left them, locking the gates behind him. The Prince's followers, having no means of crossing the river, could do nothing to help their master; and learning that he was a prisoner, they dispersed and hid themselves.

Meanwhile the King, in great anxiety as to the whereabouts of his son, continued his march to Lahor. As he neared the city, the two Fathers in charge of the church there came out to pay their respects to him. They had been in great peril from the Gentiles, who had threatened to destroy them as soon as the Prince entered the gates.[15] After proceeding about two leagues, they met the King at the head of his army. He was riding between two lines of troops in fine array, and was attended by many great lords. He was preceded by an advance guard, who cleared the way before him, allowing none to remain on the road. The Fathers, however, were permitted to pass on until they came to the King, who, on seeing them, drew rein, and the whole army came to a halt. They approached and embraced his feet; and His Majesty, with a very amiable countenance, enquired after their welfare, and took into his hands the small present which they offered to him; then signing to them to withdraw, he continued his march.

Towards evening he received news that his son was a prisoner, and a Captain, with a guard, was at once dispatched to bring him to Lahor. Having entered the fortress where the Prince was, the Captain, without any display of courtesy or respect, produced fetters, covered with velvet, and said that he was commanded by the King to put them on his feet. Having thus secured him, he brought him away, together with his fellow-captives, under a strong guard. On their return, the King sent an elephant, meanly harnessed, to carry the Prince across the river, and ordered him to be brought to the pleasure-house where he then was, for he had not yet made his entry into the city. On being informed of his arrival, he withdrew into the house, perchance to give way, like Joseph, to the natural feelings of a father. But in a little while he came out, and ordered him to approach.

The whole court awaited in suspense the sentence of the King. The spectacle of the poor Prince, chained hand and foot, being led into his father's presence, moved all who witnessed it to compassion. As soon as he saw the King he made signs of submission and reverence. His Majesty ordered him to approach and place himself amongst his Captains. Then turning on him a countenance full of wrath, he upbraided him in the most bitter terms. The two chief Captains of the Prince were also made to come before him. One of these had been a great Captain under this, as well as under the late King, whom he had served in many important offices. The other had held the post of Treasurer, and had been Governor of Lahor. As these two stood before him, heavily manacled, His Majesty spoke mockingly to them of the King they had chosen to follow, and of the fine Captains their King had chosen to aid him in his exploit. Finally he made over the Prince to one of his Captains with orders that he was to be kept in chains and closely guarded. As to the two Captains, the foremost, having been stripped naked, was enveloped in the skin of a newly slaughtered ox, and the other, the Chief Steward, was similarly arrayed in the skin of an ass, also newly slain for the purpose. The skins were sewn tightly over them so that they were put to extreme torture as they dried and shrank. They were left thus throughout the night, and in the morning they were paraded through the city, clad in the manner described, and each riding upon an ass, with his face turned towards the tail.

The sight of these two great nobles, the one having the horns of an ox fixed to his head, and the other the ears of an ass, caused the greatest astonishment amongst the people, who were accustomed to see them so differently arrayed. When they returned to the pleasure-house where the King was, the Captain was so overcome by the ignominy to which he had been exposed in the streets, where he had formerly gone in state with his elephants and horses and retainers, that he had no strength left in him, and fell to the ground as one dead. The King ordered his head to be cut off and sent to Agra to be fixed to the gate of the city. His body was cut up into quarters which were hung up on the roadside.

The Treasurer was left sewn up in his case; but the King, as a great favour, gave permission that his servant might moisten the skin so that it should grip him less severely. But this relief had its drawbacks, for the moisture engendered fleas and other vermin, so that he was tormented worse than before, and he counted himself happy whenever he could crush some of them in his fingers and get rid of them. At the same time, owing to the heat of the sun, the skin began to putrefy, and gave forth such an evil smell that none would go near him. In the end, however, he was set free; for a courtier who was desirous of marrying his daughter interceded for him to such good purpose that he obtained his pardon; but for this he had to pay His Majesty something over a hundred thousand crowns. On the same evening that he paid this sum, he was unsewn, and conducted to the city. After a few days, he began to go about as usual, and the King restored him to his office as though nothing had happened.[16]

Many of the Prince's followers had also been captured; and on the day that the King made his entry into the city, two hundred of these captives decorated his route, on either side of which they had, by his orders, been impaled or hanged. Amongst them were many who were related to his chief favourites; but none dared to interfere in their behalf, lest he should be accounted a partisan of the Prince.[17] The King, mounted on a magnificently caparisoned elephant, entered the city in triumph. As he passed along the route, he turned his head from side to side to regard his victims, listening to what was told him of each. A little behind, the fetters still on his feet, and mounted on a small elephant devoid of harness or trappings, came the Prince, a spectator by compulsion of this tragic sequel to his ill-judged adventure.

After entering Lahor the King confined the Prince in his palace. He still kept him in chains, but of a somewhat lighter description than before. To make his degradation complete, he deprived him of his titles and his right to succeed to the throne, transferring these to his second son. A hundred thousand crowns came to the King through the Captain whose head he had cut off, and other large sums through the other offenders.[18] All this he kept for himself; but the horses and other things that he took from his son, he conferred on those whom the unfortunate Prince looked upon as his greatest enemies, thereby rendering his vexation the more acute.

While the Prince was flying from Agra, he passed the spot where there dwelt one whom the Gentiles call Goru,[19] a title equivalent to that of Pope amongst the Christians. This person was looked upon as a saint, and was greatly venerated. On account of his reputation for holiness, the Prince went to see him, hoping apparently that this would bring him good fortune. The Goru congratulated him on his new royalty, and placed his tiara[20] on his head. Although the Prince was a Moor, the Goru deemed it lawful to bestow on him this mark of dignity, proper only to a Gentile, since he was the son of a Pagan woman; and the Prince accepted it, believing the Goru to be a saint.

When, after his son's capture, the King heard of

this circumstance, he ordered the Goru to be apprehended, and for some time kept him a prisoner. However, certain Gentiles interceded on behalf of their holy man, and in the end he was allowed to purchase his freedom for a hundred thousand *crusados*, for which sum a wealthy Gentile became his surety. Now this man thought that either the King would remit the fine or that the Goru would himself provide, or at any rate find some means of raising, the sum required. But in these hopes he was disappointed, and in consequence he proceeded to take from the wretched pontiff all his worldly possessions, including the furniture of his house, and even the clothes of his wife and children; for these Gentiles regard neither Pope nor Father where money is concerned. And when this did not suffice to pay the fine, he subjected him to every kind of ill-usage, causing him to be beaten with slippers, and preventing food from being given to him, in the hope that his victim, to escape from his sufferings, would produce the money which he still believed him to possess. But neither the Goru nor those about him could meet the demands of his tormentor; and at last the poor man died, overcome by the miseries heaped upon him by those who had formerly paid him reverence.[21] The Gentile sought to escape his obligations by flight, but he was taken, and having been deprived of everything that he possessed, was thrown into prison, where he died.

CHAPTER II

How the King began his Reign. He compels Two Christian Children to become Moors[1]

Having put an end to these disorders, the King occupied himself with the government of his kingdom. He displayed so great a love for justice that, calling to mind what one of the ancient kings of Persia had done, he gave orders that a silver bell with a chain twenty cubits long should be suspended close to his own apartments, so that all who felt that they had grievances and were unable to obtain redress at the hands of the law or the officers of the State, might pull this chain, when the King would immediately come forth and deliver justice verbally.[2] He also gave orders that merchants were no longer to pay the tolls demanded from them by his Captains in various places through which they passed; and he restored to their heirs the goods which, according to the orders of his father, came into the King's possession when the owners died. Out of this arose trouble for the Fathers. For the late King had during his lifetime given to them some houses which had belonged to a certain Gentile, in which they had established their church and taken up their abode. The heirs now demanded the restitution of these houses, as well as of some others in which Christians were living. The matter was brought before the King, and the claimants, thinking to achieve their object the more easily, said many evil things about the Fathers.[8] But the King paid no heed to them, telling them that if their allegations had been true, complaints would have reached him long before; and in the end he confirmed the gift of the houses, and said that he would listen to no more complaints regarding grants made by his father to the Christians. The Fathers gladly endured the difficulties and dangers to which this dispute exposed them, and which, for love of their church, they faced so resolutely. They have made their church very beautiful, so that every day Moors and Gentiles newly arrived in the city ask to be allowed to see it, and are greatly astonished at its perfection. The buildings have the appearance of a college. There are verandahs, and fine upper rooms for winter use, and lower ones for the summer. There is a separate apartment for every office, very conveniently arranged, and there is also a porter's lodge with a bell for the use of those who pass in and out. Thus, in the heart of this Moorish kingdom, there is a Company established as though it were in a Christian land, exercising all its functions, and regarded with such respect that whenever the Fathers go abroad the children in the streets cry '*Padrigi Salamat*,' that is, "God keep you, Señor Padre," which rejoices the hearts of the Fathers, leading them to hope that God will one day give these children grace to know Him, since they show such affection for His servants.

After the difficulty about the houses, another circumstance occurred which caused the Fathers no less anxiety. It came about in this manner. The new

King, having taken the sceptre into his hands, bethought himself of the oath which he had sworn to the Moors. Now there was in his household a young Gentile, the son of a great Captain who had been much favoured by the late King. Some years previously this young man had for certain reasons been circumcised; and one evening, when he was in the royal presence, the King referred to this circumstance, and said that since he had been circumcised he was no longer a Gentile, and that he ought to take another law. This he at first declined to do; but the King insisted, and finally said, " If you wish to become a Moor, here are the Mullas, who will teach you their law. Or if you would rather become a Christian, I will send for the Fathers, who will baptise you." Finding himself forced to make a choice, and worked upon by those who were present, he elected to take the law of the Moors, which he did, and was paraded through the city on an elephant with great state, and amid much rejoicing, to the great contentment of the Moors and the mortification of the Gentiles.

Seeing how he had pleased the Moors, the King determined to try a similar experiment with a Christian, choosing for his purpose a young Armenian of a very honourable character. This young man had likewise been made much of by the late King, who had his two sons brought up with his own grandsons, showing them great affection, which they well merited, for there were no children so well behaved in the royal palace. Some years ago this Armenian had, under pressure from one of the King's wives, and by order of the King himself, married the sister of his deceased wife who was the mother of his two children.[4] From that time the Moors maintained that the Armenian had made himself one of them, since he had followed a Moorish custom and married two sisters, though in truth he was not, and had never admitted himself to be, a follower of their faith. It chanced that about this time he came from the province which he governed[5] to pay his respects to the new King, and to submit his accounts to the controller of the royal treasury. Now the King, having made up his mind to make this man a Moor, took counsel with the Treasurer with whom he had business, and the latter, aided by his friends, did all in his power, partly by threats and partly by promise of favours, to bend the Armenian to the King's will. But the young man's constancy to his faith remained unshaken, to the great joy of the Christians, and especially of the Fathers, to whom he recounted his difficulties and trials, saying, "There is nothing I desire more than to die for the faith which I follow, as an atonement for the sins of which I have been guilty, and the scandal which I have occasioned."

It was at this juncture that the King was overtaken by the storm of troubles occasioned by the flight of the Prince from Agra; and on his departure in pursuit of his son, the Armenian seized the opportunity to return to his province, taking his two sons with him. After the defeat of the Prince, the King, having taken up his quarters at Lahor, enquired for the children, and when in course of time they arrived at the palace, he received them very kindly. He enquired after their father, and told them they were to remain with him as before. In the evening of the same day, they were spoken of in the presence of the King; and when many things had been said in their praise, a certain Moor who was present remarked to the King, "It is a pity that children of such excellent parts are not Moors." This set the match to the fire. The King asked them what law they followed, and they answered that they were Christians like their father. "Their father is not a Moor," said the King. "But he is, Sire," said one of those present, "because after the manner of a Moor he has married the sister of his first wife." But the children insisted that they were and always had been Christians. "Then," said the King, "since you are Christians you shall eat hog's flesh." When the King said this, both the children shuddered, for they had been brought up by one of the Queens, from whom they had imbibed various Moorish notions, and they loathed hog's flesh like the Moors themselves, so that their father had never been able to induce the elder child even to taste it. They told the King that though their law did not forbid them to eat hog's flesh, it did not oblige them to do so.

Nothing more was said on the subject that night, and the next day the children went to the Fathers and told them what had taken place. The Fathers fortified them with advice and encouragement, for they knew the King's nature, and that he would never allow the matter to drop; and the next evening the children had to withstand a fresh assault. Again one of those present insisted that they were Moors. "They have been brought up as Moors," he said, "and it is only reasonable that they should be Moors." These words were greeted with cries of "Hear, hear!" while the King forbade the children to leave the palace, and ordered them to be confined to a certain place as though they were prisoners, thinking that with no one to encourage them they would be the more easily overcome. News of this was carried to the Fathers by some of their relatives, one of whom, declaring that he was ready to give his life for Christ, drew his dagger from his belt and entrusting it with what money he had to the Fathers, entered the palace and made his way to the children's side. When they again came before the King, the battle about their faith and the eating of hog's flesh began anew. The younger lad said they would eat as the King ordered if the Fathers told them it was their duty. The King would have summoned the Fathers to put them to the test; but one of his courtiers, enraged at the lad's reply, gave him two severe blows, saying, "Do you answer thus? How dare you refer to the Fathers when His Majesty gives you an order!" Upon this, the King, putting aside the question of the hog's flesh, went to the root of the matter. "Listen to me!" he said. "You are to become Moors. Repeat the *Calima*,"[6] which is the confession of the law of Mafamede. But the two lads remained silent; whereon the King sent for the whip used for scourging criminals, and ordered them to be flogged. Terrified into submission by the prospect of this torture, the children repeated through their clenched teeth the words demanded by the Moors. After this they were allowed to go, and they returned downcast and miserable to their apartment. In the morning, the King sent a barber to circumcise them. But to this they refused to submit, and they made so loud an outcry that the barber left them and went to tell the King, who at once sent for them and asked them the meaning of their refusal. They replied that they were Christians and that they would remain Christians, and would not be circumcised. The Fathers, who had been each day to the palace to see the lads, had prepared them for this last struggle with counsel and exhortations. They had also tried to gain access to the King that they might speak to him on the children's behalf; but the Moors were so watchful that they had no opportunity of doing so.

The King, on hearing what the children said, tried to make them yield by promises of countless favours to come, and when these proved unavailing, by threats of punishment. Thus sorely pressed, and seeing that their answers and their resistance were unheeded, one of them cried: "Sire, we implore you, for the love of Alazaraht Ieam (i.e. the Lord Jesus),[7] do not compel us to be circumcised!" To this the King, who before his accession was greatly devoted to our Lord, and wore on his breast a richly enamelled crucifix, replied: "It is for love of Him that I do so." "But that will never please Him," said the child. Then the cruel King, to put an end to further words, ordered them to be held hand and foot, and despite their protestations and cries, had them circumcised then and there, in his presence. "Now," he said, "you are Moors. Repeat the *Calima*!" The struggle recommenced with even greater fierceness on the King's part, for the sight of the innocent blood seemed to make him all the more determined to carry out his purpose, and satisfy those who were instigating him. The more the children resisted, the more determined he became. At last the whips were brought, and the two lads were beaten without mercy. Many of those present were moved to compassion to see them, still bleeding from the circumcision, suffer these cruel stripes, which, because of the presence and rage of the King, exceeded in severity those ordinarily inflicted on criminals. The elder, who was fourteen years of age, yielded after the fourteenth stripe and said what was required of him, though by no means in the manner the Moors desired. The younger, who had not yet completed his eleventh year, continued to hold out even when he saw his brother give way. He was therefore beaten with increased severity. At each stroke of the whip he cried out, "Ah, Hazaraht Ieão, Señor Iesu!" for he had this holy name always on his lips, and his hands clasped the reliquary he wore about his neck. All were filled with astonishment at his constancy, and even the King showed signs of compassion and became silent. One of the courtiers, however, continued to urge on those who were beating him, crying, "Smite him! Smite him!" so that they gave him thirty stripes severe enough to overcome the strongest man. The cruelty of this last onslaught deprived the poor child of strength and spirit, and to escape further torture he repeated the words of the *Calima*, after which he was given three or four more stripes for not having yielded sooner. Perchance if he could have held out a little longer, he would not have had to suffer worse. But it was much that so young a child had endured so long, with no one near to encourage him, but only ravening wolves who thirsted for the blood and soul of this innocent lamb, and the maddened King. Had the wrath of the latter been directed against those who instigated him, it would have needed many fewer stripes to make them abandon the law of Mafamede and accept that of Christ which they hold in such abhorrence, so greatly do they stand in awe of and fear their King.

Content with his fictitious victory, the King ordered the children to be taken to their quarters and carefully tended. The same evening the Fathers, ignorant of what had taken place, went to see them. They found them lying on the ground silent and miserable. As soon as the Fathers entered the younger cried out: "Padrigi, I am a Christian! I am a Christian! Let them cut me how they like, it makes no difference. It was all against our will. If they had not beaten us, do you think we would have given way? We have borne these blows willingly;" and they showed on their bodies the marks of the whip, which were pitiful to behold. The Fathers could not find it in their hearts to admonish them for their fall, but comforted them and praised them for the constancy they had shown, that they might not think of themselves as vanquished or as Moors. And indeed, from that time, the children openly declared that they were Christians as they had always been, and that what they had done was by compulsion and because of the torture that had been inflicted on them. The King sent a Mulla to dress their wounds and teach them their prayers. But they said whatever they liked of Mafamede before him. After their recovery they were taken to the King, who gave them each a dress and permission to leave their lodging; but he forbade them to see or converse with the Fathers. The children paid little heed to this order, and went about publicly proclaiming themselves Christians, and saying so many things against the Moors and their law that they had more need of the rein than the spur. The elder lad, who had shown himself the weaker of the two, of his own accord took a dagger and cut the figure of a cross, the length of a span, on his left arm. He must have endured much pain, for the flesh was permanently marked. The top of the figure was at the wrist, so that each time he raises his arm the cross was uplifted. Thus day by day were these lads filled with new zeal. For the rest, the King treated them in private as he had formerly done; whilst the Moors continued to wonder at their constancy, admitting that all the force they had used had been wasted, for the lads' hearts had never been conquered. When the father of the children heard these things, he refused food for three days, and sent one of his personal attendants to find out the meaning of all that had happened. The Fathers wrote to him bidding him beware of a continuance of the attack on himself which the King had commenced before he set out from Agra. The Armenian bravely replied that he was ready to behave in such a manner as would cause the Moors to respect the Christian faith. But the King, as if nothing unusual had taken place, resumed his former friendly attitude towards the Armenian and his children and the other Christians, and even dispatched some business on behalf of the Fathers with every sign of good will. But he never gave them an opportunity of speaking about the Armenian children.

CHAPTER III

SOME CONVERTS TO THE FAITH

TOUCHING the fruits of this Mission, the number of new Christians made was small. This was partly because few persons asked to be baptised, and partly because the Fathers could place so little reliance on the people of this Moor-ridden land that to convert them was like building with worm-eaten timber.

In Agra about twenty persons were baptised. These included the family of a highly respected Armenian, who had lived many years amongst the Moors, far from all Christian intercourse. [When a Father happened to pass through his neighbourhood, the Armenian, though he went to see him with his present, entreated him not to visit him; and he told other Armenians that if the Father came there, he would pretend not to know him.][1] This was apparently on account of his relatives and neighbours, amongst whom he did not wish to be known as a friend of the Christians. Some years later, by the help of God, the Fathers prevailed on him to bring his family to Agra, where they could live amongst Christian people. He came with his wife and sons and daughters, who, together with most of his household, were baptised. He himself made confession and was married to his wife according to the rites of the Church, after living eighteen years as a Moor; so that we may count him amongst the converts as well as his wife and children. One of the latter, a little innocent girl, was called to our Lord soon after receiving baptism. Another case was that of a man who had for many years lived a Christian life, confessing and receiving communion with the Christians, but who, the Fathers discovered, had never been baptised. The rite was administered to him in secret, to his great consolation.

In the city of Lahor an aged Moor, a native of Baçora, became a Christian. He had been a man of importance in his own country; but after the Turks took Baçora he wandered from place to place seeking a livelihood. He went to Veneza and other Christian places, and at length found his way to Lahor, and meeting with the Fathers, begged them to make him a Christian. He importuned them much on account of his age; but the Fathers would not baptise him at once, and he left them, full of hope, to go to the lands which the late King had given him. It was not long before he returned, insisting more than ever that he should be baptised, for he was too old to wait longer. So the Fathers acceded to his request, though few were aware of his conversion, as he did not wish this to be made public. But he made another old man, who was his companion, promise that on his death he would not permit the Moors to touch his body, but that only the Fathers and the Christians should prepare it for the grave, and bury it with Christian rites. He would have done better had he publicly acknowledged his conversion. But so evil-minded are the Moors that he would have been unable to live with those of his house, had they known that he was a Christian. It is the fear of similar ill-usages that deters many from embracing our faith.

There lived near the Fathers a Brahman Gentile whose son, as has already been told,[2] had endured much through becoming a Christian. Now it happened that a daughter of the same Brahman fell sick, and her sister, seeing that she was near to die, began to mourn for her. The Father heard her cries, and not knowing what the matter might be, sent for her brother who was a Christian and told him to go to her. On learning the cause of his sister's lamentations, he persuaded his mother to allow the sick child to be made a Christian. She was accordingly brought to the church, and the Father baptised her. She died as she was being taken away, and her soul entered the abode of eternal bliss, of which her sister was the occasion, and her brother the instrument.

Many received help in their temporal as well as their spiritual necessities. Thus, five or six strangers who had come from Christian countries, and had been seized and held as captives by the Moors, were succoured by the Fathers, who obtained their liberation and sent them back to their homes. On another occasion, a young lad, who was in the service of a respectable Italian, ran away from his master in Sind, and became a Moor. Having come to Agra, where he failed to find the assistance he had hoped for, he was reduced to beggary. The Fathers came to know of him and gave him shelter in their house, where he remained quietly until an opportunity came for sending him on his way.

A certain Moor, a captain of high rank, had in his service two Cafres[3] who had come from a Christian land. He treated them well; but in spite of his indulgence they were not content to live amongst Moors. To induce them to settle with him, the Moor arranged marriages for them; but the day before these were to take place they made their escape and took refuge with the Fathers, who sent them from Agra to Lahor, from whence they travelled to Sind, and finally to Goa. On their way to Lahor they were recognised by some of the Moor's people; but they managed to defend themselves and put to flight those sent to apprehend them. At Lahor they lived like good Christians in the house of the Fathers; but they were again recognised by someone belonging to the Moor; so the Fathers concealed them in the house of a certain Portuguese Christian, until the time should arrive for them to depart. There was in the same house a certain man, a native of Goa, who, thinking he saw an opportunity of gaining the favour of the King, went to one of his Captains and told him about the two Cafres, saying that they were very clever fellows, and that one of them could play the organ and sing Portuguese music; and he offered to deliver them into his hands, which he actually did, luring them from the house by saying that the Fathers had called them. He led them, all unsuspecting, to a spot where a number of persons, some on foot and some on horseback, awaited them. By these they were taken under strong guard to the Captain, who in turn took them to the King. His Majesty at once took them into his service on very good terms. Nothing was said about their becoming Moors, so they remained in the Church, and lived with the Fathers. But the affair did not end here; for the Portuguese, in whose house the youths had been lodged, determined to punish him who had tricked them; and this they did, taking into account another of his misdeeds, which alone merited the good blows which they gave him, having tied him up securely to render his chastisement the more effective. One of his servants escaped through a window crying out that they were killing his master. His cries reached the ears of the Merinho Mor, who sent some of his men to the house, where they found the man still tied up. As soon as they had liberated him he vociferated loudly that his assailants meant to kill him and bury him secretly. He made them take the two who had beaten him into custody, and told them that it was the Fathers who had incited them to attack him. The Fathers were with the King on other business when the two men and their accuser were brought to the palace. The latter, on coming before the King, tore open his clothes from his belt upwards to show the marks of the blows he had received, while he poured forth with many tears a long tale of his wrongs, and ended by saying that the whole affair had been a plot of the Fathers, who had come to the house at midnight disguised in turban and cabaya, and that they had acted against him thus because of the two Cafres he had taken away and delivered to His Majesty. The King signed to the Fathers to speak. "Sire," they said, "ask these men if we have ever, up to this day, been to their house." But the other ceased to press his charge against the Fathers, seeing that the King paid little heed to what he said against them, and turning his attention to the two unfortunate captives, he said, to obtain the sentence he desired, "Sire, do justice to me in this matter, and I will become a Moor." On this, the King said, "I deliver them to you. You may do what you will with them, and I will make you a Captain." It would take long to describe the injuries and insults which the two Portuguese had to suffer in the streets at the hands of this mad fellow.

When the King retired, the Fathers were admitted to his presence. He laughingly asked them what it was the Feringhes were quarrelling about, and they told him all the circumstances. He expressed great surprise and said, "I did not understand the matter. Enquire into it well, and bring the man to me, and you shall see what I will do with him. Nevertheless they did wrong to beat him. They should have brought him to you for punishment, or to me. It was for this reason I handed them over to him, so that he in his turn might beat them." For such is the justice of this King and this land. The Fathers said that the two men had already been well punished, and begged the King to order their release, which, after some further enquiries, he did. They also requested that if this man brought any charges against them, he should be made to prove the truth of his words; and they added that, if proof were forthcoming, they would submit to whatever His Majesty should order. "Oh, you are in a different class," was the King's reply. "There is no need even to speak of it." Such is this King's opinion of the Fathers. As to that unholy man, the devil seemed to be in him; for in his determination to discredit and defame the Fathers, he circulated a thousand false stories about them; but these served only to enhance the good reputation of those against whom they were directed; for no one believed his words, and he became an object of general contempt, even the Moors declaring they would not have such a man in their sect. He heard nothing more of the promotion which had been promised him by the King.

The next day the King sent for the Fathers, and received them in an inner apartment to which very few are admitted. He enquired how many Christians there were, and whether there was much distress amongst them, and said that he would be very glad to contribute something towards the assistance of those who were in need. He also asked about the church, saying that he would like to come and see it, and that the Fathers must let him know when there was to be a festival; and when they told him that the church needed white-washing, and more pictures for its adornment, he promised to provide funds for both these purposes. Before taking leave of him, they showed him a version of the Gospels in Arabic in which he showed great interest, saying, however, that he would like still more to see a Persian translation of the same. The Fathers said that they had a copy of the Gospels in Persian, and that they would bring it to him. At this the King expressed much pleasure, so they revised the translation and presented it to him. This took place in the month of September, 1606.

CHAPTER IV

SOME EVENTS OF THE YEAR 1607[1]

THE King set out for Cabul,[2] taking with him his son, whom he still kept as a prisoner, though with less strictness than at first. When the Fathers went to take leave of him, he begged them to commend him to God. They presented him with a copy of the Holy Gospels in Persian, which he accepted very graciously. He would allow no one to hold it for him, but kept it in his hand until he withdrew. The Fathers passed their days as peacefully as though they lived in some secluded college, devoting themselves to their spiritual studies and the performance of their religious exercises, and celebrating with the other Christians the times and feasts of the Church.

This year, their commemoration of our Lord's Passion included, for the first time, a public procession of disciplinants, which took place on Maundy Thursday. One of the Christians, who had no suitable vestment, fashioned himself one out of his own garments, and joined the procession. Another, who had never been in a Christian country, nor was it known who had taught him, came forth with his arms bound to a large beam, as though it were a cross. The procession was headed by a crucifix, after which came a band of children singing litanies. The streets were crowded with Gentiles who gazed in astonishment on this new spectacle. They shuddered at the sight of the blood so willingly spilled, and, eager to see what the end would be, they continued to follow the procession while it made its circuit of the city and returned to the church. The Fathers and the Christians, greatly comforted by this act of penance, determined to repeat it with increased devotion year by year, in despite of the devil who could ill endure to see such a spectacle in a land which he looked upon as his own, and where he was so strongly entrenched. On the evening of Easter Day, the Fathers illuminated the roof of their church, where there is a terrace, with lamps and candles, and let off many kinds of fireworks, which they make very well in this country, and of great brilliancy. In the early morning there was another grand procession, headed by a cross adorned with roses and other flowers, and accompanied by musicians with hautboys, which they had learnt to play in Goa, having been sent there for that purpose; and as these instruments had never been heard or seen in the country before they attracted many people and caused much astonishment. The Christians followed the musicians, clad in festal garments and holding candles in their hands. The Fathers accompanied them wearing their surplices and singing their best as they marched along. One of them carried a very beautiful picture of the infant Jesus, which had come from Portugal. These novel scenes were watched by countless crowds of people, through which the small band of Christians moved as serenely and devoutly as though they were commemorating the triumph of Christ in the land of the most catholic of kings, instead of being surrounded by Moors and Gentiles, who would have rejoiced at their destruction.

These feasts were followed by that of Corpus Christi, on which occasion one of the Fathers carried through the streets the holy Sacrament enclosed in a glazed tabernacle under a canopy. A band of Christians surrounded him bearing torches and candles, while others followed, some playing on pipes and some singing, as they went in procession to the church. At one spot where the priest stopped, a little child, neatly clad, approached and kneeling down worshipped the holy Sacrament, declaring in a voice that all could hear his faith in the real presence of Christ the Saviour and Redeemer of the world; then standing up he recited a story about the Sacrament which took the place of a sermon, and gave great joy to the Christians.[8]

As to the two lads who had been forcibly circumcised, the King, seeing them one day at play with other children, called them to him and asked them whether they wished to be Moors, or to follow the law of their father. They answered that they would remain Christians; upon which the King, turning to his courtiers, said: "It is a bad thing not to follow the law of one's father. These lads through fear said that they were Moors; but they were really Christians." Then turning to the children he said: "Continue to follow your own law!" The lads made their salaams to the King, and ran eagerly to tell the Fathers, shouting as they went that they were Christians. Those who had been foremost in inciting the King against them did not escape punishment. One of them soon afterwards incurred His Majesty's displeasure and was deprived of all his revenues; and though a few months later he was restored to favour, he lived in a state of perpetual fear. Another, who was the greatest noble in the kingdom, and was for that reason called the King's brother, fell into a lingering illness and became paralysed in both legs. After a short time, the disease mounted to his head, and his memory became so bad that he forgot his own words, and repeated whatever he said again and again, as though he had never said it. On this account, the King's affection for him cooled, and at last he took from him the royal seal, together with his estates, revenues, and dignities, which he conferred on another, leaving him only a few lands for his maintenance, and he is now recovering with expectations very different from those which he once entertained.[4]

When the King was in Lahor, one of his courtiers told him that the King, his father, had given orders that a portion of the pension which he had granted to the Fathers who lived at Lahor should be withdrawn. His Majesty at once replied that the Fathers were to continue to receive the whole amount, which was fifty rupees a month. On another occasion, the Fathers reminded him of the alms he had promised for the Christians, whereon he ordered them to be given each month another fifty rupees, and, in addition, thirty rupees for the church. This enabled the Fathers to give assistance to many poor Christians.

The King at this time began to show himself much less of a Moor than at first. He declared it was his intention to follow in his father's footsteps; and his actions confirmed his words. God grant that his end may be better. He allowed the two young Cafres, who, as already mentioned, had been delivered to him, to remain with the Fathers and the Church, and also four pipers who had been sent from Goa. The latter had likewise been delivered over to him, the Venetian who was conducting them from Goa having died on the journey. Nevertheless, though he desired to keep them in his service, he contented himself with making them play before him; and even when some of his courtiers told him that these negroes had belonged to the late King, who had sent them to the Fathers for instruction, he did not compel them to stay with him, but only asked them if they were willing to do so, at the same time offering them good pay. When he saw that they preferred to go to the Fathers, and that they showed great constancy to their faith, answering well the questions he put to them, he ordered them to be handed over to the Fathers, who decided that, on His Majesty's return from his journey [to Cabul], they would present them to him for his service, so that they might earn their livelihoods, and at the same time serve the Church.

His Majesty continued to show himself worthy of the name, "The Just King,"[5] which he had taken at the commencement of his reign; so that there were no aggrieved parties throughout his dominions; and woe to that Governor or Captain who was found to have taken tolls or other things from the merchants who passed through the lands in his charge. At Lahor, one of the King's officers was stationed on the far side of the river, in order that he might conduct any merchants coming from Caxemir or Cabul to the royal palace, so that His Majesty might purchase from him whatever he wished, and enquire what things he desired to take from his country. When, on one occasion, this officer was found to have exacted some trifling toll, the King gave orders that his head was to be shaved, and that he was to be dragged, thus disgraced, through the streets of the city. The poor fellow has never shown his face since.

On another occasion it was found that the Governor of Ahmadabad, the royal city of Cambaya, who was a great Captain with an income of five hundred thousand rupees a month,[6] which is equal to two hundred thousand *crusados*, had, with his two sons, been guilty of many acts of tyranny. They were therefore, summoned to appear before the King at Lahor. The two sons arrived first, their father, they said, having been delayed by sickness. So, for a time, the King dissembled; but, as soon as the father appeared, he placed them all under arrest. He had the sons frequently beaten, sometimes in his own presence; and he kept the father in confinement until he had paid two hundred thousand rupees which he owed to the Crown, and had compensated all those whom it was proved that he had despoiled. Having thus punished him, he appointed him Governor of Lahor, where he lives in much reduced circumstances. The sons he continued to keep as prisoners.

To show that in the things of the law he was following in his father's footsteps, he issued, as the latter had done, a decree forbidding the eating of flesh on certain fixed days. During one of these periods of prohibition, he and his two sons, disguised as poor men, went by night into the city, where they saw in a certain quarter that meat was being sold. Knowing that this could only be with the connivance of the Merinho Mor, the King, early the next morning, sent for that officer and, after seeing him soundly flogged, caused him to be led with much dishonour through the streets of the city riding on an ass. A day or two later he again sent for him, and presented him with a horse and a dress as a sign of his restoration to favour, and reinstated him in his office.

He similarly pardoned and restored to favour the great Agiscoa [Aziz Khan Koka], the foster-brother of King Achebar, and a member of a very distinguished family. This noble had a very great revenue amounting to at least a million rupees, and his daughter was wedded to the eldest son of the King, who used to call him his uncle. It happened that one of His Majesty's Captains, whilst serving in the Deccan, found a letter which had been written by Agiscoa during the reign of the late King,[7] in which he reviled that monarch for forsaking the law of the Moors, which they call the law of salvation, and becoming a heretic. The Captain put this letter into the hands of the King, who one night asked his uncle if he had written it. On his confessing that the letter was his, the King flew into a violent rage, heaping a thousand curses on him and calling him a thousand bad names, while his courtiers, following his example, reviled him in like fashion; so that he, before whom all had been wont to tremble, was stunned by the indignities he was made to suffer. He was placed under a guard and brought twice each day to the palace, that he might hear the reproaches which the great lords, in their desire to please the King, heaped upon him. And this he felt the more, because, as is the way with those who have been accustomed to, or rather enslaved by worldly honours, he had never in his life dreamt that such misfortune could befall him. He now began to distribute huge sums in alms amongst the poor of his faith; indeed, it is generally believed that at this time he gave away more than a hundred thousand *crusados*. On account of these good works, God succoured him and caused the King to look on him with kindness. After some marks of indulgence, His Majesty restored to favour him whom he had so bitterly mortified, and they commenced to live on good terms as before. This story reminds us that even those who cross the waters of life on the highest bridges do not always remain dryshod.

And now, leaving the King, let us speak of the slender harvest which the Fathers gathered on the land of their sowing. A Hungarian Christian, more than a hundred years old, who in his youth had been made captive by the Moors amongst whom he had lived in various places with his sons and grandsons, seeing that his end was approaching, had all his household baptised, except one son who had not yet made up his mind to become a Christian. After receiving the sacraments, this good old man passed away with the Fathers at his bedside. At his burial there was a very imposing service in the church, which was a great consolation to the Christians, all of whom attended with candles in their hands. The service was also witnessed by many Moors and Gentiles, who were much impressed by the solemnity of the Christian rites, which, they confessed, far surpassed their own.

A certain Christian lady, belonging to a Moorish family of high rank, fell sick during the absence of her husband, and fearing she was about to die, sent for the Fathers. When they came to her, she showed them the shroud which she had made for herself before she fell sick, and the cloth which was to be placed on her bier, and which was afterwards to be given to the poor, together with whatever else she should leave them for that purpose. She then showed them the best of her clothes and ornaments, which she had set aside for her daughter; and having sent for the child, and also for her little sons, all of whom she had carefully instructed in the Christian faith, she said to the Fathers, "Look upon them not as mine, but as yours! I leave them in your hands, to do with them what you will. I do not entrust them to my brothers or sisters or other relations, because all of them are Moors. I know only the Fathers; and to them I entrust my soul, my children, and all that I possess." After the children had been dismissed, she made confession, and said that it was her intention to go to the church the next day to communicate. When the palanquin in which she was carried to the church was opened, she was discovered speechless and unconscious, with her lips closed. Seeing her in such a condition, the Fathers were preparing to administer extreme unction when, by God's will, she came to herself. As soon as the service began, she insisted on being taken from the palanquin; and when those who stood around hesitated to move her, she attempted to raise herself; so they lifted her out of the palanquin and placed her on the ground with a pillow to support her head. At the time of the elevation of the Lord, she threw aside the pillow; and when they brought the Lord for her to communicate she received it with the same faith and reverence as the other communicants. From that moment she began to regain strength. As she left the church she said: "I thank God for the grace He has bestowed on me, and the Fathers for their trouble." And she returned to her house and was cured.

Sickness also overtook the infant son of a certain Christian, who, finding his remedies unavailing, brought the child, whom he dearly loved, to the church. One of the Fathers, who had in his possession a relic of the blessed widow Margarilla de Chaves, placed this in a little water which he gave to the child to drink, at the same time commending him to the Saint. In a few moments the little sufferer showed signs of recovery, his fever abated, and the happy father, giving thanks to God, took him back to his home.

Amongst those who were baptised during this year was the son of a certain Moor of high position. This young man also fell ill, and when it became evident that he was dying, a Christian, who was a friend of his father, came to see him, under the pretext of giving him some remedy, which, indeed, he did, but it was the remedy which bestows eternal life, for, having taken with him a little holy water, he straightway, and without the father being aware of what he did, baptised the young man, who, two or three days later, died and went to heaven, where he joined his two brothers, who some years previously had been baptised under similar circumstances by the same Christian. About this time, some other children, who had been sold by their parents for trifling sums, were also baptised. One of these cost but a quarter of a *larin*,[8] which is equivalent to a *tostao*.

The Fathers often went on Fridays to the mosques of the Moors, where they discoursed to the Moorish doctors on the teaching and life of Christ our Lord. The Moors heard them attentively until they began to confute the law of Mafamede, when they lost all patience, refusing either to listen, or to be drawn into a disputation.

CHAPTER V

THE FATHERS ACCOMPANY THE KING TO AGRA[1]

THE Mission to Mogor was still in the hands of the four Fathers of our Company who had gone there some years previously,[2] and who continued to labour and to bear their life of exile with patience and hope: with patience, because the fruit of their labours was as yet small in comparison with their desires, so dense is this Moorish forest that it seems impossible to penetrate, or even to enter it: and with hope, because of the good-will of the King; for they felt that, with the benevolent protection of so powerful a monarch, they need not despair of a rich harvest in the future.

The King remained for some months in Cabul. The Fathers did not accompany him on this expedition, but remained all four of them at Lahor, where during his absence they enjoyed much spiritual peace, performing the services of the Church and ministering to the Christians with as much security as if they had been in some catholic city of Europe. On the King's return,[3] they went forth two leagues from the city to welcome him. His Majesty received them with marked kindness, stopping his horse for some moments, as did also his sons and all the others. He greeted them after his usual manner by placing his hands on their shoulders, and enquired very kindly after their welfare. The Fathers presented him with a book which they had composed, containing the lives of the Apostles in Persian, with numerous pictures of their labours [*registros de seus passos*],[4] a gift which he greatly appreciated.

After his arrival at Lahor, the King decided to send an ambassador to the Viceroy of India, and selected as his representative an officer of very high authority. He also summoned the Fathers, and having told them of his decision, said that he would be very glad if one of their number, to be selected by themselves, could accompany his ambassador. The Fathers could not refuse to comply with this request. Moreover, it was to the advantage of the Mission that one of its members should proceed to Goa;[5] so they made arrangements accordingly, their choice falling on Father Manoel Pinheiro.[6] They set forth without delay, and were already in India, but had not arrived at Goa.

The embassy had for its object nothing more than the maintenance of friendly relations with the State, while the ambassador was instructed to bring back with him any rare and curious objects he could procure in India from the Portuguese.[7] The King entrusted Father Pinheiro with numerous presents to be given in his name to the Fathers in India; and he also provided the Fathers at Lahor with gifts to send to their friends at Goa.

It was just before Christmas that the embassy left Lahor.[8] The Fathers who remained behind celebrated the festival with all the devotion possible. They decorated their church so splendidly that even the Moors could not help saying how different it was from their own mosques. On the altar there was a small manger so beautifully made that it attracted large numbers of people to the church. The King did not come to see it himself, but he sent some choice candles of white wax to be burnt before it, and some of his own beautiful pictures to add to its adornment. This was highly appreciated by the Christians, though it gave offence to many of the Moors. All the Christians made confession at this festival, and attended the midnight mass [*missa do Gallo*],[9] which was celebrated with singing and the playing of flutes and shawms [*charamelas*].[10] Before the service commenced, amidst the din of tambourines and drums [*com grande estrondo de atambores & atabales*],[11] there was a display of fireworks in the 'compound' of the church, which was seen from a long distance. These things could not have been done more openly in a Christian country; and that they took place in an infidel city in the heart of this Moorish land, must be accounted a thing greatly to the glory of our Lord, and the exaltation of our holy faith.

Amongst the many respectable Moors who came to see the fireworks was one who refused to go away until he had attended the service of matins, which on this occasion was choral, one verse being sung, and the next accompanied by the music of flutes. After he had been present throughout the service, and the sermon which followed it, he was politely asked to withdraw, as mass was about to be celebrated. He very courteously complied, but a moment or two later returned, and, without the Fathers knowing it, was present throughout the celebration. He was so much impressed by what he saw that he went to the Fathers and said that he was at heart a Christian, and that they must therefore permit him to attend their prayers and divine services. Since then, though he has not yet been baptised, he has displayed great affection and respect for the Christians.

After Christmas, the King announced his intention of going to Agra, which is the second royal seat of his empire, and he informed the Fathers that it was his desire that one of them should remain in Lahor, and that the other two should accompany him on his journey, and he gave orders that they were to be supplied with a horse and four camels to carry their effects. The King set out first,[12] accompanied, according to custom, by his army. On his way he devoted himself to hawking, and hunting with cheetas and other animals, as well as shooting with bow and arrow. His progress was consequently very slow, so that the Fathers, who set out some time later, overtook him in a few days. On one occasion, to make a feast for them, he sent to their tent on an elephant two large boars which he had killed himself. As it was Shrove-tide, this gift was very welcome to them and those with them. Eight or ten days later, he called them to his tent where they found him surrounded by his Captains. He showed them fifteen boars and a number of deer which he had slain that day, and told them that they might take as much meat as they pleased. They thanked him for his kindness, and told him that what he had sent them before had come at a very opportune time; but now they could not make themselves a feast as they had entered upon the season of Lent, during which Christians do not eat flesh. He then asked many questions about Lent, and the manner of fasting amongst Christians, showing great interest in all that they told him about these things. During the remainder of their journey the Fathers observed the season of penitence in a very real manner; for as they could not eat flesh, their fare consisted solely of lentils and rice, which they were obliged to take at night after reaching their encampment, for the whole day was spent in travelling, so that they had no opportunity to prepare their scanty meal. But more than all, they suffered from lack of water; for the King's army fouled every pool, tank, or stream to which they came, so that throughout their journey they only drank when necessity or sheer thirst compelled them. It was only by God's mercy that they obtained even such water as this. Nevertheless, in spite of these difficulties, they reached Agra safely, a month and a half after their departure from Lahor.

After the King had captured the Prince, his son, as we have narrated in a previous chapter, he took him on all his journeys as a prisoner, with chains on his feet, and carried in a cage on the back of an elephant. It was thus that he now took him from Lahor to Agra; and on reaching the spot where the battle between them had taken place, to punish his son for his disobedience, he caused him to be blinded by the application to his eyes of the juice of certain herbs, which had the appearance of milk.[13] He did the same to a great Captain who had formerly been his close favourite, but who had joined in a conspiracy against his life. This Captain, whom he took about with him heavily manacled, and riding on a meanly harnessed mule or ass, he caused to be blinded on the same spot, and in the same manner as the Prince.

On arriving at Agra, the Fathers installed themselves in the house and church which they had there, which was the same church that the King, when Prince, had ordered them to build,[14] and occupied themselves in ministering to the small Christian community which had grown up in that place. But of more importance were the discussions which here took place before the King, and of these an account will be given in the following chapters.

CHAPTER VI

The Fathers Dispute with the Moors before the King

The Fathers had long been anxious for an opportunity of disputing with the Moors before the King, that they might demonstrate the truth of our faith, and the falseness of the law of Mafamede. This opportunity they found soon after the King had settled down at Agra, and it extended over more than a month, during which many notable disputes took place. In these the Moors were completely defeated by the Fathers; and though they were not converted, for their obstinacy and perversity would not allow them to admit the truth of our faith, nevertheless the same was made manifest, to the great glory of Christ our Lord.

The occasion arose out of the pleasure which the King took in looking at the coloured pictures of sacred subjects which the Fathers, knowing his interest in these things, had presented to him. It happened one evening that he called for a number of these, and finding he did not understand them, sent for the Fathers that they might explain them to him. It happened that the first picture which he showed them was one of David on his knees before the prophet Nathan, who had just uttered the words, *Dominus transtulit peccatum tuum a te.* The Father had scarcely begun his explanation of the picture when a Moorish Captain who was present interrupted him, and began to relate the version of the story which is found in the Alkoran. Seeing that this contained many untruths, the Father begged the King to allow him to repeat the story as it is written in the holy Scriptures, which, on receiving His Majesty's permission, he proceeded to do. The Moors listened to him until he began to speak of David's adultery with Bathsheba, when they cried out, "It is a lie! It is a lie! The prophets never sinned, and could not sin." "What!" said the Father. "Do you not admit that David wept?" "Yes!" they replied. "But it was not because he had been guilty of adultery, but of homicide." "Then," said the Father, "if you admit that he was guilty of homicide, it is manifest that he sinned, which is contrary to what you have just said, that the prophets did not, and could not sin. You cannot deny that he who commits one kind of sin may commit another. Moreover, David, you say, had the desire to sin, which means that in the eyes of God he did sin; for the desires of the heart are as manifest to Him as the works of the hand are to us. Again, if the angels, whose natures are perfect, and who are endowed with so many natural and supernatural gifts, are not without sin, how much less were the prophets without sin, who were but men. And more than all, how can you deny of David what he so many times confessed of himself in his psalms, never ceasing to lament the sins he had committed against God?" The Moors were put to complete confusion by the Father's words, and were unable to make any reply.

Amongst those in attendance on the King was a

very grave and learned man whose duty was to read to His Majesty before he retired to rest at night, or when he took his ease during the day-time; an office very similar to that of the person referred to in the Book of Esther, whose business it was to read aloud to King Ahasuerus the chronicles of his kingdom. The old King, the father of him who is now reigning, had held this man (who had served him in the same capacity) in great esteem, partly on account of his learning, and partly because he was of the lineage of the Prophet. He was also well versed in all branches of history.[1] When the Father had concluded his arguments, the Reader, who was present on the occasion, said, "Sire, the versions of the Gospels, the Psalms, and the Books of Moses which the Christians possess are all corrupt." "That is not so, Sire," said the Father, "for the Christians would give up their lives a hundred thousand times rather than allow a single word of their holy Scriptures to be altered." Another Moor then said, "I can well believe, Father, that such a thing has never been done by you, or your predecessors, or by the people; but your Kings do it." Again the Father said, "That is not true! Our Kings," he added, "do not interfere either with our law or our Scriptures, which they respect and obey like all others."

The King spoke next, asking the Fathers to enlighten him on various points. Though it cannot be said that he spoke with kingly gravity, his questions deserve to be recorded, seeing that they were asked by so great a monarch, and were evidently meant to put our faith in a favourable light. Moreover, they serve to show his genuine interest in religious matters, and also the good which resulted from these disputes.

"What do the Christians say of Mafamede?" was his first question.

"They say," was the reply, "that he was a man who took upon himself the rôle of a prophet."

"Then he was not a prophet?"

"That is true, Sire."

"In other words, he was a false prophet?"

"Yes, Sire."

At this the King laughed.

"Tell me," he said once again, "was Mafamede a false prophet?"

"Yes, Sire," said the Father, "he was a false prophet."

Now all this the King did to bring ridicule on Mafamede, and on his Moorish courtiers, who, during this conversation, stood grinding their teeth with rage against the Fathers. At last the King's Reader, unable any longer to restrain himself, came forward and said, "The Fathers speak falsely. For Mafamede is mentioned in their own Gospel, where it is stated that he will come a second time into the world."

"Is that so?" asked the King, turning to the Fathers.

"No, Sire," was the reply. "The Gospel tells us that no true prophet will come into the world with a new law until the day of judgment."

The King expressed great astonishment at these words, and made the Father repeat them several times, after which he again asked him if he regarded Mafamede as a prophet.

"No, Sire, I do not," replied the Father, repeating these words also over and over again.

Upon this, the King's Reader altered his demeanour. He said that it was wrong to liſten to such things, and that he who did so was an unbeliever; and so saying, he withdrew in anger, and was not seen again that night.

The following evening the King reopened the discussion by again asking the Father in loud tones what he thought of Mafamede, adding that his Reader was very angry with him on account of what he had heard him say, though there was much truth in his words. The Father replied as on the previous evening; whereon the King, who seemed to delight in hearing evil spoken of their prophet, beckoned to his Reader, who had kept himself at a diſtance, saying, "Come here, Nagibuscao" (for such was his name). "Do you hear what the Fathers say, that Mafamede is a false prophet?"

"Such men," said the Moor, "ought to be put to death rather than liſtened to." And with that he ſtopped his ears and haſtened away.

This greatly diverted the King, who laughed and slapped his thighs with merriment, at the same time calling to his Reader to come back.

"Sire," said the Father, "this queſtion is one to be settled by discussion and sound reasoning, not by the threats and calumnies of Nagibuscao."

"The Father speaks truly," said the King. "So

now, Nagibuscao, prove to us that Mafamede was a prophet."

Thus called upon, the Reader proceeded to narrate a number of stories and other nonsense from the Alkoran; and after he had spoken for some time, the King stopped him, and told the Father to answer him. The latter replied that all these stories were false; and he was proceeding to support his words by argument, when a Moorish Captain interposed and said, "We cannot prove anything by these stories, because the Christians do not hold our stories to be true." Then, in support of his own faith, he narrated a miracle which they ascribe to Mafamede, which is, that the moon once fell to the earth and was broken to pieces, and that Mafamede put it together again, and passed it through his sleeve.[2] The Moor seemed to think that this was the last word, and that no further vindication of his prophet could possibly be required. The King asked the Father what he had to say to it. The Father answered that it was a prodigious lie. "For Your Majesty knows well," he said, "that the moon is so great that, if it had fallen from the sky, it would have overwhelmed not only the kingdoms of Indostan and India in the East, but many parts and kingdoms of Europe, where there would undoubtedly be some record of the occurrence, had it ever taken place in the manner described; for it would have been the greatest marvel in the history of the world, and even the enemies of Mafamede would have to describe it as an amazing miracle. But as the Moors are the only people in the world who have heard tell of it, it is manifeſt that it is a ſtory of their invention. The moon, you say, was small when it reached the earth. To this we reply that whatever it may have been that gave rise to this ſtory, it was not the real moon, which could not dislodge itself and fall from the heavens, but that it was a delusion and a trick by means of which Mafamede sought to impose on the world."

This reasoning ſtrongly appealed to the King, who turned to those present and repeated what the Father had said. Many opinions were then expressed, now on this side, now on that. The King liſtened to all who spoke, and the Father answered their arguments, His Majeſty always appearing satisfied with his words. At laſt, one of the Captains said, "Our difficulty is that the Fathers are not to believe in our books, but we are to believe in theirs. How is it possible for us to dispute with them?" Another was about to speak when a third Captain ſtopped him, saying, "Do not join issue with these, who are very clever and possess much knowledge." There was also a Gentile Captain present, to whom the King now turned, asking him if he regarded Mafamede as a prophet. "Sire," was the reply, "how can I know anything of Mafamede?"

"Do you regard him as a false prophet?" asked the King.

The Gentile, perceiving that it pleased His Majeſty to ridicule Mafamede, replied, "Yes, Sire! He is a false prophet," at which the King laughed exceedingly.

Whilſt these things were taking place, a young

noble was carrying on a conversation with one of the Fathers who stood near him, asking him various questions about Christ, and also speaking against the King for mocking at Mafamede. His Majesty looked at him, and, bidding him approach, asked him what he was saying to the Father. Trembling with fear, the young man replied that he was speaking of the Lord Jesus. Distrusting his reply, the King turned to the Father and asked him what the youth had said. The Father made the best of it, and said that he was speaking of Christ our Saviour.

"Very well," said the King, "let us hear you dispute with the Father."

The poor young man, not knowing what to do, said, "Sire, I am only a youth, and he is a learned man. How can I dispute with him?" He asked the Father if Christ was the Son of God, and then stopped, unable to proceed any further. However, a short time afterwards he went to the Father and thanked him for not telling the King he had spoken ill of him, begging him never to let this be known, as it would surely lead to his destruction. After this he took every opportunity of showing his gratitude. Indeed, he was so frequently in conversation with the Father that one of his relations, who was the chief of the King's nobles, rebuked him, saying, "Why do you, who scarcely know your A.B.C., converse and dispute with those who are a very sea of learning?" None the less, the young man, though he spoke little to the Fathers in public, continued to visit them in secret, enquiring often about the mysteries of our law, which, being a youth of much intelligence, he learnt to understand very well.

These disputes about Mafamede were soon talked of throughout the city, and the Moors began to regard the Fathers with intense hatred, following them with evil looks wheresoever they went, *stridebant dentibus in eos*, so that each time they returned by night from the King's palace to their own house, they prepared themselves for what they so earnestly desired, namely, death for confessing Christ. But God did not permit the sons of darkness to work their will; for it seemed to be His purpose still to use the Fathers for the greater manifestation of the light of the world, and the glory of His only Son. It is very remarkable, the good Fathers write, how these Moors close their ears to whatever is said against Mafamede. They will listen to all that is told them of our faith; but this is the one thing they cannot endure; and if it were not for their fear of the King, we should have died a thousand times. To have a further opportunity of speaking of these things, they went one Friday to a large mosque. The Moors at first listened, but when it was said of Mafamede that he was not a prophet, they would not hear another word, but arose and departed, saying that it was wrong to listen to such men.

CHAPTER VII

A Dispute on the Divinity of Christ

One evening, the King was looking through a portfolio containing the pictures of which we have already made mention, while the Fathers stood by him explaining their meaning. Presently he came upon one representing Jesus Christ crucified, which the Fathers, when he handed it to them, adored with great reverence, removing their caps and placing it on their heads. After they had explained the picture, a Moor who was present asked them why, if they and the Christians loved Christ so much, they permitted him to be represented thus dishonoured. One of the Fathers replied, " By keeping Him before our eyes in this form, we do Him the highest possible honour, because He suffered thus not for His fault, but for our sake, of His own free will giving up His life to expiate our sins, and to teach us to give up our lives for Him. Whenever we think of this, our hearts are filled with gratitude to Him, and we are never weary of gazing upon Him thus upon the cross. For if," the Father continued, " one of your Majesty's vassals, in order to preserve your life, voluntarily submitted to torture and ignominy, you would consider that you were showing him the highest respect by recounting the sufferings he endured for your protection; and the contemplation of them would stir you to gratitude and to honour him and his children.

How much more then ought we to be grateful to our God and Lord who created us, that being God, He became man and suffered persecution and shame to save us who so little merit salvation. Are we not bound to love Him with all our hearts, and to be ready to lay down our lives for Him? That such is our duty there can be no question; and hence it is that the most beloved representation which we have of our Lord in life is that which shows Him, as here, on the cross; and so highly do we esteem it, that if we were to see, side by side, our Lady the Virgin Mary and the image of Christ crucified, we should do reverence to the latter before doing reverence to the Virgin."

"Do you mean," said a Moorish Captain, "before doing reverence to an image of the Virgin, or before doing reverence to the Virgin herself?"

"Before doing reverence to the Virgin herself," replied the Father.

That is not reasonable," said the Moor.

"Do not be astonished," said the Father, "for we do not venerate these pictures because of the materials of which they are made, which we know are nothing more than paper or cloth and some colours, but because of that which they represent, which is the person of our Lord Jesus Christ. In the same way you do not place the firmans of His Majesty the King on your head because they are sheets of paper with ink on them; but because they represent the commands of His Majesty and what it is his will that you should do."

The King heard the Father quietly and with approval,

observing, when he had finished, that he had reasoned very justly. But the Moorish Captain said, "If Jesus Christ died on a cross with so much ignominy, how can you say that he was God?" This led to a discussion on the divinity of Christ, a subject which always provokes the Moors to anger. As the King was as yet unable to comprehend such matters, lacking the light of the true faith, and being anxious, as it seemed, to explain or qualify the Christian doctrine, said by way of defending it, "The Fathers, in calling Christ God, use, as it were, a figure of speech, meaning thereby to show their great love for him. In just the same way I may call any one of whom I am very fond my brother, or my soul, though, in fact, the person is nothing of the kind. In the same way the Christians call Christ God because they love him, though he is not so in reality." This was his answer to all the instances and proofs which the Fathers brought forward. He held forth with so much impetuosity that the latter could not get a word in, though they repeatedly begged to be allowed to speak. At length, to pacify them, he said, "Leave it to me, Fathers! I am on your side."[1] And continuing he said, "As to their calling Christ the Son of God, that is because he had neither father nor country, and was miraculously born of the Virgin Mary." Here one of his courtiers interrupted him by saying, "In the same way, Sire, we might call the worms that are engendered in the flesh the sons of God, for they have no country." "That is unreasonable," said His Majesty, "for these are creatures which live only four days, and have no qualities for which they can be called sons of God." Then, evidently very proud of his oration, he asked the Fathers if his explanation of their doctrine was not correct. They told him that it was not, at which he was a good deal annoyed, as he had been endeavouring to speak in their defence. But the subject was a grave one, and the Fathers could not dissimulate. He asked them if they had understood what he had said. They replied that they had, and repeated the words he had used.

"Then what do you say to it?" he asked.

"We say," replied one of the Fathers, "that Jesus Christ was the actual Son of God, and that He is in very truth God."

"Is that in the Gospels?"

"Yes, Sire."

At this point, one of the Moors said, "If Jesus Christ had done miracles which no other ever did, one might say that he was God. But all the miracles which he performed were also performed by others; so you have no reason to call him God." The Fathers disposed of this argument by instancing many miracles which were performed by our Lord and by no others.

The King asked if, in the Gospels, Christ said of himself that he was God.

"Many times," was the reply; whereon the King repeated his favourite argument, that the Fathers said this because of their great love for him.

"Sire," said a courtier, "what you say is very reasonable; but these people will never confess as much. They do nothing but say that Christ is actually

God. Ask the Father, and Your Majesty will see what he says."

"There is no need to ask them," said the King. "They cannot help speaking of Christ in this manner because of their love for him. If they were threatened with death they would still say the same, because they have consecrated their lives to him."

"Sire, not only these who are consecrated to him, but all the Christians say the same. How do you explain this?"

"It is," said the King, "because they are all, from their infancy, brought up to love the Lord Jesus Christ, and to believe that he is God. Nor is this very strange. Here in our own mountains there are, as you know, certain Darures (a class of devotees who profess to serve God) who, after drinking two cups of *Bange*,[2] which is a kind of beverage that gives pleasure while it destroys the senses), begin to perform such feats and antics that all the people run after them and acclaim them saints. If we were to see anyone raise the dead as easily as did Jesus Christ, there is no doubt that we should call him a god. And if I who have not seen the miracles which Christ did, love him much only because I have heard of them, and commend all my affairs to him,[3] why is it surprising that those who with their own eyes saw him raise the dead, called him God?"

All his nobles applauded these words, saying that the King had spoken truly, and that they were heathens [*sem ley*] who did not believe in Jesus Christ [*que não criam a Jesu Christo*].[4]

CHAPTER VIII

THE KING'S REVERENCE FOR JESUS CHRIST

THROUGHOUT the discussions of which we have spoken, the King always showed his deep regard for Christ our Lord. He also spoke very strongly in favour of the use of pictures, which, amongst the Moors, are regarded with abhorrence; and on coming from Lahor, and finding his palaces at Agra very beautifully decorated and adorned both inside and outside with many pictures which had already been completed, and others that were being painted, in a balcony [*varanda*] where he sits daily to be seen by the people—:[1] nearly all these pictures were of a sacred character, for in the middle of the ceiling there was a painting of Christ our Lord, very perfectly finished, with an aureola, and surrounded by angels; and on the walls were some small pictures of the Saints, including John the Baptist, St. Antony, St. Bernadine of Sena, and some female Saints. In another part were some Portuguese figures of large size, also very beautifully painted. On the outside of the wall, where is the window at which the King sits when he shows himself to the people, there had been painted life-size portraits of some of his favourites; but these he ordered to be obliterated, and in place of them he had painted a number of Portuguese figures, very well arranged, and of huge stature, so that they could be seen from all parts of the maidan [*por todo o terreiro*].

There were three figures on each side of the window. Above those on the right was a representation of Christ our Lord with the globe of the world in His hand, and on the left of our Lady the Virgin, copied from a painting by St. Luke; and to the right and left of these were various Saints in a posture of prayer. The window where the King sits, being in the form of an oriel [*charola*], every part of which is coloured, he had painted on the flanks of the same wall life-size portraits of his two sons very splendidly attired. Above one of them is a representation, on a smaller scale, of our Lord and a Father of the Company with a book in his hand, and above the other, of our Lady the Virgin. On the vault of the *charola* are pictures of St. Paul, St. Gregory, and St. Ambrose.[2]

It is a great consolation to the Fathers, when they come here to wait upon the King, to tell their beads before the picture of our Lady, and to commend themselves to Christ our Lord; and they give constant thanks to God that these sacred pictures, which fill the Moors with astonishment every time they look upon them, are thus publicly displayed in this infidel King's chamber, which resembles the balcony [*varanda*] of a devout Catholic King rather than of a Moor.

In the interior of the palace the walls and the ceilings of the various halls are adorned with pictures illustrating the life of Christ, scenes from the Acts of the Apostles, copied from the Lives of the Apostles which the Fathers had given him, and the stories of SS. Ana and Susana and many other Saints. All this the King did of his own accord, without a suggestion from anyone. He himself selected, from his own collection of pictures, the figures to be painted; and he ordered his artists to consult the Fathers as to the colours to be used for the costumes, and to follow their instructions in every detail.

The King's way of decorating his palace was very offensive to the Moors, who regard pictures of all kinds with such disfavour that they will not tolerate portraits of their own saints, much less those of the Christian faith, which they hate so bitterly. As they deny altogether the passion of our Lord, they greatly resented a large picture, a copy of a painting of Christ *a coluna*, which the King had made at this time. It was his intention that this should serve as a pattern for a curtain [*pano*] which he had ordered to be made of pure silk, and on which were to be woven, as on arras, the same figure of Christ *a coluna*, with the inscription, worked in a like manner, in Persian characters.[3] On a wall of one of the halls he had painted figures of the Pope, the Emperor, King Philip, and the Duke of Savoy, whose portraits he possessed, all on their knees adoring the holy cross, which was in their midst, as in a picture which he had.

The Father Ioão Aluares, Assistant of Portugal, sent His Majesty from Rome a picture of our Lady and the Adoration of the Magi. It would be difficult to say how greatly he prized this picture. As it reached him direct, without passing through the hands of the Fathers, he sent for them as soon as he received it, and having shown it to them in the presence of his courtiers, asked them to explain its meaning. When they had done so, he repeated what they had said to those present, telling the story of the birth of our Lord and the Adoration of the Magi just as though he were a preacher in a pulpit, holding up the picture the while that all might see it. Afterwards he sent it to the Fathers to be suitably adorned and mounted on a board [*sobre hua tauoa*],[4] that it might not become damaged by being constantly unrolled. The Fathers decorated the border which surrounded the picture with ornamental designs in black and white, copied from some of our books and paintings. The King was delighted with their work, and had his own portrait inserted in the design, himself choosing the place for it.

By means of these pictures, and what the Fathers have told him about them, the King is well versed in most of the mysteries of Christ our Lord and our Lady the Virgin, and openly prides himself on his knowledge. One evening when the Fathers were with him, he took up a picture of the Circumcision of our Lord, and making a sign to them not to speak, asked some of his nobles if they knew what it meant; and when they said that they did not, he explained it to them, and then asked the Father if what he had said was correct. On being told that it was, he was greatly pleased, and said: "I understand these things very well." In brief, so high is his esteem for Christ and our Lady, that all the orders and letters which he sends, whether to Moors, Gentiles, or Christians, though bearing on the inside the royal signet, are sealed on the outside with their effigies. For he has an instrument like a small forceps made of gold, on the points of which are set two emeralds, square in shape and as large as the nail of the thumb, on which are engraved the figures of our Lord and the Virgin, and these are impressed on the wax with which the letters are fastened.[5]

By these and other signs one cannot but recognise the sincere devotion of this King to Christ and our Lady, for whom he himself confesses his great love. And though the fruit the Fathers so earnestly desire to gather has not yet matured, he daily gives them new grounds for hoping that the good Jesus and his most holy Mother will look with compassion upon him, and bestow on him that which he lacks. Moreover, he is a man who, having once formed a resolution, does not shrink from carrying it out before the whole world; so that his determination to join our faith would be a splendid consummation, for it would doubtless lead to the establishment of a great Christian stronghold in these parts.

But while he has so high a regard for Christ and the holy Virgin, and for all that appertains to the Christian faith, he is held back by the severe discipline which our law imposes, and more than aught else because it forbids a man to take more than one wife, which is a stumbling-block not only to the Moors, but to all the Gentiles of the East; indeed it is, as they themselves say, on account of this prohibition that they find our faith so hard to accept. The King, who often discussed the subject with the Fathers, mentioned it on one of those evenings when they were disputing with the Moors. In reply to his remarks, one of the Fathers said that to overcome the difficulty of which he spoke, all that a man had to do was to embrace the law of Christ; for God would thereupon endow him with such grace that what before seemed difficult to him would be made easy.

"Sire," interposed one of the Moors, "the Father speaks thus now; but a short while ago he proved the contrary with the example of David, who though a great prophet, and possessing so many wives, nevertheless sinned."

"The sin of David," said the Father, "is an example of human frailty. Moreover, in David's day, the law of Christ had not been established, and men had not experienced the great strength of the divine grace. But since Christ came into the world, and gave us His holy law, the efficacy of that grace has been proved by the number of Christian kings, and the millions of other Christians scattered over the whole world, who have lived, or are still living, content with one wife."

"What you say is very well," said the King; "but allowing that this thing is difficult, and that if it were not so we should all be ready to embrace your law, I ask you—If a King like me, who has many wives, should desire to become a Christian, what would you have him do?"

"His Majesty means, Father," interposed a Moorish Captain, "any king whatsoever."

"I do not mean," His Majesty said, "such a king as I am; but one who like myself is a king. What would you say to him?"

"The first thing I should say, Sire," replied the Father, "would be that out of his many wives he must select one, and leave the rest."

"That would not be an easy matter," said the King. "But supposing he is left with only one wife, what, I ask you, is he to do if she is blind?"

"Let him not marry the one who is blind; but choose another."

"But suppose she becomes blind after marriage!"

"That presents no difficulty; for blindness does not prevent the act of marriage."

"That is true enough," said the King, "but the heart would not be drawn to her."

"And suppose," said one of the Moors, "that after marriage she becomes a leper!"

"Then," replied the Father, "it would be necessary to have patience."

"Oh, that would be impossible!" said the King.

"It would be possible, Sire, with the aid of God's grace, which makes all things easy."

"I do not doubt," the King said, "that to you, who have been accustomed from childhood to abstain from women, it would be easy; but those who are not like you—what are they to do?"

"Sire, even with custom such things are not without difficulty; and amongst Christians, too, sins are committed. But for this, the law of Christ our Lord provides the remedy of penitence."

"And what penitence," asked the King, "is required of those who sin against the law of chastity?"

This gave the Father the opportunity of discoursing

on the doctrines of penitence and grace, and the means which Christians use to overcome the temptations of the flesh. The Moors, being a carnal-minded race, disputed with him at great length, but the Father answered them in such a manner that though they did not admit defeat, they were convinced and put to shame by his words.

Amongst the Christians who are here, many things have been done in the service, and to the great glory, of our Lord. This is what befell a young Cafre Christian who was in the King's service, and who, by His Majesty's orders, lived in the house of an Abexim [Abyssinian] Moor, who was one of the royal favourites. One day the Moor sent for him and tried to make him abandon his faith, and pay homage to Mafamede. But the young man said he was a Christian, and that he would never do such a thing. The Moor first tempted him with soft words and fair promises, and then, finding these unavailing, sought to overcome him by blows, which were administered with such fierceness that the Cafre's *cabaia* was rent in pieces. He then attempted to seize the string of beads which he saw about his victim's neck; but the latter gripped them so tightly with his hands that he was unable to succeed. He next ordered fire to be brought, saying that he would burn the beads on his neck. "Do not make too sure," said the Cafre; "you shall burn me before you burn these," and when the Moor threatened to throw him on the fire, which had already been kindled, he answered: "You may do with me what you will; but I will never become a Moor." All who were standing by marvelled at his constancy, while his sufferings excited so much compassion that a water-carrier, indignant at what he saw, threw the water he was carrying on the fire and extinguished it. As the young man still showed no signs of yielding, the Moor put iron chains on him, and shut him up in his house like a prisoner.

When this came to the ears of the Fathers, one of them went straightway to the house. On entering the courtyard he encountered a Gentile who had witnessed all that had taken place, and who, on seeing the Father, exclaimed: "How bravely your Cafre bore himself, and what blows he endured in defence of his law! I swear that if they had done as much, or even less, to any Moor or Gentile, they could have made him submit to anything. What courage, what constancy he showed!" The Father then spoke to the Moor, with the result that the latter handed over to him his prisoner, who was in so weak and exhausted a state that he had great difficulty in walking to the Father's house. His tattered *cabaia*, and the marks of the stripes on his flesh, gave him comeliness in the sight of God, and in the eyes of the Fathers, who envied him not a little his triumph. One of them went at once to the palace to give an account of the affair to the King. At the entrance, he encountered the Moor, who, guessing the purpose that had brought him thither, begged his forgiveness, making a thousand excuses and apologies for his behaviour, and vowing that he would never do such a thing again. He pleaded so hard, while other nobles came up and pleaded for him, knowing that it would go hard with him if the affair came to the knowledge of the King, that the Father could not help yielding to their entreaties. He refrained from speaking to the King, and earned thereby the lasting gratitude of the Moor.

An Armenian belonging to a certain village had caused the death of a little Gentile girl. The father of the girl took him before the officers of justice and charged him with murder, and as soon as he had been put in prison, went his way. While he was in prison, a Moorish Captain came to see him, and sent others many times to him, promising him, in the King's name, his life and many rewards and favours, if he would abandon the Christian faith and accept the law of Mafamede. But this good Christian paid no heed to their allurements and remained true to his faith. At length he, and four others who were prisoners with him, were sentenced by the King himself to have their right hands cut off. The Merinho Mor sent for him, and he too promised to obtain his pardon if he would become a Moor. But then was fulfilled the promise of the Saviour of the world to those who, for His sake, are arraigned before the tribunes of princes and kings, "*Dabo vobis os, & sapientiã, &c.*"; for by no means could the Merinho Mor persuade him. When the hand of this brave soldier of Christ was placed on the block, and the executioner was ready to sever it at a blow, the Caciz even then offered to save him if he would accept his law. But the Armenian answered him angrily, and turning to the executioner, said: "Do your office. My choice is made: though I lose my life, I will not give up the faith which I profess." Seeing that he was wasting his time, the Caciz ordered the sentence to be carried out; and the Armenian's right hand, and the right hands of the four others, were cut off, after which they were taken back to prison.

As the Fathers were not allowed to enter the prison themselves, they sent one of their servants to minister to the brave Armenian. Such was the inhumanity of the Moors, that they showed no kind of pity for these mutilated victims of the law. No surgeon was called to stanch the blood which was flowing from their veins, and two of them bled to death. The Armenian was carefully tended by the servant of the Fathers, who made him plunge his arm in boiling oil, which stopped the flow of blood, after which he dressed it as well as he could. A day or two later, Father Xauier with great difficulty obtained his release from prison, and took him to his house where he was well looked after. The Father paid a surgeon to attend him, and provided sustenance for his wife and children as well as a house for them to live in; for when the Armenian was sent to prison, his property was confiscated by the State. But at this time he received news that his brother had died at Chaul in the house of the Santa Misericordia,[6] and had left him five thousand *larins*[7] (a *larin* is worth four *testons* of Portugal), with which sum he was able to repair his fortunes. Thus, by the death of his brother, our Lord recompensed him for rejecting pardon, freedom, and worldly honours, for His sake.

Another case was that of a Frenchman, a man of

many parts, who held an important post in the gun-foundry. Some years previously he had been captured by the Turcs in the Mediterranean Sea, not far from Marseilles, and had been taken to Argel [Algiers], where he was forced to become a Moor. Subsequently, while serving in the galleys of Argel, he was made a prisoner by the Christians and was confined in the convent of St. Francisco of Valenca, in Aragao. From here he contrived to escape; and after traversing Spain, Italy, Egypt, Ethiopia, and parts of India, found his way with his wife and children to Lahor and Agra, and the King took him into his service and made him a Captain of two hundred horse. He was very fond of telling the Moors about the Christians, and especially about the miracles of our Lady of Monseratte.[8] He spoke with such affection of the Christian faith that the Moors, amongst whom he had acquired considerable influence, were greatly impressed by his words. At Agra he fell sick; and as he had already become acquainted with Father Xauier, he sent for him and told him that he was a Christian, and that he had never found any satisfaction in the law of Mafamede. The Father exhorted him to make a general confession, telling him how this should be done, at the same time giving him a book in which he might study the Christian doctrines. He spent several days ministering to the spiritual needs of his patient, who was thus brought back to the holy Mother Church. He received the sacraments with devotion and tears of penitence, and passed from this life with every hope of salvation.

Our Lord was greatly glorified in this heathen capital, where all the people are His enemies and the King is an infidel, when on Maundy Thursday He was raised upon the cross and carried in procession through the streets of the city, before the very eyes of His enemies. The procession started from the church and was preceded by an officer of justice who had charge of those parts of the city through which it passed. He had others with him who cleared the way, and kept back all who attempted any interference. There was also a certain Captain who assisted in the same way. He came on an elephant, which he stopped as the procession approached, and watched the whole company file past him, marvelling to see the good order which the Christians kept, and the multitude of lights which they carried. One of the Fathers held aloft the holy crucifix, and another wearing the cope of the asperges,[9] chanted litanies to which the children of the *doutrina* responded. Amongst those who followed were twelve disciplinants, who scourged themselves until the blood ran down their bodies, a spectacle which greatly astonished the Moors, who had never seen the like before. After the procession was over, they were heard to say amongst themselves: "Are these the people we call heathens? We have nothing to compare with this."

On one occasion, Father Xauier brought to the King a rosary of walrus ivory [*cavallo marinho*][9] with a cross attached to it. This the King presented, as a mark of his favour, to one of his great Captains, who, being a Moor, removed the cross. Presently, the King, seeing the beads without the cross, asked the Captain what had become of it. "I removed it, Sire," he said, "because it is heavy, and because the Christians say that it is a representation of that on which Jesus Christ suffered, in whom we do not believe." This roused the King to such anger that he then and there deprived the Captain of his office, disgracing him in the eyes of all who were present. He afterwards banished him to Mecha.

CHAPTER IX[1]

The King Sends an Embassy to Goa

The Great Mogul had determined to send an ambassador to Portugal,[2] who was to take with him a present for His Majesty worth, it was said, two hundred thousand *crusados*, and another for the Pope. But certain reasons of state, combined with the advice of his councillors, led him to abandon his intention. He resolved, however, to send an embassy to the Viceroy of India, choosing as his representative a great Captain from Cambaya, named Mocarebecam [Muqarrab Khan],[3] whose advice he took in all important matters. This powerful lord had an income of fifty thousand *pardaos*, besides a hundred and fifty thousand which he received from the King. His Majesty asked Father Ieronimo Xauier, Superior of the Mission, to allow Father Manoel Pinheiro, who resided at Lahor, to accompany the Mission, to which he readily assented; and the Father set forth with the ambassador on the 13th September,[4] 1607.

They reached Cambaya in April, 1608; but as the Count de Feira, who had been newly appointed Viceroy, had not yet reached India,[5] the ambassador decided not to proceed at once to Goa, but to await in Cambaya the news of his arrival, that his embassy might receive a more distinguished reception.

During these days there came into the hands of the Father a picture of the Wise Kings,[6] which had been sent from Rome, and was on its way to the King. As it was a work of unusual excellence, the Father displayed it publicly in the church, placing it on the altar, which was beautifully decorated for the occasion. The fame of the picture soon spread through the city, and Moors and Gentiles alike flocked to see it, so that it was estimated that in the thirteen days during which it was on view no less than thirteen thousand persons visited the church. Many seemed unable to take their eyes off the picture, and had to be sent away to make room for others. To avoid a mixed crowd, it was arranged that men should enter at one time and women at another. The Nuabo, who is the Chief Judge, was amongst those who came; and he, too, gazed on the picture as though spell-bound by such perfection. The ambassador begged that it might be sent to him, that he might show it to the ladies of his household, who greatly desired to see it. The Father replied that he could not allow the picture to go out of his keeping; but that his Lordship could come and see it as often as he wished. So he came, with all his family. On being shown the picture, he saluted very reverently the Infant Jesus and his holy Mother; and so deeply was he impressed with the majesty visible in their figures, that he said that it would be better not to have lived at all than to have lived without seeing so marvellous a work.

It happened at this time that the son of the ambassador was attacked by a severe illness. As the doctors were unable to give him any relief, recourse was had to enchanters, who endeavoured to drive the disease away with their charms and superstitious remedies. When their efforts also proved unavailing, the ambassador begged the Father to come and treat his son, whose condition was growing daily worse. The Father read the Gospel of St. Mark over the patient; then, taking a cross containing some relics, he placed it on his eyes and forehead, whereon it pleased our Saviour to deliver him from his fever, and in a short time he was completely restored to health. Not long afterwards, the ambassador himself fell sick, and the Father was able, by God's help, to cure him also. When the King heard of this, he sent the Father his thanks, and the ambassador, too, was filled with gratitude for all that had been done for him.

There were in Cambaya some Armenians who were living sinfully with some Moorish women whom they kept in their house. The Father pointed out to them the depravity of their conduct, and remonstrated with them to such good purpose that the women became Christians, and were married to the Armenians according to the law of the Church. These and many other things the Father did there in the service of God, until he was summoned to Goa, where he spent a great part of the winter. He had, however, to return to Cambaya to transact certain business with the Mogor ambassador, the nature of which we shall now explain.

For the better understanding of the Father's Mission, some reference must be made to the circumstances which led to it. These were briefly as follows. After the ambassador and Father Pinheiro had set out for

India, an Englishman, the captain of two ships which a year or two previously had arrived at Surrate, came to Agra where the King was holding his court.[7] He carried letters of recommendation from the Captains of Surrate, and arrived at court in great state, very richly clad, and styling himself the ambassador of his King, from whom he brought a letter written in the Spanish language.[8] He conversed with the King in Turki, for he could both speak and understand this language. Religion was one of the first subjects they discussed, the King enquiring specially about the most holy Sacrament. In reply, the Englishman, like the heretic he was, told him much that was contrary to the truth and to the Catholic doctrine of this mystery, which the Fathers had fully explained to him during one of their disputes with him and the Moors. The King next asked him why he had come to his kingdom. The Englishman presented the letter he had brought, and said that he had come as the ambassador of his King to ask permission for English ships to trade at his ports. The King at once granted this request, being influenced to a large extent by the presents which the ambassador brought him. These must have been worth as much as twenty-five thousand *crusados*, for a single precious stone that he brought was valued at twenty thousand. As an additional mark of his favour, the King made him a captain of four hundred horse with the pay of thirty thousand rupees,[9] which are equal to fifteen thousand *crusados*. He thus became bound to the imperial service, so that he could not return to his own country without permission. To please the King he dressed himself after the fashion of the Moors,[10] but he made it known that though he had adopted their costume, he had not accepted their law.

After this, the heretic grew insolent in his behaviour. He treated the Fathers with contempt, deeming himself to be higher than they were in the favour of the King. He brought with him to Agra two servants,[11] both heretics like himself. One of these was his minister. The other died whilst at Agra, and as the Fathers refused him burial amongst the Christians, the heretic was much offended. He was afterwards still more offended with them because they refused to marry him to the daughter of an Armenian. When he requested them to perform the ceremony, they excused themselves by saying that they could have no dealings with him in divine matters, since he was a heretic. But the other, for the sake of his own honour, as well to please his father-in-law in this matter, continued to urge his request that one of them should be his priest. At last, in order to be rid of him, the Fathers said that it should be as he wished, provided that he would publicly acknowledge the Pope to be the head of the universal Church. This condition the heretic refused to accept, and in the end he was married to the daughter of the Armenian by the minister whom he had brought with him.[12]

One day, whilst the Englishman was still basking in the royal favour, the King asked him by what means the fortress of Diu could be captured from the Portuguese. He answered that with fourteen English ships on the sea, and a land army of twenty thousand men, the Portuguese would be forced to capitulate through sheer hunger. Just at this time, some other Englishmen arrived at Cambaya. They had left London in March of the year 1607 with two ships,[13] and a crazy pinnace which they fitted out in the bay of Saldanha [Table Bay], where they wintered. Off the Cape of Good Hope they encountered a severe storm which lasted twenty days, in the course of which the admiral's ship, a very large vessel, became separated from the others and was not seen again. The remaining ship and the pinnace, after rounding the Cape, sailed to the island of Socotra, and thence to Aden where they anchored. The Turks made them land their merchandise, and having taken the best part of it at their own price, ordered them to re-embark the remainder, making them pay a duty of fifteen per cent. for landing it, and the same for being permitted to take it away. From Aden they went to Moca; but the Xarifi would not allow them to land, saying that they were Corsairs; so they returned thence, and sailed for Cambaya. In making for the port of Surrate in Cambaya they struck upon a sandbank which extends from before Medafaual to Danu,[14] where they were wrecked. They managed to save their lives and some money in two boats; but they left at the bottom of the sea seventeen chests of *reals* and much merchandise. The two boats, containing about seventy persons, reached Surrate, and the Captain of the place, looking to make some profit out of the strangers, gave them a friendly reception.

News of this event, and of the reception which the English had met with at Surrate, reached the Governor of India,[15] Andre Furtado de Mendoça, soon after he had assumed charge of his post. Connecting the coming of these people with what he had heard about the English ambassador, who, as we have said above, had been very honourably received at the Mogul court, and had obtained from the King permission to set up a factory at Surrate, he held that the treaty of peace between the Portuguese and the King had been broken; and though at the commencement of his governorship, and before knowing these things, he had written to the Mogul ambassador saying that he anticipated his visit with great pleasure, he now wrote to cancel what he had written, telling the ambassador that as the treaty of peace with his King had been broken, it was not desirable that he should come to Goa. At the same time he issued orders both at Goa and in the fortresses of the North, prohibiting all persons from entering Cambaya. This caused much discontent, especially amongst the traders, both Moors and Gentiles, and even amongst the Portuguese. There was an immediate outbreak of hostilities in the lands of Damao, and seizures were made on both sides. But there were soon signs that the breaking of the peace and the stoppage of trade were very unwelcome to the Moors. On this account, and because there were on our side many reasons for not entering upon a war before seeking every means of avoiding it, the Governor and his Council decided that, before the rupture became more serious, a messenger should be sent to the Mogul ambassador to arrange with him for the dispatch of a complimentary letter which it was their desire to send to his King, pointing out to him the reasons why he should preserve the peace and friendly relations which he had established with the King of Portugal, and cancel anything he had done to disturb them.

To negotiate an affair of such importance the Governor and his Council judged that there was no one better fitted than Father Pinheiro, who was then at Goa; so having obtained the Provincial's consent to his employment, the Governor gave him letters to the ambassador and authority to decide either for peace or war, sanctioning whatever he should do. At the same time he authorised him to notify in all the fortresses of the North that merchants were free to proceed to Cambaya as before.

The Father had to endure many hardships on his journey, for it was the winter season, which is very unfavourable for travelling. After being twice forced by storms to return to India, he managed to get as far as Tarapor[10] some twenty-three leagues from Goa, where he entered the river to await more favourable weather. In the meantime, sand closed up the entrance to the river, so that it became impossible for him to put to sea. As the business on which he had been dispatched was very urgent, he continued his journey by land through the country of the Moors, travelling sometimes in a litter and sometimes on foot, and encountering many difficulties owing to the rivers which had to be crossed, and the mountains over which he had to pass. The Moors, knowing that he was of the Company, showed him much courtesy and kindness; but the Captain of Danda,[17] in the country of Daquini, detained him, saying that his embassy would be prejudicial to his King who was at war with the Mogor, at whose court he, the Father, had so long resided; and it was only his tact and his knowledge of the Persian language which enabled him to extricate himself from this predicament. As he passed through the fortresses of the North he announced, on behalf of the Governor, that merchants could go to Cambaya as before. The Father was warmly welcomed not only in the domains of the Portuguese, but in all parts of Cambaya, both Moors and Gentiles expressing their gratitude to him for coming to restore peace. The ambassador received him with every sign of pleasure, for they had long been on friendly terms. The Father negotiated with him in such a way that everything was arranged to their mutual satisfaction, and to the advantage of the State of India and the kingdom of Mogor.[18] As a state of war had actually existed in Damao, and reprisals had been made, orders were issued that everything that had been seized by either side should be restored. Both the ambassador and the Father wrote reports to the King, urging the necessity of peace with the Portuguese, and the removal of all obstacles to its continuance.

The King agreed to everything, and revoked the permission he had given to the English to establish a factory at Surrate. This was to the great discomfiture of the unfortunate English ambassador, who was, as we have said, at the Mogul court, for he at once fell from the favour of the King, who sent him to the country of Bengala, far away from Cambaya, where he had no opportunity of communicating with his countrymen.[19] The Mogul ambassador, as Governor of this kingdom [Cambaya], sent immediate orders to the Captain of Surrate that he should no longer give shelter to the English in that city. The latter asked permission to build, or hire, a ship to take them to their own country; but they were told to apply to the Viceroy of India. Finding themselves reduced to such straits, these poor people endeavoured to make their way to the King of Mogor; but on the road they were attacked by a band of horsemen, for there are many robbers in this country, who plundered them and slew the greater part of them, including their Captain.[20] Those who were left at Surrate went to Goa with Father Pinheiro, from whom and from others of the Company in that city they received the charitable treatment which those of the Society are always ready to extend to their fellowmen.[21]

The ambassador was awaited at Goa by the Viceroy, Ruy Lourenço de Tauora, who had also arrived, and had written to say that he might now come to Goa with all security. At the same time orders were given for one of our ships to bring him. But as he was at this time recalled by the King, he was unable to come. His duties as the Mogul's ambassador were therefore carried out by Father Pinheiro, who shared his office. The Father arrived at Goa on St. Catherine's day, and on the following Sunday the Viceroy received the letter of the King, upon which guns were fired and other public demonstrations took place to celebrate the peace which had been confirmed with so many testimonies of good-will. On behalf of the ambassador the Father presented to the Viceroy the present which he had brought; and the Viceroy thanked the Father for having conducted the negotiations so greatly to the honour and advantage of the State.

NOTES

NOTES TO CHAPTER I

The Rebellion of the Prince against his Father, and the Consequences thereof

[1] This chapter belongs to Part IV of the *Relations* (fols. 148a-151b). Guerreiro's authority was Father Xavier's letter to the Provincial at Goa, dated 25th September, 1606.

My references to the *Memoirs* of Jahangir are throughout to the translation by Mr. Alexander Rogers (*Tuzuk-i-Jahangiri*, Royal Asiatic Society, 1909).

[2] Cf. *Memoirs*, I, p. 1. "By the boundless favour of Allah when one sidereal hour of Thursday, Jumada-s-sani, A.H. 1014 (October 24th, 1605), had passed, I ascended the royal throne in the capital of Agra, in the 38th year of my age." Akbar died on October 17th (old style). The Fathers, who reckoned by the new style, which is ten days in advance of the old, give October 27th as the date of Akbar's death. The reformed calendar came into use in Roman Catholic countries in the year 1582.

[3] i.e. *Padshah salamat*, the Persian equivalent of 'Hail, King!' or "God save the King!"

[4] The note on this word in my *Scenes and Characters from Indian History* is wrong. I was misled by du Jarric, who incorrectly renders Guerreiro's words, *as ramesas & oraçoes dos mouros*, by the phrase, *leurs Ramesas, qui sont les prières des Saracens*. The reference is evidently to the fast of *ramazan*; and the passage means that Jahangir reinstituted the fast, and the prayers of the Muhammadans in the royal palace, where their observance had been discontinued by the orders of Akbar.

The people of Spain and Portugal gave the name *Mouros*, or 'Moors,' to Muhammadans in all parts of the world, the name having come into use when the Muhammadans of Mauritania overran the Peninsula in the middle ages. Their example was followed by the Dutch and the English, though in other countries of Europe the older name 'Saracen' was more generally employed. To the Portuguese the people of India were either Moors or Gentiles (Gentios), the latter term being applied to all Hindus, irrespective of race or caste.

[5] i.e. Nur-ud-din (Light of the Faith), Muhammad, Jahangir (Conqueror of the World). The two first words do not constitute a single

phrase, as the text implies. Jahangir explains his name as follows: "An inspiration from the hidden world brought it into my mind that, in as much as the business of kings is the controlling of the world, I should give myself the name Jahangir and make my title of honour Nuru-d-din, inasmuch as my sitting on the throne coincided with the rising and shining on the earth of the great light (the sun). I had also heard, in the days when I was a prince, from Indian sages, that after the expiration of the reign of King Jalalu-d-din Akbar one named Nuru-d-din would be administrator of the affairs of the state. Therefore I gave myself the appellation of Nuru-d-din Jahangir Padshah" (*Memoirs*, I, p. 2).

6 Nevertheless, says Father Xavier in his letter of September, 1606, the Gentiles continued to show respect to the Fathers, remembering the favourable treatment they had received from the late King, "de modo que viuiamos do credito passado que com o Rey morto tivemos, e com elle [Jahangir] antes que fora Rey."

7 By the old reckoning, April 4th.

8 i.e. the *Kotwal*, or Chief Constable.

9 The Persian word *jah* signifies 'mighty.'

10 It is interesting to turn to Xavier's account. Many suggestions, he says, were made as to who should be sent to capture the Prince. But the King, knowing the courageous spirit of his son, and having little confidence in his advisers, whom he suspected of being privy to his designs, decided to take the matter into his own hands; and before dawn, and without giving his escort time to get ready, he dashed off, practically unattended, in pursuit of the fugitive. All was confusion in the palace. The great nobles hastily armed themselves and galloped after the King, while all were dismayed at his precipitancy, and reproached those who had permitted him to set forth in such fashion. Nevertheless, observes Father Xavier, if the King had not gone himself, the Prince would never have been taken, for he was a general favourite with the people, who would gladly have espoused his cause, and many were ready to follow him; while Jahangir, whose liberality had fallen short of the promises made at his accession, was far from popular. The passage in the letter runs as follows: "Ouvio varios conselhos sobre o que faria, e quem mandaria apos elle, toda via como quem conheçia os espiritos do filho, e a pouca confiança que tinha dos seus que temeo que erão sabedores da fugida se resolueo de ir elle mesmo apos elle, e assi em amanhecendo parte, eis subit[te] reuolta a terra, huns caualgão apos el Rey que saio so'o sem guardos & com os grandes que em poucas horas da noite se poderão aparelhar, outros se vem desaparelhados para tal presa quasi todos notauao el Rey de mancebo e mal aconselhado, e culpouão aos que não pegauão delle para lhe impedir a tal saida, mas na verdade sayo o conselho certo que se o mesmo Rey não fora apos seu filho nunca a ouuera os mãos; porque estaua el Rey mal quisto por não

moſtrar a liberalidade que antes de ser Rey prometio, e ao contrario o filho com essa tinha de sua mão os corações de muitos e folgauão muito de o acompanhar."

[11] The name of this Captain was Husain Beg Badakshi, who, says Jahangir, "was of those who had received favours from my revered father, and was coming from Kabul to wait on me. As it is the temperament of the Badakshis to be seditious and turbulent, Khusrao regarded this meeting as a godsend, and made Husain Beg the captain and guide of 200 or 300 Badakshan Aimaqs who were with him" (*Memoirs*, I, 55). Husain Beg had rendered Akbar very valuable service in Afghaniſtan, in return for which he had been placed in charge of Kabul, and had been given Fort Rohtas in the Panjab as a *jagir*. According to the *Ain-i-Akbari*, it was he who persuaded Khusru to seek refuge at Kabul, which, he said, had always been the ſtarting-place of the conquerors of India. He also said that he had four *lakhs* of rupees in Rohtas which were at the Prince's disposal.

The second captain who joined Khusru was Abdur Rahim, afterwards dignified with the title Khar (Ass). He was Diwan of Lahore. Jahangir says that Khusru gave him the title of Malik Anwar, and made him his Vizier.

[12] In his *Memoirs* Jahangir says that, at the critical moment of the battle, "the men of the right wing raised the cry of *Padshah Salamat* ("Long live the King!") and charged, and the rebels, hearing the words, gave up and scattered abroad to various hiding-places."

[13] The battle was fought at Bhairawal (Bhaironwal, Bhyrowal) on Friday, Zi-l-hijja 27th (April 24th). The dates in the *Memoirs* are not always correct; and it is frequently difficult to tell whether Jahangir is referring to a Hijri or an Ilahi month. Fortunately, however, he generally mentions the day of the week, so that it is possible to reconſtruct the course of events with tolerable accuracy. Jahangir reached Sultanpur, on the southern bank of the Beas, the day before the battle, i.e. on Thursday, Zi-l-hijja 26th. In the *Memoirs* this date is wrongly given as Thursday, 16th. On the previous evening he had received news that Khusru was marching from Lahore with the intention of making a night attack on his vanguard. "Although," he says, "it rained heavily in the night, I beat the drums of march and mounted. By chance at this place [i.e. while he was at this place] and hour the victorious army encountered that ill-fated band." Khusru, he says, was captured on Sunday, Zi-l-hijja 24th. This is again clearly a miſtake for Sunday, Zi-l-hijja 29th (April 26th). The news of his capture reached Lahore "on Monday, the laſt day of the month," that is on Zi-l-hijja 30th (April 27th), and he was brought before Jahangir "on Thursday, Muharram 3rd (April 30th), in Mirza Kamran's garden." Jahangir tells us that he took up his abode in the garden "on the laſt day of Zi-l-hijja," and waited there for nine days "because

the time was unpropitious." He entered Lahore "on Wednesday, Muharram 8th"—*i.e.*,on the 5th May. (The dates are "old style.")

Thus in less than a month Khusru's rebellion was completely stamped out. I do not think Jahangir has been given sufficient credit for the energy he displayed in this crisis. And a crisis it was; for Khusru was popular with all classes of the people; and had Jahangir allowed the grass to grow under his feet, the rebellion would soon have assumed formidable dimensions, and the positions of pursuer and pursued might easily have been reversed. From a military point of view his pursuit of Khusru was a notable performance; and it speaks well for the organisation of his troops that they were ready, at a moment's notice, to set out on what promised to be an arduous, if not a prolonged campaign. What force Jahangir took with him from Agra we do not know; but it must have been a strong one, since the vanguard alone was sufficient to overcome the rebel troops. Accompanied by this considerable army, Jahangir marched from Agra to the banks of the Beas, a distance of nearly 400 miles, in 17 days. On the morning of the 18th day, before they had had time to draw breath, his advanced troops met and defeated the rebels in a desperate and bloody encounter. Victory was followed by pursuit; and within 24 hours most of Khusru's followers had been rounded up or slain. Effective measures for intercepting the flight of Khusru had been taken some days before the battle was fought (*vide Memoirs*, p. 66), and two days after his defeat the Prince was a prisoner.

In point of actual speed Khusru's movements were much more astonishing than his father's. Nine days before the battle of Bhairawal, he invested Lahore. He must, therefore, have arrived before that city on April 16th at the latest, having covered the distance from Agra, i.e. about 450 miles, in 12 days. It is true that he set out with only a few followers; but Husain Beg, with his Badakshi contingent, met him at Muttra, and many others fell in by the way; so that during the latter part of his march he must have had with him a force of several thousand men. In such circumstances the maintenance of an average speed of close on 40 miles a day was a performance that cannot often have been surpassed. Akbar once traversed 600 miles in 11 days; but fresh horses awaited him at every stage of his journey, and the few who accompanied him were mounted on swift camels (*vide* V. A. Smith's *Akbar*, p. 118).

[14] Khusru was captured whilst attempting to cross the Chenab by the ferry at Sodra, not far from the town of Gujrat.

[15] Xavier's letter makes this plainer. Some Armenian merchants had, we are told, stored their goods in the Fathers' house; and the Gentiles had determined to kill the Fathers during the confusion of the Prince's entry, and possess themselves of the merchandise: "Estauão em Lahor então os Pres Manoel Pinheiro e Frano Corsi que no tempo do cerco tinhão gozado da estreiteza do tempo no comer e prouisão,

e cada dia estauão temendo a morte porque os gentos lhes tinhão tão boa vontade que tinhão feito conselho de matalos como entrasse na cidade o principe para lhes tomar o fato que tinhão visto recolher a nossa casa dos Armenios mercadores que estauão fora dos muros da cidade."

[16] The statement that Abdur Rahim resumed his office a few days after his punishment is hardly consistent with what Jahangir wrote four years later in his *Memoirs*: "On the 14th Zi-l-hijja 1017 A.H. [March 10th, 1610], having pardoned all the faults of Abdu-r-Rahim Khar, I promoted him to the rank of *yuzbashi* (Centurion) and 20 horse, and ordered him to go to Kashmir &c." In a note on this passage Mr. Beveridge says, "On being released he became one of the personal servants, and served His Majesty till by degrees the latter became gracious to him (Note of Sayyid Ahmad)." Guerreiro's statement is, however, taken from Father Xavier's letter, where it is expressed even more definitely: "Aquella mesma tarde foi leuado a cidade e solto, e daly a poucas dias passeaua por ella, e tournou a seruir el Rey no mesmo officio que seruia e tinha seruido no tempo del Rey morto, e agora serue como se nunqa ouuera passado nada."

[17] Xavier describes the scene as follows: "Determinou el Rey entrar a 4 F[ra] [quarto feira, i.e. Wednesday] seguinte na cidade e quis que lhe armassem o caminho da horta ate a cidade de sentençeados a dextris e a sinistris, manda pois a espetar e enforcar alguns duzentos por ambas las partes do caminho, certe era hum horrendo espectaculo via homem aly enforcado fulão Capitao, espetado fulão irmão de fulão, filho de fulão que quasi todos erão principois e conhecidos, vimos alguns muito parentes de muitos pruiados del Rey que actualmente o seruem, não havia respeitar a ninguem, nem havia quem ousasse rogar por ninguem temendo que não tiuessem a elle por da parte do Principe."

[18] At this time, says Father Xavier, the utmost terror prevailed in the city. Many were arrested, others were deprived of their goods, and others were put to death. None could trust even his own friends, and ill betided all who attempted to conceal the wealth of the King's victims. Of the property of the Captain who was put to death, more than a hundred thousand *crusados* were discovered; and it is affirmed that the total amount seized from him and from others amounted to millions of *crusados*. Some endured personal suffering as well as loss of property; others loss of property only, and in every case the punishment was very heavy. It is amazing, the Father adds, what vast quantities of money were discovered at this time; and all for the King. The passage in the letter runs: "Neste tempo andauão todos cheos de medo, a huns prendião, a outros confiscauão as fazendas, a outros matão, amigos de amigos não se fiauão quem sabia do fato dalguns destes sentenceados cuitado se o não descobria. Daquelle Capitao que dixe descobrio hum soo cento e tanto mil cruzados e delle e outros se affirma que ouue

alguns contos de cruzados que huns erão castigados na pessoa e na fazenda, outros somte na fazenda e todos com penas grauissimas he marauilha a quantidade do dinheiro que sa descobriu nestes tempos e tudo para el Rey."

19 This was Guru Arjun, the fifth of the Sikh *gurus*, and the composer of the *Granth Sahib*.

20 Guerreiro has blundered here, and his mistake is repeated by du Jarric. It was not a tiara which the *guru* placed on Khusru's head, but the *tika*, the mark made on the forehead of Hindus either as a sign of sovereignty or to bring success in some great undertaking. As Khusru was the son of a Hindu princess (his mother was the daughter of Raja Bhagwan Das of Jaipur), the *guru* considered him entitled to this distinction. Jahangir refers to the circumstance as follows (*Memoirs*, I, p. 72): "He [the *guru*] behaved to Khusrao in certain special ways, and made on his forehead a finger-mark in saffron, which the Hindus call *qashqa*, and is considered propitious." As Mr. Beveridge points out in his note on this passage, *qashqa* is a Turkish word; the word in use amongst Hindus is *tika*; and this is the word which Xavier himself uses in his letter: "elle lhe deo o parabem do nouo reynado e lhe pos o tiqa na testa."

21 For the Sikh account of Guru Arjun's death, which differs considerably from Guerreiro's, the reader is referred to Macauliffe's *The Sikh Religion*, III, pp. 70-101. The *Memoirs* present us with another version of the story, which is probably the most reliable of the three. Jahangir had long been suspicious of Guru Arjun, who "in the garments of sanctity" had captivated so many of his Hindu, and even of his Muhammadan subjects. Many times it had occurred to him "to put a stop to this vain affair"; and as soon as he was informed of the meeting with Khusru, he caused the holy man to be arrested. "When this came to my ears," he says, "and I clearly understood his folly, I ordered them to produce him and handed over his houses, dwelling-places, and children to Murtaza Khan, and having confiscated his property commanded that he should be put to death." Xavier states that Jahangir afterwards sent for the brother of the Guru, and gave him a post in his service.

NOTES TO CHAPTER II

How the King Began his Reign. He Compels two Christian Children to become Moors

[1] In this chapter (from Part IV of the *Relations*, fols. 151b-155a), as well as in Chapter III (*ibid.*, fols. 155a-157b), Guerreiro is still following Father Xavier's letter of 25th September, 1606.

[2] This is a very inadequate description of the famous chain of justice, if we may trust Jahangir's own account of his contrivance. "After my accession," he says, "the first order I gave was for fastening up of the chain of justice, so that if those engaged in the administration of justice should delay or practise hypocrisy in the matter of those seeking justice, the oppressed might come to this chain and shake it so that its noise might attract attention. Its fashion was this: I ordered them to make a chain of pure gold, 30 *gaz* in length and containing 60 bells. Its weight was 4 Indian maunds, equal to 42 Iraqi maunds. One end of it they made fast to the battlements of the Shah Burj of the fort at Agra and the other to a stone post fixed on the bank of the river" (*Memoirs*, I, p. 7).

[3] We learn from Xavier's letter that the Fathers were accused of making converts by force, and of kidnapping and selling little children: "Foi o negotio a el Rey e chamados nos e diante de nos dixerão de nos que faziamos X[tos] por forca, e que mandauamos meninos a terra de X[tos] a vender." A similar attempt on the part of the 'Gentiles' to deprive the Fathers of their houses had been made shortly before the death of Akbar, and it was largely through the intervention of Jahangir, then Prince Salim, that their designs were frustrated. (See *Akbar and the Jesuits*, pp. 197-100.)

[4] This account of the Armenian and his marriage is very different from that given by Father Xavier in his letter of the year 1599 (see *Akbar and the Jesuits*, p. 85). In that letter we are told that the Armenian did his utmost to force the Fathers, and to induce Akbar to force them to consent to his incestuous union, and that when they refused to countenance so great a sin, he basely deserted his faith, and became a follower of the *Din Ilahi*.

The elder of the two children whose ordeal is described in this chapter eventually attained a position of some importance in the service of the state. In the fifteenth year of his reign (1600), Jahangir made him a *faujdar*, and the circumstance is thus referred to in the royal diary: "Zu-l-Qarnain obtained leave to proceed to the faujdarship of Sambhar. He is the son of Iskandar (Sikandar), the Armenian, and his father had the good fortune to be in the service of Arshashyani (Akbar), who gave him in marriage the daughter of Abdu-l-Hayy, the Armenian, who was in service in the royal harem. By her he had two sons. One was Zu-l-Qarnain, who was intelligent and fond of work, and to him, during my reign, the chief diwans had entrusted the charge of the government salt works at Sambhar, a duty which he performed efficiently. He was now appointed to the faujdarship of that region. He is an accomplished composer of Hindi songs" (*Memoirs*, II, p. 194).

The father, 'Iskandar,' died in 1613 at Agra, whither he had gone shortly before Christmas, 1612. Father Xavier, in his annual letter dated 23rd September, 1613, says that 'Iskandar' had contracted a lingering disease, and being unable to find a remedy, "had decided to come and live, or die, here in Agra where there are Fathers and a church." After his death, his body was taken to Lahore, "where is his sepulchre." The letter gives a detailed account of the Armenian's many charitable gifts, which included Rs. 3000 for the 'Holy House' at Jerusalem, and other large sums for the church and poor Christians at Agra.

As Sir William Foster has pointed out (*Early Travels in India*, p. 267) Zu-l-Qarnain was in all probability the "noble and generous Christian of the Armenian race" who entertained and assisted Thomas Coryat during his sojourn at Ajmir in 1616. Detailed reference is made to him by Botelho, and he is mentioned by Manucci, Edward Terry, Peter Mundy, and other writers of the times. A full account of him and his family, written by the Rev. H. Hosten, can be read in the *Memoirs of the Asiatic Society of Bengal*, vol. v, pp. 115-191.

5 Doubtless the district of Sambhar, to which his son was afterwards appointed

6 The *Kalimah* (lit. 'the word') is the Muhammadan confession of faith, namely, *la ilaha illulahu Muhammad-ur-rasul ullah*, "There is no God except the one God, and Muhammad is the prophet sent by God."

7 Muhammadans generally refer to Christ as *Hazrat Isa*, of *Al-hazrat Isa*. The Arabic word *hazrat*, meaning literally 'the presence' is much used as a title of respect, and, when applied to an apostle or prophet, signifies the sacredness of his office.

NOTES TO CHAPTER III

Some Converts to the Faith

[1] The words in the original are: "Acertando hum padre de passar por onde elle eſtaua, poſto que o veo ver com seu pre-rogar que o nam fosse visitar, & disse a ontros, que se o padre la hia, auia de fingir que o nam conhecia." This sentence is manifeſtly corrupt, several words having been omitted. I have therefore followed the corresponding passage in Father Xavier's letter, which runs: "Acertando eu a pasar por onde elle eſtaua, poſtoque me veo a ver com seu presente todauia me mandou rogar nao no fosse visitar e dixe a outros Armenios que se la hia auia de fingir que me nao conhecia etc." Xavier, it will be noticed, was the Father in queſtion.

[2] The conversion of this young Brahman is described in Part I (ch. viii) of the *Relations*. For du Jarric's version of the ſtory, see *Akbar and the Jesuits*, p. 134.

[3] The word Cafre, or Kafir, was in common use amongſt writers of the period to denote a negro who was neither a Chriſtian nor a Muhammadan, nor a 'Gentile.' The word was also used by Muhammadans as a term of contempt for a Chriſtian, or a Jew, or for anyone who was not of their own faith. There were many 'Kafirs' in Goa, "blacke people," Linschoten calls them, "of the land of Mosambique, and all the coaſt of Ethiopia, and within the land to the Cape de Bona Speranza." Great numbers of them, the same writer adds, were brought to India from Mosambique, "and many times they sell a man or woman that is growne to their full ſtrength, for two or three duckets. When the Portugals ships put in there, then they are dearer . . . and because the Portugals have traffique in all places it is the cause why so many are brought out of all countries to be sold, for the Portugals doe make a living by buying and selling of them, as they doe with other wares."

NOTES TO CHAPTER IV

Some Events of the Year 1607

[1] This chapter, belonging to Part IV of the *Relations* (fols. 157b-162a), is based on Father Xavier's letter to the Provincial at Goa, dated 8th August, 1607.

[2] Jahangir states in his *Memoirs* that he set out for Kabul on the 25th of March, 1607 (7th Zi-l-hijja, 1015 A.H.). He returned to Lahore in December of the same year.

[3] In catholic countries the procession of the Blessed Sacrament on Corpus Christi Day (the Thursday after the festival of the Holy Trinity) is looked upon as the most joyful solemnity of the year. The procession usually traverses the whole town in which it takes place, setting out from, and returning to the principal church. The entire route is strewn with flowers, and at intervals halting-places are arranged, with altars on which the 'sanctissimum' can be rested. A full account of the festival can be read in Adrian Fortescue's *Ceremonies of the Roman Rite described*, pp. 352-4.

[4] The Fathers seem to have taken a special pleasure in recounting any misfortunes which overtook those who were against them. Such misfortunes are invariably held up to us as manifestations of the divine wrath, and not infrequently, as in the present case, the 'punishment' is considerably exaggerated. The person here referred to is Sharif Khan, on whom the King had, a short time previously, conferred the splendid title *Amir-ul-umara*, 'Lord of Lords.' He was one of Jahangir's oldest friends. "He had lived with me," we read in the *Memoirs* (I, 14), "from his early years. When I was prince I had given him the title of *khan*, and when I left Allahabad to wait on my honoured Father I presented him with a drum and the *tuman-togh* (standard of *yak* tails). I had also promoted him to the rank of 2,500 and given him the government of the province of Bihar. I gave him complete control of the province, and sent him off there. On the 4th of Rajab, being fifteen days after my accession, he waited on me. I was exceedingly pleased at his coming, for his connection with me is such that I look upon him as a brother, a son, a friend, and a companion. As I had perfect confidence in his friendship, intelligence, learning, and acquaintance with affairs, having made him Grand Vizier, I promoted him to the rank of 5,000 with 5,000 horse and the lofty title of Amiru-l-umara, to which no title of my servants is superior." There is no evidence to show that Sharif Khan ever forfeited Jahangir's favour and regard, or that he lost his office through any other cause

than his illness, by which he was for a time completely incapacitated. In his *Memoirs* (p. 103), Jahangir says: "As I had handed over the administration of all civil affairs to the Amiru-l-umara, and his illness increased greatly, and forgetfulness came over his faculties to such an extent that what was settled in one hour he forgot in the next, and his forgetfulness was increasing day by day, on Wednesday, the 3rd Safar, I entrusted the duties of the viziership to Asaf Khan." That Jahangir heard of Sharif Khan's recovery with genuine satisfaction is evident from his own words: "On the day when I mounted my elephant for the purpose of leaving Kabul, the news arrived of the recovery of the Amiru-l-amara and Shah Beg Khan. The news of the good health of these two chief servants of mine I took as an auspicious omen for myself" (*ibid.*, p. 121); and again, "On the 6th Shaban, at the halting place of Chandalah, the Amiru-l-umara came and waited on me. I was greatly pleased at obtaining his society again, for all the physicians, Hindu and Mussalman, had made up their minds that he would die" (*ibid.*, p. 130). In the following year (1609), Sharif Khan was made joint commander in the Deccan with Prince Parwiz; but his sickness returned, and he died three years later. In recording his death, Jahangir laments the fact that he left no son on whom he could bestow his patronage.

[5] Father Xavier says that Jahangir was called 'Adel Pasiah,' i.e. *adil padshah*. The Arabic word *adil*, meaning 'just,' 'upright,' is in common use amongst Indian Mussalmans.

[6] This was Shaikh Farid, who commanded the force which defeated Khusru at the battle of Bhaironwal. In recognition of his services on this occasion he received the title Murtaza Khan. His delinquencies as governor of Gujarat are briefly referred to in the *Memoirs* as follows: "As it was again represented to me that oppression was being committed by the brethren and attendants of Murtaza Khan on the ryots and people of Ahmadabad in Gujarat, and that he was unable properly to restrain his relations and people about him, I transferred the Subah from him and gave it to Azam Khan." This took place towards the end of the year 1608. In 1610 he was given charge of the Panjab. Jahangir gives the 21st of the Ilahi month *Mihr* (about the 2nd October) as the date of his appointment, on which day, he says, "I promoted Murtaza Khan to the subahdarship of the Panjab, which is one of the largest charges in my dominions, and gave him a special shawl." His death, which took place in 1616, is recorded in the *Memoirs* as follows: "On the 3rd of this month (Khurdad) the news of the death of Murtaza Khan came. He was one of the ancients of this State. My revered father had brought him up and raised him to a position of confidence and trust. In my reign also he obtained the grace of noteworthy service, namely the overthrow of Khusrau. His mansab had been raised to 6,000 personal and 5,000 horse. . . . I was much grieved

in mind at this news: in truth, grief at the death of such a loyal follower is only reasonable. As he had died after spending his days in loyalty, I prayed to God for pardon for him."

[7] We learn from the *Memoirs* (I, p. 79) that this was a letter which Aziz Koka had once written to Raja Ali Khan of Khandesh. It will be remembered that in 1597 Raja Ali Khan was killed at the battle of Supa, while fighting on Akbar's side, and that, when he fell, his camp was plundered by the imperial troops. The letter was subsequently found in Burhanpur, amongst the Raja's effects, by Khwaja Abul Hasan, who was acting as Diwan to prince Daniyal, when the latter was sent to administer the conquered lands of the Deccan. Jahangir had no cause to love Aziz Koka, who had done his best to secure the Mogul throne for Khusru, who was his son-in-law. When, therefore, Abul Hasan placed the letter in his hands, Jahangir gave way to uncontrollable fury. "In reading it," he says, "the hair on my head stood on end. But for the consideration and due recognition of the fact that his mother had given her milk to my father, I could have killed him with my own hand. Having procured his attendance I gave the letter into his hands and told him to read it in a loud voice to those present. When he saw the letter I thought his body would have parted from his soul, but with shamelessness and impudence he read it as though he had not written it and was reading it by order. Those present in that paradise-like assembly of the servants of Akbar and Jahangir and heard the letter read, loosened the tongue of reproach and of curses and abuse." Jahangir himself upbraided the Khan in the most bitter terms, after which he says, "his lips closed, and he was unable to make any reply. What could he have said in the presence of such disgrace? I gave an order to deprive him of his jagir. Although what this ingrate had done was unpardonable, yet in the end, from certain considerations, I passed it over."

A few years later, after holding various important offices, Aziz Koka again incurred the royal displeasure and was confined in the fortress of Gwalior. On this occasion he was pardoned at the instance of none other than Akbar himself, who appeared to Jahangir in a dream, and said: "Baba, forgive for my sake the fault of Aziz Khan, who is the Khan Azam." "Though he had been guilty of many offences," says Jahangir, "and in all that I had done I was right, yet when they brought him into my presence and my eye fell upon him, I perceived more shame in myself than in him. Having pardoned all his offences, I gave him the shawl I had round my waist."

[8] A *lari*, named from the district of Lar, bordering on the Persian Gulf, was a coin much used in Western India. It was worth about a shilling. Yule (*Hobson-Jobson*, p. 506) quotes the following from P. della Valle: "The *lari* is a piece of money that I will exhibit in Italy, most eccentric in form, for it is nothing but a little rod of silver

of a fixed weight, and bent double unequally. On the bend it is marked with some small stamp or other. . . . In value every 5 lari are equal to a piastre or patacca of reals of Spain, or 'piece of eight' as we choose to call it." The *tostao*, or 'tester,' was worth about 6d; so a *lari* (according to Guerreiro) was equal to 2 shillings. Fitch valued it at one-sixth of a ducat, Linschoten at 'halfe a gilderne,' and Whithington at a shilling."

Regarding the practice of selling children in India, see *Akbar and the Jesuits*, p. 244.

NOTES TO CHAPTER V

The Fathers Accompany the King to Agra

[1] This, and the remaining chapters, belong to Part V of the *Relations* (fols. 6a-22b). Guerreiro's authority for Chapters V to VIII was Father Xavier's letter to the Provincial at Goa, dated 24 September, 1608.

[2] These were the Fathers Jerome Xavier, Emanuel Pinheiro, Francis Corsi, and Anthony Machado. The first two came to 'Mogor' with the 3rd Mission in 1595. Corsi joined the mission in 1600, and Machado in 1602. The last named was sent to take the place of Benoist de Goes, who, in 1603, set out on his mission to Cathay.

[3] Jahangir gives the date of his entry into Lahore as the 13th of *Shaban*, equivalent to the 1st or 2nd December.

[4] The Rev. H. Hosten translates these words "pictures of his [Akbar's] palaces" (*Journal of the Punjab Historical Society*, 1918, VII, p. 5). The word *paço*, 'a palace,' was frequently written 'passo'; but it seems improbable that the Fathers would have illustrated the lives of the Apostles with pictures of Akbar's palaces. The word here used I take to be the ordinary Portuguese word meaning 'a step,' 'a pace,' or, metaphorically, 'going backwards and forwards,' 'trouble,' 'pains,' 'labour,' etc. In a subsequent passage (*vide* p. 64) Guerreiro, in describing the mural paintings at Agra, says that some of these consisted of scenes from the Acts of the Apostles, "taken from the Lives of the Apostles which the Fathers had given him." This seems to put the meaning of *passos* beyond question.

[5] Xavier wrote: "paraceo nos boa occasião esta para ir la hum de nos que de palaura podesse enformar a V. R. do estado desta Missão que ate agora em tantos annos toda a enformação foi por cartas."

[6] Xavier says that Jahangir was much pleased at their choice for; he had a great affection for Father Pinheiro, whom he had known for many years. The Father's departure was deeply regretted by the Christians of Lahore, many of whom had been brought up by him. "Foi eleito o Padre Manoel Pinheiro, e dando lhe conto disso folgou muito porque ha annos que o conhece e ama. Ja neste tempo estaua pera partir o dito Capitão e assi foi necess[o] aprezar o P[e] a partida, el Rey o despacho cedo deo lhe alguas pecas que leuasse aos P[es] e a nos alguas que mandassemos a alguns amigos. Muito sentirao os X[tos] a partida do P[e] por ser elle em Lahor o mais conhecedo e que criaua os mais que aly estauao. De nos que diremos? Mas como hia por nosso S[or] e para bem desta residencia nos consolauamos, foi despedido de todos com muito amor."

[7] Muqarrab Khan appears to have carried out his instructions in a highly efficient manner. His return to Agra is thus referred to by Jahangir: "On Friday, the 7th [i.e. 7th Maharram 1017 A.H.= 2nd April, 1610] Muqarrab Khan came from the ports of Cambay and Surat, and had the honour of waiting on me. He had brought jewels and jewelled things, vessels of gold and silver made in Europe, and other beautiful and uncommon presents, male and female Abyssinian slaves, Arab horses, and things of all kinds that came into his mind. Thus his presents were laid before me for two and a half months, and most of them were pleasing to me" (*Memoirs*, I, p. 167).

[8] In a subsequent passage (p. 77) Guerreiro gives the 13th September as the date of the departure of the embassy to Goa, which is obviously incorrect. The month we know to have been December, for the embassy was dispatched after the King's return from Cabul, and before Christmas. The day of the month may have been the 13th, but the 23rd would seem to be a more likely date.

[9] The *missa do gallo* is the mass celebrated at midnight on Christmas Day, at which time the cocks (*gallos*) are supposed to crow.

[10] The *charamela* was a double-reed instrument of the hautboy, or oboe type. Lacerda gives 'bag-pipe' as the equivalent; but the resemblance must have been confined to the sound.

[11] In other words, with much beating of tom-toms. *Tambur* is the Arabic name for a kind of guitar; but in India the word is applied to a drum. *Tabal*, another Arabic word, also denotes a drum, but a smaller instrument than the *tambur*.

[12] According to Father Xavier the King left Lahore on Sunday the 7th January. "He asked us," says the Father, "whether we would prefer to accompany him, or to remain at Lahor. I said that I would not be separated from him on any account. He then asked what would happen to our church if we left it. I replied that there were three of us, and that if it pleased His Majesty, two of us would accompany him, whilst the other remained with the church and the Christians at Lahor. Accordingly he ordered us to be supplied with a horse for the journey, and four camels to carry our goods. The King set out first and we followed later, that is, Father Corsi and myself, leaving Father Machado alone at Lahor. We left Lahor on the 10th February, and arrived at Agra on the 18th March, leaving the King at a spot some five or six leagues from the city, where he awaited an auspicuous hour for his entry."

[13] This must be regarded as the most authentic account we possess of the blinding of Prince Khusru; for, though Father Xavier may not have been in Jahangir's camp at the time the punishment was inflicted, he must have reached it a few days afterwards, and must have heard a great deal about it. He states in his letter that the juice of the 'leiteira' was applied to the victim's eyes. 'Leiteira' is the

Portuguese name for plants of the spurge family (*Euphorbiaceæ*), nearly all varieties of which are to a greater or less degree poisonous. The Captain who was blinded at the same time, and who was, we are told, the chief of those who had instigated the King to persecute the two children of the Armenian Sikandar, succeeded in saving his sight by constantly bathing his eyes with some healing lotion. We are also told that after the blinding Khusru was taken about with a bandage over his eyes, from which Xavier inferred that he was not totally bereft of sight. As so many different versions of the story have come down to us, it is as well that Xavier's account, which Guerreiro has considerably abridged, should be quoted in full. It runs as follows: "No caminho passou hua cousa notauel e ha que como tinha el Rey ainda preso com ferros a seu filho morgado Soltão Xhocero (que he o que nos chamamos Codraos ?) assi o truxa com ferros no caminho e muito bem recado, e quando chegou ao lugar onde pelejara o ditto Principe com a gente de seu pay em pena de tal desobediencia aly mesmo lhe fez çegar os olhos remolhando lhos com leite de leiteiras e o mesmo fez a hum mouro seu priuado de quem ja escriui o anno passado que fora consentidor dos que conjurarão para matar el Rey. e o fez trazer de Cabul a Lahor em ferros sobre hum burro ou muleta bem mal concertado e o teue preso em Lahor, e neste mesmo lugar fez çegar da mesma maneira, mas elle lauandose muito os olhos com certas cousas diuertio a peçonha da quella leite hum pouco e fiqou com algua vista e agora o mandou preso a fortaleza que chamão de Goalier [Gwalior] a onde uão os grauamente culpados, este he o principal que mouia a el Rey a fazer mouros os filhos de Alexandre Armenio bem paga seu peccado, e elles estão muito firmes en seu ley. Assi que digo que ao Sultão em aquella lugar o mandou çegar. Alguns affirmão estar de tudo çego, outros que não, o certe he que ainda depois que dizem que o çegou sempre vinha no caminho sobre hum elefante em hua charola coberta por todas as partes e com muito gente de caualo de hua parte e outra, e o que mais he que tem bandados os olhos, e no noo da banda esta posta chapa del Rey por sua mão, destas cousas colligem não estar de todo çego. Nullo modo se falla della diante del Rey nem na terra como se não ouvesse tal homem."

[14] This was in 1602, when Prince Salim, after his reconciliation with Akbar, took up his abode in Agra. Seeing that there was no place at Agra where the Padres could hold their services, he obtained Akbar's permission for the building of a church, and gave a thousand crowns towards the cost of its construction (see *Akbar and the Jesuits*, p. 191).

Father Xavier says that on reaching Agra they went to take possession of the house which Jahangir, thinking the owner to be dead, had given them. On their arrival, however, they found that the owner had reappeared, and had renovated the houses, which were now occupied by the members of his family. So they had to take up their abode in a place near by, which had been intended for their servants. They commenced to put their church in order; but they were able to use only the chapel, as the body of it extended to the aforesaid houses. They made what shift they could with the chapel; but as it did not afford sufficient accommodation for all the Christians, they determined if the King remained in Agra, to ask him to pass an order that the houses were to be sold to them.

NOTES TO CHAPTER VI

The Fathers dispute with the Moors before the King

[1] The name of Jahangir's reader was Ghiyas-ud-din Ali; but he was generally known by his title, Naqib Khan. He was the son of Abdul Latif who had been tutor to Akbar. He was one of those who received promotion on Jahangir's accession. We read in the *Memoirs* (I, p. 28), " I promoted Naqib Khan, who is one of the genuine Sayyids of Qazwin, to the rank of 1,500. My father had distinguished him with the title of Naqib Khan, and in his service he had complete intimacy and consideration. He has no equal or rival in the science of history and in biographies. There is in this day no chronologist like him in the inhabited world. From the beginning of Creation till the present time, he has by heart the tale of the four quarters of the world. Has Allah granted to any other person such faculty of memory ?" Naqib Khan died in 1614.

[2] This appears to be an elaborate variation of the tradition that when the unbelievers demanded a sign of the Prophet, the moon was cleft in two. The 1st verse of the fifty-fourth *Sura* of the Quran is supposed by some to refer to this miracle: " The hour of judgment approacheth; and the moon hath been split in sunder: but if the unbelievers see a sign, they turn aside, saying, This is a powerful charm." Others regard this verse as prophetic, and maintain that the words rendered " hath been split " actually signify " will be split "; the cleaving of the moon being one of the signs which are to precede the day of judgment.

NOTES TO CHAPTER VII

A Dispute on the Divinity of Christ

[1] To this, says Xavier, the Father replied, "God preserve your Majesty! I could not have a better advocate."

[2] 'Bhang,' said to be derived from the Sanskrit *bhanga* (see *Hobson-Jobson*, p. 59), is the name given to the seeds and dried leaves of the Indian hemp, which when eaten or smoked, produce intoxication.

[3] In Part II of his *Relations* Guerreiro relates that Jahangir, before he ascended the throne, once asked a number of his Captains to whom they would appeal for help in time of danger; and when some answered in one way and some in another, he said, "As for myself, I should call on none other but the Lord Jesus" (see also *Akbar and the Jesuits*, p. 187).

[4] Guerreiro would have done better had he kept to his 'copy.' Father Xavier wrote "que não querião a Iesus X^{to}," i.e. "who do not *love* Jesus Christ."

NOTES TO CHAPTER VIII

The King's Reverence for Jesus Christ

[1] Abridgment has here resulted in confusion. Guerreiro's sentence is incomplete; and he leads us to suppose that the words "in the middle of the ceiling" refer to the verandah where the King showed himself to his people; whereas Father Xavier's letter makes it plain that these words refer to another apartment, where he used to sit prior to appearing in the outer verandah. The passage in the letter runs: "Quando elle veo de Lahor achou o paço muito bem concertado e pintado com varias pinturas que ja erão feitas, e eſtauão para se fazer assi dentro como fora em hua varanda onde se assenta cada dia *ad populum*, no meio della eſta soo assentado, nas duas bandas os seus filhos, e despois delles alguns criados de seruiço, que todos os capitoes e grandes estão em baixo, e quando chama algun em cima, vai e logo se dece. Da banda de dentro onde sae de noite, e se assenta antes quando quera sair a eſta janela ou varanda de fora, tem hua varanda larga, no alto do foro della, etc." Or in English: "When he came to Lahor he found his palace very beautifully decorated, and adorned with many paintings which had already been completed, and others which were yet to be completed both on the inside and the outside of the verandah where he sits to be seen of the people. In this verandah he only is seated. His sons ſtand on either side of him, and behind them some of his personal attendants. The Captains and nobles stand below; and if one of them is ordered to go up, he goes and descends quickly. Within, and to one side, where he goes at night and where he sits before he wishes to appear in the outer verandah, he has [another] large verandah, on the ceiling of which, etc."

[2] As Xavier's own description of the balcony, or *janela de fora*, contains some additional details, it is as well that the reader should have it in full: "Da janela de fora que direi? Nas elhargas do lugar onde el Rey se assenta quando sae *ad populum* eſtauão pintados muito bem alguns dos priuados del Rey ao natural, poucas dias depois todos os mandou borrar e mandou pintar em lugar delles huns soldados Portugueses muito bizaros armados grandes de eſtatura de homem de maneira que se vem por todo o terreiro, eſtão tres de cada parte, e em cima delles a banda da mão dereita eſta pintado X^to^ N. S^or^ com o globo do mundo na mão esquerda, e da outra banda N^a^ S^ra^ muito bem pintada, mas despois que vio hua S^ra^ de S. Lucas que temos na nossa igreja fez borrar aquella e pintar eſta; as ilhargas de X^to^ N. S^or^ e N. S^ra^ eſtão huns S^tos^ como em oração. Na charola da varanda como janela

onde elle se assenta às ilhargas na mesma parede estão pintados seus dos filhos muito ricamente ao natural, em cima de hum delles esta X^{to} N. S^{or} em figura piquena e aly junto hum P^{re} com hum livro na mão, e sobre o outro N. S^{ra}; no mesmo vao da charola estão S. Paolo S. Gregorio S. Ambrosio, estes por serem piquenas e dentro da charola pouqo se vem dos que estão em baixo, mas as outras de todos se podem ver." The figures of Christ and the Virgin here mentioned appear to be the same that are referred to by William Finch in his description of a 'small court' near the King's durbar, "Where aloft in a gallery the King sits in his chair of state, accompanied with his children and chiefe Vizier (who goeth up by a short ladder forth of the court), no other without calling daring to goe up to him, save only two punkaws to gather wind; and right before him below on a scaffold is a third, who with a horse taile makes havocke of poore flies. On the right hand of the King, on the wall behind him, is the picture of our Saviour; and on the left, of the Virgin" (Foster's *Early Travels in India*, p. 182). This reference of Finche's to the pictures of Christ and the Virgin appears to have been overlooked by the Rev. H. Hosten, who in his account of Guerreiro's fifth *Relation* (*Journal of the Punjab Historical Society*, Vol. VII), remarks on the complete absence of allusion to the mural paintings at Agra by the various European travellers who visited the city in 1609 and the following years of Jahangir's reign.

3 In Xavier's letter the passage runs: "E o que mais he, a imagem de X^{to} N. S^{or} a colunna fez tirar de hum registro pequeno em hum painel grande com suas coras muito bem por q fosse por mostra por fazer hum pano de seda fezido com aquellas figuras como pano de ras, e o letreiro deste papel mandou fazer em Parsio por tecer no pano como mesmo feitio."

4 Xavier says they were to stretch it on a wooden frame: "pola em hum quadro de pao estirada." The picture was evidently worked on silk, and appears to be the same that is referred to on p. 77, *infra*. It was probably this picture which Jahangir mentions in his *Memoirs* (I, p. 44). He says that on the 16th Safar, 1007 (1st June, 1608): "Muqarrab Khan sent from the port of Cambay a European curtain (tapestry), the like of which in beauty no other work of the Frank painters had ever been seen."

5 Count Von Noer, who appears to have seen fragments of Guerreiro's work, wrongly attributes this method of sealing letters to Akbar (see his *Kaiser Akbar*, ch. v, and also my *Akbar and the Jesuits*, p. xxxiv).

6 The Casa da Santa Misericordia, the Holy House of Mercy, was established in Goa soon after the conquest of the city by Albuquerque. It was maintained by a pious association of laymen who administered various charitable institutions in Goa.

7 See note 8, p. 99.

NOTES TO CHAPTER VIII

[8] The reference appears to be to the black image of the Virgin, standing in the Benedictine Abbey on the slopes of Monserrat in Barcelona, which attracts many pilgrims.

[9] The *capa de asperges* is the cope, or pluvial, worn by the priest when performing the asperges, that is, the rite of sprinkling the congregation with holy water before the celebration of mass.

NOTES TO CHAPTER IX

The King sends an Embassy to Goa

[1] This chapter appears to be based on a letter, or letters, written by Father Pinheiro immediately after his return to Goa at the end of November, 1609. That Guerreiro possessed no information of a later date is proved by the incorrect statements he makes regarding Hawkins and the survivors from the *Ascension* (see note 20, *infra*). Moreover, letters written at a later date could hardly have come into his hands in time to be included in his book, which was completed before the end of the year 1610.

[2] This was in 1606, for Father Xavier refers to the circumstance in his letter of that year. It was, he tells us, just after his persecution of the two children of Sikandar the Armenian, that Jahangir declared his intention to send an ambassador, accompanied by a Padre, to the King of Portugal. He selected as his representative a Moor who was distinguished as a man of letters, and who had the post of Chronicler (nomeou o embaxador que he hum muito bom letrado dos Mouros, e seu cronista, e não mal feito aos Portugeses). He told Xavier that he was to accompany the ambassador; but Father Pinheiro submitted that Xavier was too old to support the fatigues of the journey, and asked that he might be sent in his stead, to which the King readily agreed (dixe que ficasse eu e yria o P[e]). A few days later he asked Xavier to give him in writing a list of articles, unobtainable in Portugal, which he could send as presents. "I sent it to him," says the Father, "written in Persian, and he ordered the articles to be collected." But after all, Jahangir's plan, like the similar plan formed by his father (see *Akbar and the Jesuits*, pp. 114, 259-260), came to nothing. It may be doubted whether either Akbar or Jahangir ever seriously contemplated sending an embassy to Europe. Very possibly the proposal was in each case nothing more than a piece of bluff, designed to impress the Portuguese authorities.

[3] His real name was Shaikh Hasan. Jahangir thus refers to him in his *Memoirs* (I, p. 13): "From the days of his childhood to this day he has always been in my service and in attendance on me, and when I was Prince was distinguished by the title of Muqarrab Khan. He was very active and alert in my service, and in hunting would often travel long distances by my side. He is skilful with the arrow and the gun, and in surgery he is the most skilful of his time." In a later passage Jahangir tells how Muqarrab Khan once bled him. The disease of *Khun-para*, he says, had affected his health. "By the advice of the

physicians, I drew about a *sir* of blood from my left arm. As a great lightness resulted, it occurred to me that if they were to call blood-letting 'lightening' it would be well. Nowadays this expression is made use of. To Muqarrab Khan, who had bled me, I gave a jewelled *khapwa* (dagger)." In 1616 Muqarrab was made Governor of Gujarat, and a Captain of 5,000. Subsequently he became Governor of Agra. He remained in the public service throughout the life-time of Jahangir, and was pensioned off soon after the accession of Shah Jahan. He was ninety years of age when he died. Whatever his faults, and from all accounts they were plentiful enough, he seems to have played his cards skilfully, and to have served Jahangir well.

[4] See note 8, p. 102.

[5] The Count de Feyra died on his way to India. He set out, Faria y Sousa tells us, "on the 29th of March, 1609, and died on the 15th May. His body was sent back, and brought to Lisbon the 24th July" (*Asia Portuguesa*, tr. Stevens, III, p. 153).

Since the death of Dom Affonso de Castro in 1606, the administration of the Portuguese settlements had been in the hands of Dom Alexius de Menezes, Archbishop of Goa, who continued to hold office till the 28th of May, 1609, when he was succeeded by Andrea Furtado de Mendoça, who had formerly been Governor of Malacca. Mendoça was Governor (neither he nor the Archbishop assumed the title of Viceroy) for a little over three months, and was succeeded on September 5th by Ruy Lorenço de Tavora, who arrived from Portugal on that date.

[6] See note 4, p. 108.

[7] William Hawkins, the Englishman referred to, sailed from London in March, 1607, and reached Surat on the 24th August, 1608. He set out for Agra on the 15th February, 1608, and reached that city on the 16th of April.

[8] It is difficult to understand why the King's letter was written in Spanish. But this was evidently the case; for Hawkins says that when he presented the letter, Jahangir "called for an old Jesuite [doubtless Father Xavier] that was there present to reade it." And he adds that the Jesuit "told him [the King] the effect of the letter, but discommending its stile, saying that it was basely penned, writing *Vestra* without *Majestad*. My answere was unto the King: And if it shall please your Majestie, these people are our enemies: how can this letter be ill written, when my King demandeth favour of your Majestie? He said it was true."

[9] This agrees with Hawkins's own statement. The King, he says, promised "he would allow me by the yeare three thousand and two hundred pounds sterling for my first, and so yearly hee promised mee to augment my living till I came to a thousand horse. So my first should be four hundred horse." The value of the rupee in Jahangir'

reign was constantly fluctuating. Roe gave it as 2s. 2d. Its average value was about 2s. 3d.

10 This is borne out by Jourdain, who says that Hawkins, in his house, "used altogether the custome of the Moores and Mahometans, both in his meate and drinke and other customes, and would seem to be discontent if all men did not the like."

11 These were his 'boy,' Stephen Gravener, who died in Agra, and his 'man,' Nicholas Ufflet, who returned to England with him. Ufflet appears to have been a person of some education, and is said to have written an account of the city of Agra. See Foster's *Early Travels in India*, pp. 84 and 185.

12 Hawkins does not say that he asked the Jesuits to perform the ceremony, though it is very likely that he did so. His own account is as follows: "I tooke her and, for want of a minister, before Christian witnesses I marryed her. The priest was my man Nicholas Ufflet, which I thought had been lawfull, till I met with a preacher that came with Sir Henry Middleton and hee, shewing me the error, I was new marryed againe."

13 These were the *Ascension* and the *Union*, which left England in March, 1608, under the command of Alexander Sharpeigh. Others on board the former ship were John Jourdain, William Rivett, and Robert Covert. A full account of the voyage can be read in Jourdain's *Journal*. The ships reached the bay of Saldanha, or Table Bay, in July, and remained there until the following September, "our time," says Jourdain, "being long at Saldamia by reason of setting upp our pinnace." Off the Cape of Good Hope a violent storm was encountered, and the ships became separated. The *Ascension* reached Aden in April, 1609, where a week or two later she was joined by the pinnace. The difficulties encountered at Aden, and later at Mocha, are much exaggerated in the text account (see *The Journal of John Jourdain*, Hakluyt Society, 1905, pp. 127 *et seq.*). The *Ascension* arrived in Indian waters at the end of the month of August, and was wrecked off Surat on the 4th September. Sixty-two persons found their way to land, taking with them about £3,000 out of the £15,000 which the ship carried.

14 Medafaual, or as it is spelt on Levanha's map of Gujarat, Madrefauat, was a small port on the western shore of the Gulf of Cambay, to the north of Diu. Danvers identifies it with Mahava (*Portuguese in India*, II, p. 533). Danu, now spelt Dahanu, is on the opposite side of the gulf, near to, and south of Daman. Barbosa calls this place Dinvy. It was, he says, inhabited "by both Moors and Heathens, and had a great trade in goods of many kinds."

15 This is a mistake on Guerreiro's part, another example, probably, of careless abridgment. Furtado de Mendoça became Governor of Goa on the 28th May, and laid down his office on the 5th September.

NOTES TO CHAPTER IX

The *Ascension* was wrecked on the 4th September; so that the news of this circumstance, and of the reception of the English at Surat, could not have reached Goa whilst he was Governor. The most that he could have known of the English ships at the commencement of his term of office was that they had arrived at Aden, with the intention of proceeding to India. Mendoça must, however, have known all about Hawkins's journey to Agra and of the favours granted to him by Jahangir, even before he became Governor. He was a man of very prompt action, and we shall probably be right if we assign his order placing Cambay out of bounds, and his refusal to receive the Mogul's ambassador, to the early part of the month of June. Seeing the effect of his virtual declaration of war, Mendoça lost no time in dispatching an emissary to Cambay to make a final bid for peace. The subsequent course of events, and such dates as we possess, indicate that Father Pinheiro, the emissary chosen, set out from Goa about the end of July (at which time he would be likely to encounter the full force of the S.W. monsoon). As he was obliged to travel most of the way to Cambay by land, his journey, which by sea would have been a matter of four or five days, must have taken as many weeks. We do not know the date of his arrival at Cambay; but we know that the report of his negotiations with Muqarrab Khan was not received at Goa until after Lorenço de Tavora had assumed the office of Viceroy, that is, until after the 5th September. We may assume, therefore, that Pinheiro's meeting with Muqarrab Khan took place towards the end of August. The result of their conference must have been communicated to the Viceroy and to Jahangir with as little delay as possible. With his report Muqarrab doubtless forwarded to Jahangir the Viceroy's letter, and at the same time sent his order to the Captain of Surat that the newly arrived English were no longer to receive shelter. The Viceroy's acknowledgment of the report, together with his invitation to Muqarrab Khan to visit Goa, must have reached Cambay before the end of September; for we know that, on the 7th October, Father Pinheiro, who had taken Muqarrab Khan's place as ambassador, had already arrived at Surat on his way to Goa (see note 21, p. 115). The Father reached the latter place on the 25th November, so that he must have made this journey also by land.

Although Muqarrab Khan was recalled in September, he does not appear to have left for Agra till the following January; for Jourdain says that in that month one of the merchants who came on the *Ascension* met him in Cambay. Jahangir says that he reached his court on the 2nd April (see note 7, p. 102).

[16] This is evidently a mistake. If the place where Pinheiro took shelter was only 23 leagues from Goa, it cannot have been Tarapur. The Tarapur creek is more than two hundred miles from Goa; and had Pinheiro begun his land journey here, he would not have passed through Danda.

[17] Danda, or Danda Rajpuri, is a part of the Janjira State which has for centuries been in the possession of an Abyssinian family. The Chief is still known as the Siddi of Janjira. In spite of the repeated efforts of the Moguls, and afterwards of the Marathas, to expel the Siddis and gain possession of Danda Rajpuri, the little state contrived to preserve its existence until it came under British protection.

[18] According to Hawkins, Muqarrab Khan had been heavily bribed by the Portuguese Viceroy, who had sent him a great present, together with "many toys" for the King. "These presents," he says, "and many more promises wrought so much with Mocrebchan that he writeth his petition unto the King, sending it together with the present, advertising the King that the suffring of the English in his land would be the cause of the losse of his owne countries neere the sea-coasts, as Suratt, Cambaya, and such like, and that in any case he entertaine me not, for that his ancient friends the Portugalls murmured highly at it, and that the fame is spread abroad amongst the Portugalls that I was generall of ten thousand horsemen, readie to give the assault upon Diu when our shipping came. The Vice-royes letter was likewise in this kind. The Kings answere was that he had but one Englishman in his court, and him they needed not to feare, for hee hath not pretended any such matter, for I would have given him living neere the sea parts but he refused it, taking it neere me heere" (Foster's *Early Travels in India*, p. 84).

[19] This is pure fiction. Hawkins remained for another two years at the Mogul court, and even then Jahangir was unwilling that he should depart. He left Agra on the 11th of November, 1611. At the end of December he arrived at Cambay, where he joined Sir Harry Middleton's fleet, and sailed from India in February, 1612.

[20] This also is fiction. An account of the journey of these men from Surat to Agra is given by Jourdain, and also by Robert Covert, who was himself one of the company; but neither says anything about an attack by armed brigands. The march commenced on the 21st of September, under the leadership of William Rivett, a merchant who came on the *Ascension*. The men were a most disorderly lot, and no sort of discipline was maintained. Rivett died of sickness on the way, and there were numerous other casualties. Nevertheless, the bulk of the party reached Agra safely on or about the 8th December.

The story in the text, and the previous statement about Hawkins, are not difficult to account for. Guerreiro, as I have already stated, is here using a letter written immediately after Father Pinheiro's return to Goa, probably by the Father himself. At this time all kinds of rumours are likely to have been in circulation regarding the fate of Hawkins and the crew of the *Ascension*. These would find ready credence at Goa, and Pinheiro, without waiting to verify his information, at once passed them on to Portugal. I have been unable to discover any copy, or other reference, to this letter, but it must have been written before the end of the year; for by that time it would have been known at Goa that Hawkins was still at the Mogul court.

[21] This is corroborated by the narrative of Thomas Jones, who came to India on the *Ascension*, and was one of those whom Father Pinheiro conducted to Goa. His reference to his journey with the Father, in which he gives us a very useful date, is as follows: "Whilst I was in many determinations, it pleased God of his Goodness to send a Father of the Order of Saint Paul being a Portugal, who came from Cambaya to Surat by land, with whom I came acquainted, he promising me, that if I would commit my selfe into his hands, hee would send mee home into my country, or at leastwise into Portugal, which promise he did accomplish most faithfully. In company of this Father, my selfe and three more of our company, departed from Surat the seventh day of October" (*Purchas, his Pilgrimes*, Vol. I, p. 231). Similarly Jourdain, in reference to those who went to Goa, says, "I had letters from them of there kind usage by the Jesuits which carried them theather" (*Journal*, p. 136).

PART II

THE TRAVELS OF BENEDICT GOES

CHAPTER I

Introductory

N.B.—This chapter is taken from the *Hiſtoire* of Father P. du Jarric (Part II, pp. 494-498). Guerreiro's narrative commences with the next chapter.

One day, before the King [Akbar] left the city of Lahor to go to Agra,[1] the Father Hierosme Xauier was with the Prince, his eldeſt son, when there came to the palace a rich merchant, about sixty years of age, and of the Muhammadan seſt, who having done reverence to the Prince, and being asked whence he had come, replied that he was juſt returned from the kingdom of Xetay [Khitai],[2] which is the same, according to Father Xauier, as that which is called Catay, of which Marc Paul the Venetian makes mention in his account of his travels, and Ayton the Armenian[3] in his hiſtory. It is also mentioned by certain of our modern authors, who place it in Tartarie, or thereabouts.

In reply to the Prince's enquiries about this kingdom, and how long he had resided there, the merchant said that he had been there for thirteen years, living in the capital city, which he called Xambalu, being the same that is called Cambalu by the writers above referred to, some of whom say that it is twenty-four, and others as much as thirty-two miles in circuit. It is also, the Merchant said, the usual residence of the King, whom he had seen many times, and who, according to his account, is a very mighty monarch; for he has in his kingdom as many as fifteen hundred towns, and all very populous. He said that no one ever addressed the King except in writing, submitting a memorial of whatever it was desired to communicate to, or ask of him, to which he responded through the medium of one of his eunuchs, who are his courtiers. Being asked how he had been able to enter the country, he replied that he had gone there in the character of an ambassador of the King of Caygarem [Kashgar], but that, notwithstanding this, he was detained by the governor of the first frontier town to which he came, until the king had been informed of his arrival. This was not done until the seals of the letters which he carried had been examined, when a message was sent to the King by a courier, who returned within a month bringing permission for him to proceed to court.[4] The journey, he said, was easily accomplished, though the distance was very great; for they changed horses at each post, as in Europe, and were thus able to cover each day ninety or a hundred *cos*, which would represent as many Italian miles, or from twenty-five to thirty of our ordinary leagues. Throughout the journey they were free from molestation, for justice is very strictly administered in those parts, and robbers are never pardoned.

Questioned further as to the appearance and manners of the inhabitants of the country, he said that he had never seen handsomer people, preferring them to the Rumes, that is to say to the Europeans (for thus the people of the East designate the European Turks of Constantinople and Greece, because of the Romans who once ruled over the whole world, and particularly over Europe), that the men usually wore long beards, and that all of them, both men and women, were of a white complexion. As to their religion, he said that they were for the most part Isauites, or Iesauites, meaning Christians, who are so called by these people from the name Jesus, just as we say Jesuites, or just as, at the commencement of the Church, men were called Christians from the name Christ. Asked if all the people were Christians, he replied that this was by no means the case; for many of them were Mussauites, that is to say, Jews (the people of this nation being so named because Mussau, in the language of these people, means Moses). There were also, he added, others who were Muhammadans. "And their King," asked the Prince, "is he a Muhammadan?" "Not yet," answered the merchant, "but it is hoped that he will become one soon."

At this point the conversation was interrupted; but to please the Father, who had been much interested in hearing about these things, the Prince told the merchant that he must come again and tell him more about this kingdom, and he fixed a day for the interview. But the Father, being anxious to enquire more particularly about the religion of the people of Catay, went before the day appointed to see the merchant in his lodging, who again said that the people were for the most part Iesauites, adding that he had been intimately acquainted with many of them. He told the Father that they had many churches, some of them very large, in which were to be seen pictures both printed and coloured. Amongst these he had seen one of the crucifix, to which the people paid great reverence. Belonging to each church there was a priest much respected by his parishioners, from whom he received many presents. Father Xauier then asked if they had any bishops. The merchant did not clearly understand this question; but after it had been explained to him, he said that there was certainly one of the priests who was the superior of the others. Continence and chastity were strictly practised by the priests; and there were schools in which children who were to be advanced to the priesthood were taught. All such children were maintained and fed by the King, who also built the churches and kept them in repair.

The merchant said that the Fathers (meaning the priests) wear black robes, and a bonnet on the head "very like yours, but a little larger." When they salute anyone, they do not remove their bonnets, but join their hands in front of them, and raise them, with the fingers interlaced, to their heads. They also wear cloaks, and on feast-days clothe themselves in red. As to those Christians who are not priests, they, too, for the most part dress in black, exchanging it for red on feast-days. He had often seen the King go to church, for he was a Christian. Amongst the Christians there are many, both men and women, who withdraw altogether from the world, and take up their abode in secluded houses where they lead solitary and austere lives, and never marry; while there are others who practise the same austerities in their own homes.

The merchant said that the people of Catay were,

as a general rule, well off, and that the country contained many silver mines which were a source of great wealth. The King maintained an establishment of four hundred elephants trained for war. These were brought to him from Malaca. Merchants also came there to trade from Pegu, which was distant a six months' journey.

All the above has been taken from a letter written by Father Xauier from the city of Lahor on the 26th July, 1598, to the Father Provincial of India. After reaching Agra, whither he followed the King, the Father obtained information from others who had been to this same country, and finding that their reports confirmed the information he had received from the merchant, he wrote further on the subject to the Father Provincial, in a letter dated the 1st August, 1599. In this he said that Catay could be reached by travelling through Bengala and the kingdom of Garagate [Ghoraghat],[5] where the empire of the Great Mogul terminates; but that the easiest route, and the one usually followed by merchants, was that which commenced at Lahor, and led through Caximir and Rebat [Tibet], whose King was on very good terms with the Great Mogul, straight to Caygarem [Kashgar], whence it was but a short distance to the first town of Catay, which the merchants say is inhabited by Christians.

In these letters the Father refers to a conversation he had had with the King, to whom he said: "Sire, our Superior has been told how in the kingdom of Catay, there are many who profess the Christian faith, of whom no sure tidings have been received in Europe for more than three hundred years, partly because they are so far separated from other Christians, and partly because of the wars that have taken place in the countries through which it is necessary to pass in order to reach them. It is now the desire of our Superior to send three or four Fathers[6] to see in what state these Christians are, and aid them to attain salvation; for it is our mission in life to travel the world, taking no account of dangers, in order to show men the way to eternal life." The King said in his own language, "Rahat met xoda" [*Rahmat-i-Khuda*], that is, "God's blessing be upon you!" and added other words in praise of the Company. Father Xauier then said that the Father Provincial, knowing that there was no good road to Catay except by passing through his territories, desired to know if His Majesty was agreeable to his sending some Fathers to Lahor, that they might journey thence under his protection. In reply the King said they would be welcome, and that he would send an ambassador with them, with whom they could travel in safety. "This," wrote the same Father, "will be a great advantage, since all that lies between Cambaya and Lahor belongs to the Great Mogul, and from there one enters the kingdom of Bradaxa [Badakshan], the ruler of which is a vassal of the Great Mogul, and three of his children have been brought up at Lahor.[7] Moreover, when the Fathers who first came to Lahor were teaching Portuguese to the sons of the chiefs, lords and captains of the court, these three lads were amongst their pupils. He who now rules at Bradaxa is their brother german, so that with his assistance, and with the letters of the Great Mogul, it should be possible to reach Catay easily and safely."

This is what was written by Father Xauier from the court of the Great Mogul in the year 1599. Brother Benoist de Gois has since been sent to discover this land of Catay; but as he has not yet arrived there, at any rate so far as we know, we cannot with certainty say anything further concerning it. There are, however, many who believe that Catay is no other than the kingdom of China.

CHAPTER II[1]

Lahore to Yarkand

Catayo, of which mention is made in other histories, is a great empire, of which it is reported, on reliable information, that the people are for the most part Christians, but that there are amongst them both Muhammadans and infidels. Although it has not yet been ascertained what territories and provinces are comprised in this empire, divers opinions thereon have been formed. From the stories and writings of persons worthy of credit it seems probable that Catayo, and not Abexim [Abyssinia], as has been supposed hitherto, is the real kingdom of Preste Ioam of the East, in search of whom Dom Ioam II of this realm sent men by land to India, before the Portuguese found their way there by sea.[2]

For it is known that when the King of Catayo goes on horseback, he has carried before him three crosses, the first of gold, the second of silver, and the third of some other metal. His name is Ionas. He has authority over all both in spiritual and in temporal matters. The establishment of Christianity amongst the people was due to the blessed apostle St. Thomas: not that he went in person to these parts, or ever visited Cambalu (called today Cambalab), the royal city and metropolis where the Emperors reside; but because some of his disciples went there to preach the holy Gospel. By these the people were converted;

and they kept their faith pure until their Emperors, with the desire of extending their dominions, set out to conquer the countries round about them. One of the latter went as far as Syria and the holy land of Jerusalem, and brought back with him some Christians who had been infected with the Nestorian heresy; and it was through them, as we may suppose, that certain errors took root amongst these people. By this it is seen that it is the king of this country, and not the King of Abexim, who is the real Preste Ioam of the East. The common error of supposing that it was he of Abexim originated with those whom, as we have said above, Dom Ioam II sent to discover Preste Ioam; for he commanded them to search for an Eastern King who was a Christian, and before whom a cross was always carried. So having come to Egypt and the Red Sea, and hearing of no other Christian ruler in those parts save the King of Abexim, one of their number made his way to that King's court; and when he found there both Christians and crosses, he, and others who went there afterwards and found the like, were persuaded that this was none other than Preste Ioam, and such they proclaimed him to be; and this belief has been current throughout Europe, though, as it appears, the real Preste Ioam is the Emperor of Catayo. Moreover, the Fathers who are in Mogor, who are continually receiving information about this country, understand that it is in Tartaria, and that it extends to the wall of China. They say also that it is more easily reached by way of China than by way of Mogor, which confirms what we have already said in our account of China in regard to the intercourse of the Fathers of Paquim [Peking] with these Christians.

The person chosen for this perilous mission and voyage of discovery was a Brother of our Company named Bento de Goges,[3] a native of the island of St. Miguel, a man of great courage and many attainments, and withal of such humility that, though fully qualified for the priesthood, he could not be prevailed upon to take that order. It was on account of his many virtues, and also because he was well versed in the Persian and Turkish languages, that he was selected for this important enterprise, a charge which he bravely accepted, and which, as will be seen from his letters, he undertook in willing obedience to the wishes of the Fathers and Superiors of the Company, and for the glory of God. It was considered that the best route for him to follow was that which traversed the kingdom of Mogor, as he would be able to join company with others travelling that way. He was, accordingly, sent from Goa, whither he had come with the Mogul ambassador, to Laor, so that he might commence his journey from that city. Here he made his preparations, partly with the money which had been given to him for the purpose in Goa, but mainly with the funds supplied by the King Achebar, which amounted to nearly four hundred *crusados* of our money, a gift that was greatly appreciated, and was the more remarkable as coming from a Moorish king, and one who was by no means renowned for his liberality. Even thus, his resources were all too slender for a journey which was likely to occupy, in the going and returning, at least four years; for the camel caravans, with which he was to travel, move very slowly, traversing always vast campos and sandy deserts, and seldom passing any cities on their way.

Bento Goges set out from Laor in the company of the ambassador of the King of Caygar, who happened providentially to be leaving Laor at this time. He was dressed, not as a Portuguese or a Father, but, after the fashion of the Moors, in cabaia and turban. He wore a sword in his belt, and carried also a bow and arrows; and to be able to journey with less danger through that vast Moorish region, he assumed the rôle of a merchant. He took with him a man of the Greek nation, by name Leam Grimam,[4] whom the Fathers had chosen for his companion. Besides being able to speak both Persian and Turkish, Leam Grimam was a man of affairs and a good Christian. It was solely on account of his affection for the Fathers of the Company that he consented to go on this long and hazardous journey, giving up the salary he received from the King, which was a *crusado* a day, and, what was a much greater sacrifice, leaving his wife, to whom he had only recently been married.

That the reader may the better perceive the courageous spirit in which our good Brother set forth on his mission, I shall here quote some passages from the letters he wrote to the Fathers and his Superiors at Goa on the eve of his departure from Laor, and after the commencement of his travels. In a letter to the Father Vice-Provincial, dated the 30th December, 1602, he wrote as follows:

"It has pleased God to bring me to this city of Laor, whence I am about to start for the country of Catayo. I should be neglecting my bounden duty if I departed without first writing to bid farewell to Your Reverence and my beloved Brothers in the lands of the South. I bade farewell to Father Ieronimo Xauier, and Father Antonio Machado at Agra on the 29th October. When I parted from them, I parted also from the dress I was wearing, exchanging it for the costume of the country, in which I am now attired. I will not attempt to tell Your Reverence what my feelings were when I saw myself in these strange garments. When they came to see me for the last time, Father Xauier and Father Antonio Machado remained with me the whole night giving me advice and instruction. It was with a sorrowful heart that I took leave of them and set out for Laor. On the way, some took me for a Saiyid, which means a descendant of Mafamede, and others for a grandee of the kingdom of Meca; but they little knew the school in which I had been brought up. May God be praised for all his blessings.

"I arrived at Laor on the 8th December, the day of the Conception of our Lady. I made my arrival known to Father Manoel Pinheyro and Father Corsi, but did not go to their house, as I had been instructed not to do so. Father Manoel Pinheyro came to see me, being much concerned that he could not entertain me, as is the custom of our Company. I am staying in the house of a Venetian named Ioao Galiseo, where I am playing the part of a merchant. To make my disguise more complete, I am wearing a beard reaching to my breast, and long hair, as is the fashion amongst these people. All this, my Father, I am doing for the love of the Lord, who so greatly loveth us, and suffered for us. I beg your Reverence after reading this to say a mass for me to our Lady of Victory, that she may enable me to triumph over all my enemies and difficulties; and I beg the same of all the Fathers and Brothers of these parts. They know well that those amongst whom I am going are wolves, the arch enemies of our faith; but I go confident that I have their prayers.

"I am now known as Banda Abedula, that is 'Servant of God,'[5] a name which Father Ieronimo Xauier gave to me when we parted. The seal on this letter is made with the ring which, following the custom of the country, I now wear on my finger. The King has been very generous to me. He has furnished me with many of the necessities for my journey, and has also paid me for the whole time that I was in India.[6] With this money, amounting to more than a thousand rupees, the Fathers have paid off some debts, and I have defrayed the cost of my journey from India to Agra. May God make His Majesty a Christian, which is the greatest good we can desire for him in this life. It remains only for me to send my greetings to your Reverence and to the Fathers and Brothers in those parts. May the peace of Jesus Christ be with them and with you. Amen. From Laor, the 30th December, 1602."

In another letter written before his departure to Father Ieronimo Xauier, dated the 24th February,[7] 1603, he says:

"I write in reply to the letter of farewell which your Reverence has addressed to this your Brother. My Father, our Lord alone knows how my heart overflowed with affection as I read and studied your words. Your Reverence does well to encourage his weak Brother with such letters and counsels. I cannot help repeating the words of the Apostle Paul, 'I live, and yet not I, but Christ liveth in me'; for it was by meditating on the teaching and words of Christ, that he came to say so many marvellous things in his Epistles. Therefore, reverend Father, I beg you, who are so learned in the holy Scriptures, that you will not cease to water this barren soul of mine which so sorely needs divine strength, so that I may be able to raise and bring back fruit from the lands of Catayo, whither my duty calls me; and though our Company of Jesus desires to build so lofty an edifice, with foundations as deep as its great height requires, yet I shall find support in the words of the holy Scriptures, 'God is able of these stones, etc.' Although, my Father, you are far from where I am, and from where I shall be, I cast myself, and remain always prostrate at your feet, kissing them many times, and asking pardon for my faults. I leave my soul in your hands, a living sacrifice before the most holy Trinity. May Jesus Christ grant that my eyes may yet in this life look upon your Reverence; then shall I be able to sing the song of Symeam, 'Lord, now lettest thou thy servant depart in peace.' And if it shall be that we do not see each other again, he who first enters beatitude shall be mediator before God for the other that the day may quickly dawn when he shall escape from the trials and tempests of this life.

"As Senhor Leam Grimao, whom I am well content to have as a companion, has now arrived, we have decided to take the road without delay. We have purchased camels and we start on Sunday. Today, which is the first Friday in Lent, we are carrying our belongings to the other side of the river,[8] where there is a caravan which is about to leave for Cabul. I am taking with me the memoranda and instructions which your Reverence has sent to me together with my letters-patent, and a letter for those at Catayo, and another for the Fathers at Paquim in China. I am also taking a memorandum from the Archbishop of Goa treating about the schisms which have appeared amongst these people, and in addition I have a paper on which are written all the moveable feasts down to the year 1620. I am going very well provided, needing only the offerings and prayers of the Fathers of India and Europe, to whom I beg your Reverence to write asking them to commend me to God. I carry with me, on my head, the sign and name of our reverend Father General, together with the vows that I have made before God and the whole court of heaven, as well as the signature [*firma*] of your Reverence, and of the Father Bobadilha, and of our visiting Father, Nicolao Pimenta and our Father Provincial, Nuno Rodrigues. All these I carry in a kind of Moorish reliquary, which I keep folded in a turban. On my breast I wear a cross with two evangils, one from S. Ioam, *In principio era verbum*, and the other from S. Marcos

Euntes mundun universum. These are the panoply in which I go armed. I beg your Reverence to write and obtain for me the unceasing prayers of my brother novices, who are very dear to me because of their fellowship with Christ our Lord. And because they are the tender plants in a garden which is constantly watered with grace from heaven, it cannot but be that their prayers and penances will find acceptance in His sight.

"My Father, it is time that we were on our way. I must therefore bring this letter to an end. But my thoughts of your Reverence do not end with it; for my heart can never lose the memory of the affection and kindness which your Reverence has always shown to his brother Bento de Goes; nor shall I ever lay aside the counsels which, as one experienced and schooled in the adversities of the world, you have sent to me at this hour of my departure; for those who have never suffered, who have never been cold, or hungry, or forsaken, cannot tell what such trials mean. Thus, outwardly, I bid your Reverence farewell, and crave your holy blessing; but inwardly I am still with you. Written from Laor, the 14th of February, 1603."

In another letter written after he had travelled a distance of 102 *coss* (equal to as many Italian miles) he thus replied to one he had received from Father Manoel Pinheyro:

"Your Reverence's letter written on the 4th March, containing news of the realm, reached me on the 7th of the month. I cannot describe the joy and the longings with which it filled my heart; nor can I help shedding many tears on account of the love which I have for my Brothers, whom I remember every day in my solitude. For it is my chief recreation to think about them, whereby my spirit is greatly refreshed. Owing to the difficulties and the turmoil of the journey, I am unable to observe the regular times and forms of prayer. I therefore use ejaculatory prayers [*jaculatorias*], communing with God in my heart; and thus I gain strength to bear this cross, which to others may seem heavy, but which to me seems light and pleasant, since I bear it for love of the Creator of all things. We are still fasting, taking our meal only at night. Though we have to pay much for it, our fare consists only of a little rice with ghee, some coarse cakes [*apas*],[9] and some onions; if we can get a little salt fish, we count it a treat, though it causes thirst. The cold is very severe, for we are passing mountains covered with snow. But of all these trials, which I bear with serenity, I make your Reverence, and all who belong to this Mission, partakers. Trusting in your Reverence's holy masses, etc.

" Written from the province of Gaçar, 102 *coss* from Laor."[10]

In another letter written after he had been six months on his way, he wrote that he was amongst very barbarous and savage people; but that, having God with him, he had no fear. To a barbarian king, who threatened to have him thrown under the feet of elephants, he replied calmly that he was not afraid, and that he desired nothing better than to die for the love of the true God and Creator of the universe.

CHAPTER III[1]

AT YARKAND

REGARDING the progress of this mission, the success of which is so earnestly desired, there is at this time only one letter from Brother Bento de Goes who has gone to explore this Christian country. It was written on the 2nd February, 1604,[2] when the Brother was at Hircande [Yarkand] at the court of the King who rules over Cascar [Kashgar] and other territories subject to him. In this letter he writes that as soon as it became known that an Armenian Rume had arrived, who was not a follower of their accursed prophet, all the people of the court were filled with astonishment, for they could not believe that the world contained a man of intelligence who followed any law but their own. When his arrival had been made known to the King, the Brother went to pay his respects, taking with him a present, as is customary in these parts. This consisted of one large and three smaller mirrors, a silken cloth to spread on the royal dais [*estrado*], a white cloth with coloured stripes, three loaves of sugar, and some sweetmeats.[3] The King accepted the present, and at this interview nothing further transpired. A day or two later he sent for Goes and ordered him to bring with him the holy gospel and the cross, having been told about these things by one of his vassals, or Captains, who had been to the Brother's lodging to inspect his belongings, and to see if he could find amongst them any curiosities for the King. Amongst other things the Captain saw a breviary and a richly ornamented cross, and he asked what they were. The Brother said that the book related to the holy Gospel of Jesus Christ, and that the cross was the emblem of the Christians, and was a representation of that on which the Son of God died to save the world. The Captain wanted to take these things to the King; but the Brother persuaded him not to take them away, and begged him to say nothing about them to the King. The Captain promised that he would disclose nothing; but the moment he reached the palace he gave an account of all that he had seen; and very soon afterwards the Brother was sent for, as we have already said. In compliance with this order, he made his way to the palace, where he found the King surrounded by numerous gentlemen and lords of his court, all of whom wore long beards, which gave them a very venerable appearance. After he had made his obeisance, the King expressed his desire to see the holy Gospel, that is, the breviary mentioned above. With great reverence the Brother drew it from the covering in which he had carefully folded it, and having kissed it, placed it on his head, the whole court watching him attentively. Then a courtier came forward to take it and hand it to the King. Before entrusting it to him, Brother Goes again kissed it and placed it on his head, and the courtier on taking it did the same, as did also the King when it was put into his hands. When he opened it, the King was astonished to see how small the letters were, and yet so perfectly formed. He asked the

Brother if he could read the book; and on his saying that he could, he told him to read some portion of it aloud. The first passage on which the Brother's eye fell happened to be the antiphony which is sung on the day of the Ascension of our Lord, *Viri Galilei quid statis aspicientes in cælum*, etc. These words he intoned in a loud voice, and with so much devotion that tears fell from his eyes. Observing his emotion, the Moors too were moved to tears and sighs. They asked him to tell them the meaning of the words he had recited, and the Brother, rejoicing at the opportunity thus given him of proclaiming the name of Christ in the presence of these infidels, discoursed to them on the Ascension, on the coming of the Holy Spirit on the Apostles, and, in particular, on the Day of Judgment. Then, opening the breviary again, he read the psalm beginning, *Miserere mei Deus*, which he also briefly explained to them. His words made a great impression on the infidels, who looked at one another in open-mouthed surprise, and the King in his astonishment said, "What marvellous thing is this?"

When asked to exhibit the cross, the Brother drew it forth, and kissing it with great respect, said, addressing the King, "Sire, this is the symbol of the Christians; and when we pray we place it before us." They asked him to which quarter the Christians turned when they prayed; and he answered, "To all quarters; for God is in all." They then enquired if the Christians used ablutions. He told them, not as they did, attending only to the washing of the body. Our ablutions he said, were spiritual washings, cleansing the conscience for we hold that mere outward washings cannot profit the soul while the conscience is full of sin and uncleanness. In the end they were all very satisfied with what they had heard. But none felt more satisfaction than the good Brother, who looked on the hardships and perils he had encountered as blessings, since they had enabled him to make known in the court of such a King the gospel of Christ, and His coming again on the last day.

The King afterwards sent many times for the Brother. On one occasion he showed him a number of manuscripts. Amongst them were some that were very beautifully illuminated and inscribed in round characters of a red colour. The King asked what these were about. The Brother finding that they dealt with the mystery of the Holy Trinity, commenced to speak on this subject, emphasising in particular, as did also these writings, the unity of God, and dwelling on His greatness and omnipotence; how all things that we see depend upon Him, and He on nothing; how He was the beginning of all things, though all things are in Him; and other matters of a like nature as God gave him utterance. The Moors were again deeply impressed by the Brother's words, and said one to another, "Are these the people we call Caffres, and men without a law? Their knowledge of God is no less than ours!" And the King said, "Truly this man is a Mulla."

Not long afterwards, the chief Moors of the place took counsel together saying, how excellent it would be if this man could be forced to accept the law of salvation; for it is grievous to think that one so worthy of respect must die and go to hell. But others said, what is the use of talking like this? You may strike him on the head with a sledge-hammer, but do not think you will make him abandon his law. There was one of them, however, who made the affair his own, and used every means he could devise to carry it through, until one evening the Brother went to see him in his house, and said to him, "Sir, why do you take all this useless trouble? You do not understand that my law is the essence of my being. If it is my property you want, you know where it is to be found, and you have only to go and take it. Or here is my body, which, if you like, you can tear to pieces. In either case I shall count myself as fortunate." After this, the Moor abandoned his purpose, and never spoke of it again.

On another occasion he was sent for by Merisachias [Mirza Ghyas ?], the King's chief minister and a very powerful lord, who asked many things about the Christians and their ways. The Brother answered all his questions, telling him of our customs, and of the Christian practice of self-examination which greatly surprised him. One of those present, out of pity for the Brother, asked him to repeat with him the salutation to Mafamede, so that he might be saved, for there was nothing else that he needed. He then began, with much fervour, to intone it [presumably the *kalimah*], and was much disconcerted to find that the Brother did not join in his prayer. The other Moors ground their teeth in anger, and a tumult arose, in the midst of which a sword was called for. In no way discomposed, the Brother turned to him who had summoned him, and in a calm voice said, "You ordered me to come to you, and I am here under your parole. By replying courteously to your questions, what injury have I done you?" This answer completely appeased the anger of the Moors, and many things were said in praise of the Brother.

Before reaching this city, the Brother had been able, in circumstances of which we know little (owing to the loss of the letters referring thereto), to do a service to the Queen of this country, who, while journeying from a certain place, had been robbed of her baggage containing all her personal possessions, and was thus left without even the ordinary necessities of life. Bento de Goes happened to be in the place to which she had come, and hearing of her plight, assisted her, as far as his means permitted, with funds for her immediate expenses.[4] When this became known, there was great astonishment amongst the infidels, and especially at the King's court, where all praised the Brother and thanked him for his service to their Queen, who had found in him, a stranger, the assistance she had sought in vain amongst her countrymen.

The Queen reached the court after the Brother had arrived there. Many people, with gifts in their hands, went forth from the city to welcome her. A message was sent to the Prince, her son, to whose residence [i.e. Khotan] it was an eight days' journey, and he came post-haste to see his mother. Two days after his arrival, the Brother went to see him, armed with his present. On being informed that he had come, the Prince at once came out to receive him. The Brother, following the custom of the country, would have embraced his feet; but the Prince would not permit this, and taking him kindly by the arm raised him to his feet. He then made enquiries after his health, and asked how old he was, where he had come from, and why he had left his own country. He also said that he had ordered the repayment in full of the amount he had advanced to the Queen.

This Prince is twenty-six years of age. He is of a very amiable disposition, and is well liked by the people, who will gladly welcome him to the throne on the death of him who now reigns. He was very friendly in his behaviour to Brother Goes, showing him so much favour that, besides always giving him a seat near his own, he told him that when he wished to come to his house he need not trouble to send word beforehand, but that he was to come at once into his presence and sit down without ceremony. Having been told of the breviary, he asked that it might be brought to him. His request having been complied with, he kept the book for so long a time that at last the Brother asked that it might be returned to him. The Prince at first looked somewhat abashed, and then said with a smile, "If I do not let you have it again, what will you do?" "Sire," said the Brother, "it is not the custom of Kings to use force with their subjects:" a reply which pleased the Prince and those who were with him. Some of the latter asked him to send for the book, which they were very anxious to see. But he took no notice of their request; and a few moments later he rose, and took the Brother with him to his apartment, giving orders that no one else was to be admitted. He then told a servant to bring the breviary; and when the man was about to deliver it to Goes, the Prince stopped him, and rising from his seat, himself took the book from the servant, and kissing it, placed it in the hands of the Brother, at the same time begging him to read aloud and explain some portions of it. By the manner in which he read, the Brother brought tears into the Prince's eyes. Amongst other things he spoke to him about the power of the Pope, the manner of his election, and what he represents on earth, of the way in which Christians make confession of their sins, of the hospitals and houses of mercy which they maintain, of the power and majesty of our Kings, of the bishops and cardinals, and of the government of Christian States: all of which things interested the Prince so much, that he could talk to his companions of nothing else. After some days, he went back to his estates whence he had come. He tried to persuade the Brother to accompany him, assuring him that he had nothing to fear. "My own sword," he said, "shall protect you."

In the city of Hircande, the residence of the King of these realms, there are a hundred mosques. Every Friday a Moor comes to the market-place [*praca*] and in a loud voice bids all men remember that it is Friday, and that it is their duty to attend the principal mosque and perform the ceremonies and prayers ordained in their Alcoran. Afterwards twelve men come forth from the mosque armed with leathern thongs, with which they chastise all whom they meet who have not said their prayers; and those who are beaten are absolved from their sin.[5] Each quarter of the city has its own mosque, to which all the people of that quarter are obliged to go five times a day to pray. If they do not go, they are made to pay fines. As the Brother did not attend these *namazas* [prayers], as they call them, the *cacizes*[6] tried to make him pay the fine, putting him to much trouble. So at last he went to the King and told him that the Mullas, who are the *cacizes*, would not leave him in peace and demanded his money. On hearing his story, the King and those who were with him laughed heartily; nevertheless, the *cacizes* were reprimanded, and the King told the Brother that he was free to live as he liked, and that no one should interfere with him.

God gave such grace to this Brother that there was no one who had any dealings with him who did not become his friend. There was never a feast in the city to which he was not invited. On these occasions they used to ask him questions about the Christian faith, which he thus had many opportunities of expounding. The Moors themselves used to preach every day near one of their schools. Large numbers of mats were brought for the people to sit upon, and a high chair for the preacher. Close to the chair a staff was stuck in the ground, which from time to time the preacher grasped, raising himself from his seat and continuing his harangue with many gesticulations. The sermons always dealt with stories of their false prophet, and were directed against Caffres and Christians.

Concerning the continuation of his journey for the fulfilment of his mission, the Brother made arrangements to travel in the company of an ambassador who was going from Hirchande to Trufam [Turfan], where caravans are formed for journeying to Catayo. This ambassador, who was a much-respected person, assured the Brother that he could both take him and bring him back safely, and he added that it was many years since any of our people had been to those parts. It is the custom for ambassadors to purchase [the leadership of] these journeys. The price paid by this man was 200 bags of musk, which he delivered to the King before setting out. As the ambassador can take with him [into Catayo] only seventy-two persons, merchants bribe him heavily to be included in this number. Those who pay but little are excluded; but to all who bring him presents the ambassador pledges his word, which he afterwards breaks in many cases, since all cannot enter with him. They start from this city, but travel very slowly on account of the numbers that join the ambassador, who makes a big profit.

The journey onwards to Trufam takes forty days, from thence to Camur [Camul] seven days, and from Camur to the gates of Catayo eleven days.[7] However many travellers there may be, they never allow more than seventy-two to pass in. To each of these a horse is supplied for every stage of the journey, and two attendants, as well as expenses for food whilst travelling through those parts. They say that five hundred mules are supplied for each day's march until the court is reached.

Here in Hircande the Brother found fans [*abanos*], paper, sticks of ink [*pao de tinta*], porcelain, and rhubarb, all of which come from Catayo; and by sea, from the other side, it is said that seed pearls [*aljofar*], cinnamon, and cloves [*cravo*], are brought into Catayo, while in the country itself is to be found abundance of ginger and loaf-sugar. From this it would appear that Catayo, though it is not the same as China (since what is related of the kings of Catayo is quite different from what we know for certain of the kings of China), is very near to, and closely resembles it.

The Brother was also greatly pleased and encouraged by seeing some paintings on paper which had come from Catayo. Amongst them was one representing a man wearing a biretta on which a cross was fixed, and another man stood before him with folded hands. This appeared to be the portrait of some bishop. He also saw painted on porcelain a Franciscan monk hanging by his girdle, with what looked like a tonsure on his head, though he wore the long beard of a Chinaman.

In travelling to Hircande the Brother traversed the worst roads he had met with in the whole of his journey, his route lying through the deserts of Pamech [Pamir]. The cold was so intense that five of his horses died. The country was uninhabited and no fire-wood was obtainable. The air was so bad that men could hardly breathe, while their horses suffered to such an extent that many collapsed suddenly, and fell dead for want of breath. Against this their only remedies were garlic, onions, or dried apricots, which they ate themselves and applied to the mouths of their animals. This desert is crossed in forty days when there is snow, and at other times more rapidly. It is infested with savage robbers, who lie in wait for caravans and commit many atrocities.

Since the receipt of the letter of the 2nd February, from which we learnt the particulars given above, there has come to hand another written in August of the same year from which we learn that he was able to make good arrangements for the continuation of his journey. The Captain of the caravan with which he was to travel offered to include him amongst the five who go as ambassadors; but he felt that he could not afford to live up to this position, and was content to go as one of the seventy-two passengers. He says also in this letter that while he was in the city of Hircande, the King and all the people showed him much kindness, and in particular the Prince above mentioned, with whom the Brother spent some days in the city where he lived. Christian merchants will never meet with such friendly treatment in these parts; but will find the people only too ready to rob them of their goods and drink their blood. This is well illustrated by the behaviour of a certain Moor, who was the agent of the devil himself, though all the people looked on him as a Saint. One day, this man, who gloried in his reputation, and claimed that he had caused the deaths of many people by his invocations came up to the Brother, with whom were many other people, and holding a knife to his breast bade him say the salutation to his Mafamede, or forfeit his life. His countrymen who were standing around said one to another, that it must have been revealed to him in a vision that he would be doing God a service by slaying this man; but some foreign merchants came forward and took the knife from his hands. The Brother, meanwhile, had merely smiled at the Moor's threats and violent language; and this drove him to such fury and indignation that he swore great oaths that he would have the Christian merchant's life. But God protected his pilgrim, and caused him to be looked on with such favour wherever he went that, though he did not escape the enmity of men like this Moor, there were always others ready to defend him. But in these and all other dangers he encountered his only reliance was on the fountain of all good. Thus, his manner of life was an example to all at this court, who, despite their false beliefs, admitted to one another that they had never known so righteous a man as the Brother, or any Armenian like him. It was because of the respect in which he was held that a certain merchant who had come from Moscouia, and who sometimes made the sign of the cross, came to him and besought him for a remedy for his little son who for a year past had been lying ill, with none to afford him relief. As he had been on friendly terms with this merchant, the Brother went to his house to see the child, taking his breviary with him. This he placed on the patient's head, after which he read the Gospel to him, and before departing hung a cross about his neck. Within three days, by the will of God, the child was cured.

Before his departure, a caravan arrived from Catayo. But the Moors who came with it could tell him nothing of the country except that the inhabitants were *cafares*, which means people without a law. Some called them Franks, which is a name they give to all Portuguese and Christians. The Brother also found at Hircande a captive king of Tabete [Tibet], who had been captured by a trick and brought there three years previously. His name was Gombuna Miguel [Gompo Namgyal].[8] The Brother sometimes went to see him; but he was unable to understand his language, and all that he learnt from him by means of signs was that in his country they read the Angil [Kanjur ?],[9] that is to say, the Evangelho. Amongst those who came with him, however, there was a doctor by name Lunrique,[10] who could speak Persian, and he told the Brother that in his land there was no circumcision; but that on the eighth day children are taken to their Botelhana,[11] which is their church, and that their Itolama washes them and names them after the Saints which are painted in their churches. He also said that their chief Father, whom they call Cumgao,[12] wears a mitre on his head and a robe which resembles a chasuble; that the people observe a fast of forty days during which they abstain from food till nightfall, and take neither wine nor flesh; but at the end of the forty days they make a great feast and again eat flesh; he said that they have the Angil, which is the Evangelho; that their Fathers do not marry; that they believe in a day of judgment, and in eight hells and three paradises, to all of which names are given; that each of the hells is for the expiation of particular crimes, and each paradise for the enjoyment of particular rewards. He said further that some of their grandees were in Catayo, which was a month's journey from their Tabete, and that those in Catayo would be very glad to see the Brother.

CHAPTER IV[1]

Yarkand to Suchou

In the earlier portions of our narrative we wrote all that we then knew concerning the mission undertaken by Brother Bento de Goes of our Company for the discovery of the Christians said to be living in the realms of Catayo, and of what befell him on his way. As it has pleased God that he should accomplish his mission, though the end was not what he had expected, we shall now tell what we know of the remainder of his journey and how it ended. But first, to preserve the thread of our story, we shall briefly recapitulate what we have already written.

This good Brother, then, left the city of Agra and the court of the Great Mogor on the 6th of January, 1603.[2] In order that he might not be recognised as a European, he travelled in the guise of an Armenian merchant, carrying a bow and arrows, and wearing a beard and long hair, but showing by the manner of his dress that he was a Christian. He was accompanied by a Greek deacon named Leão, and a merchant, also a Greek, named Demetrio. He also took with him another Christian Armenian named Isaac, a married man of that city, who was his faithful companion throughout the whole of his journey, and until his death. From Agra he went to Lahor, which is also the Great Mogor's capital; and from there he set out for the East with a caravan of merchants. After a journey of nearly four months they arrived at Papur [Peshawar][3] where they halted twenty days. In Cafristão,[4] which they reached in twenty marches, they halted for a similar period, after which they journeyed for twenty-five days to Zedeli [Jagdalak][5], being much troubled by brigands as they approached this city. From Zedeli they travelled in twenty days to Cabul, a large and very busy city, where they remained for eight months.[6] Some of the merchants were left behind here, and with them the two Greeks who had accompanied Brother Goes.[7]

In this city the Brother met the sister of the King of Cascar [Kashgar], who was also mother of the ruler of Cotao [Khotan]. She was known by the title, Ahchanam, which amongst the Moors, signifies "the beatified lady from Meca." To this lady, who on arriving at Cabul found herself in straitened circumstances, the Brother rendered valuable assistance, in return for which he afterwards received tokens of gratitude both from the lady and from her son. From Cabul the caravan went on to Characar [Charikar],[8] where the Brother became seriously ill, and he had not fully recovered when his journey recommenced. At the end of forty-five days the caravan reached Calca,[9] a land where the people are of a ruddy complexion and fair-haired [*ruiuos & louros*], and proceeded thence to a place called Talhan [Talikhan], which was reached in twenty-five days. On leaving here they suffered much at the hands of brigands. The Brother was amongst those who suffered loss, as well as much ill-usage at the hands of the Moors. Once when he was some distance from his companions, four brigands came down upon him. Seeing that they intended to rob him, he took a costly turban, and placing a stone in it, flung it as far away as he was able,[10] anticipating what actually happened; for whilst the thieves were quarrelling as to whose the prize should be, he put spurs to his horse and made good his escape. As they continued on their way they were repeatedly attacked by bands of robbers, who inflicted many indignities on them as well as hard blows. They also endured many hardships on account of the roughness of the roads and the snow which covered them; while the cold was so severe that many of the travellers died from its effects, and the Brother barely escaped the same fate.

At last, however, in the month of November, 1603, they reached the metropolis of the kingdom of Cascar, which is a very populous city named Hircande [Yarkand]. As caravans from Cabul do not proceed beyond this city, a fresh arrangement had to be made for the onward journey. The Brother was detained here a year, waiting for a favourable opportunity to set forth.

In this city he again met the Lady from Meca who used her influence on his behalf, so that he was well received by the King, her brother, who also afforded him assistance in preparing for his journey. On the 14th of November he set out with a caravan, the command of which the King had sold to one of the principal merchants, who was given complete authority over all the others. After travelling for nearly a year[11] they reached a city called Chalis [Kara-shahr]. On this journey they traversed many wild and rugged tracts and waterless deserts, encountering hardships as severe as any that they had previously endured. The Brother was often in great peril; but God miraculously delivered him from the hands of the Moors and infidels, who hate the very name of Christian, and whose cursed law pardons those who ill-use or slay the followers of the Christian faith.

Chalis is a small town, but well fortified. Here the Brother met some Moors who, under the pretence of being ambassadors, had been to China to sell their merchandise. These told him that at the court of Pachim (which they call Hambalac, or Cambuluc), there were some Christian strangers who had given the King a big present consisting of clocks, clavichords [*crauos pera tanger*], pictures, and other things, and that they had been well received by the King and the nobles of the realm. It turned out that these Moors, whilst at Paquim, which was in the year 1601, had been lodged next to Father Matheus Ricio and his companions, in the garden [*cerca*] where strangers are quartered, and had frequent intercourse with them. Being fond of curiosities, they had brought back with them a piece of paper with Portuguese writing on it which they showed to Bento de Goes.[12] The Brother was very glad to see this, and felt convinced that these Christian people must be the Fathers of the Company whom he knew had gone to China with the intention of proceeding to Paquim.

While in Chalis, the Brother made a present to the Lord of the country, and asked that he might be permitted to go on in advance of the caravan. This was granted, though it was contrary to the will of the

Captain. When making out his passport, the King asked him how he wished that this should be done. He replied that he should be described as being of the law of Jesus, which in the Moorish tongue would be signified by the words, Abdula issac [*Abdullah isawi*= Abdullah the Christian).[13] On hearing this, one of the oldest of the *cacizes* who were present, removing his turban and placing it on the ground, said, " This man is a true follower of his law, which he confesses in the presence of your Highness, and before all of us, who, were we to find ourselves amongst Christians, would deny our law, and through fear, or for worldly considerations, pass ourselves off as Christians, being nothing of the kind."

Having departed from Chalis, the Brother came, on the 17th of October, 1605, to Camul, where he remained for the space of a month. He then resumed his march, and in nine days' time[14] reached the walls of China. Here at last—after all the vicissitudes of his strange and perilous journey, which he had undertaken for the love of God and in faithful obedience to the wishes of his Superiors, as well as on account of his own earnest desire to discover that remote Christian community in search of which he had been sent—here at last he was finally convinced that there was in the world no other Catayo but the kingdom of China, and that the information which the Moors had brought to the court of the great Mogul, and all that they had related of the grandeur of the King of Catayo, and of the Christians over whom he ruled, were either the outcome of their ignorance or deliberate fabrications.

This was confirmed by Father Mattheus Ricio who, in a letter written on the 12th November, 1607,[15] to the Father Provincial of India, said that Christendom and the world in general need no longer be under any misapprehension in regard to the country of Catayo, which was none other than China. As to the Christians who were reported to be in this kingdom, and more particularly in the provinces of Xensi [Shen-si] and Honam [Honan], he said that he had sent Brothers of the Company, natives of China, to each of these provinces to make enquiries and clear the matter up; and that it had been ascertained by these Brothers that there had actually been many Christian families in these parts who had continued to follow their law up to the beginning of the last half-century; but that since then, fearing that the Chinese sought to kill them, as being descendants of the Tartars who five hundred years previously had subdued China, they had all dispersed and abandoned their law, and today they would not admit that they are the descendants of those Christians.

But to return to our good Brother Bento de Goes. Having reached, as we have said, the walls of China, he was obliged to wait outside them for twenty-five days whilst a messenger was sent to the Tutam[16] to obtain permission for him and his companions to pass in. When he was allowed to proceed, which was at the end of the year 1605, the names of all were written down and a list was made of the goods which they carried. The day after passing through the walls he arrived at the city of Subecheo [Su-chou],[17] and he at once dispatched a letter to the Fathers at Paquim,[18] of whom he heard further news from some Moors in this city. Of the companions with whom he had set out, the two Greeks, Leão and Demetrio, left him at Hircande;[19] only Isaac remained with him always and entered China with him. He had also some servants whom he had picked up during his journey. The caravan of Moors with which he had travelled arrived six months later.

The Brother was in this city for fifteen or sixteen months waiting for the safe-conduct which he had asked the Fathers to obtain for him, together with the passport which, as a foreigner, he required to enable him to pass through China to the court at Paquim. At the end of that time, there came to him a Brother of our Company named Ioao Fernandez, a native of China, whom Father Mattheus Riccio, on learning of his arrival, sent in search of him.

For a month past, Goes had been on a bed of sickness; and Fernandez found him completely worn-out by the hardships he had been through, and so emaciated that he appeared to be a living skeleton. Even though, during his journey through those vast interiors which he went to explore, he had suffered no other distress but that of finding in the great kingdoms through which he passed so many millions devoted to the cursed law of Mafamede, and not a single soul that knew the true faith, it would have seemed like a miracle that he lived to get as far as he did. How much more miraculous, then, does it seem when, in addition to his agony of mind, we remember the bodily sufferings which he endured, and that he was ever in the evil company of the Moors, who are so full of deceit and malice that the Brother had good reason for saying that no Christian could make by land such a pilgrimage as this owing to the treacherous character of the Moors.

No one can imagine, nor can words describe the joy of Bento de Goes on learning of the arrival of Ioam Fernandez, and on seeing once more a Brother of the Company of Jesus. He welcomed him as though he had been an angel sent from heaven. Nor did he rejoice less at the good tidings which Fernandez brought to him of the Fathers, and of the good work they had done in China. Taking the letters which had been brought to him from the Father, he kissed them reverently, and raising his hands to heaven sang the song of the aged Simeam, while his eyes filled with tears of pure devotion and joy. All that night he kept the letters clasped in his hands, giving continual thanks to our Lord for bringing him to the end of his long pilgrimage, which he had undertaken in obedience to, and for the glory of God, and the salvation of souls. For although he did not find the Christians of Catayo who were believed to be in existence, he did, in his love for them, the utmost that duty could demand. Ioam Fernandez was anxious to make arrangements forthwith for taking him to Pachim, as he had been ordered to do by Father Mateus Ricio. But the good Brother knew that this could not be; and realising that his hour was fast approaching he desired to be left in peace. Consoled by the presence of Brother Ioam

Fernandez, he spent the few days that remained to him in earnest preparation for his journey into eternity, upon which he entered on the 11th of April, 1607;[20] for on that day he died, leaving us assured that he had gone to enjoy the bliss which he had merited by a life so holy and so full of good works.

This blessed Brother was a native of Villafranca in the island of S. Miguel. He was a member of the Order for nineteen years, having entered it at the age of twenty-six. His conversion was marked by a very marvellous circumstance, and one which clearly betokened the glorious end to which he was destined. When a young man, and while serving as a soldier in India, he was sent with the fleet to the coast of Malauar, and came to Trauancor where, close to Coleche,[21] there is a church dedicated to our Lady the Virgin. He had hitherto lived a life of pleasure, devoting himself to gambling and various other follies to which youth is prone; but at this time he was seized with such bitter remorse that he lost all hope of salvation. Happening to land near this church, he entered it; and seeing over the altar our Lady the Virgin with her child in her lap, he fell on his knees before her, and implored her with tears to obtain for him from her blessed son forgiveness for his sins. At the same instant he lifted his eyes and lo! the little Jesus, lying in the arms of his mother was also weeping. As he looked, there came forth from the eyes of the little child a stream as it were of milk, which ran down until it overflowed the altar. Amazed at what he saw, Bento de Goes ran to call his comrades that they might come and bear witness to this marvel. They came and with their own eyes saw that it was as de Goes had told them; and taking a handkerchief they dipped it in the milk-like liquid, and parted it amongst themselves.[22] Then they went away and fired a salute of guns and musketry, after which they cut down branches from the trees with which they came and decorated the church until it had the appearance of a greenwood. Moved by this manifestation of the divine compassion, our soldier went forthwith to a Father of our Company and with great devotion made a general confession covering all his past life. At the same time he took the vows of religion and joined our Company, in the service of which he laboured so unceasingly and died so nobly.

On his death, the Moors who had come with him, and who were lodged in the same hostel, wished to bury him in accordance with the rites of their Alcoram, But Brother Ioam Fernandez did not permit this; and he and the faithful Isaac, having placed the body in a coffin, buried it after the Christian fashion in a quiet spot, whence on the day of judgment our Brother will arise glorious to receive a second stole, and the guerdon due to his merits.

The Brother had kept a diary in which he used to write from day to day all that took place during his pilgrimage. He had also written down in the same book the acknowledgments which the Moors gave him for the amounts which he had frequently advanced to them from his slender resources. Wherefore, the moment they heard of his death, the Moors came to his room and possessed themselves of this book, which they tore in pieces, so that no one might be able to compute their debts. Ioam Fernandez and Isaac the Armenian were greatly distressed by the loss of this diary and journal which the Brother had kept. All that they could do was to collect as many of the fragments as they could find, and these they took with them to Father Matheus Ricio who fitted them together piece by piece. It was with the help of these, and what he was able to learn from Isaac, that the Father composed the brief narrative of the pilgrimage of Goes of which we have previously spoken.[23]

The possessions which the Brother left included a breviary, a cross which he wore about his neck, a paper on which were written in his own hand the vows which he had taken, the *firmas*, or subscriptions, of the letters which our Father General, the visiting Father, and the Father Provincial of India had written to him, the patent of Father Ieronymo Xauier, and the chapter from the writings of the Apostle St. Paul which is read at mass on his day, in which the Apostle glories in the trials he endured for Christ. All these things the Father guarded with great veneration, as relics of this holy Brother, whose piety was such that amidst all the confusion and turmoil of his interminable journey he never failed to observe the holy seasons of the Church, often withdrawing himself for many days beforehand to perform the religious exercises of our Company, so that there was none who did not marvel at his devotion.

The unflagging devotion of Isaac, the companion

of Brother Bento de Goes, renders it meet that, in concluding our account of this important mission, we should say something of what befell this faithful Armenian ere he reached the end of his travels. After the death of the Brother he was greatly troubled by the Moors, who accused him before their justices of being a Moor who had turned Christian. But Brother Ioam Fernandez stood by him bravely; and on the day when he appeared to answer the charge made against him, the Brother brought some pork which he made the Armenian eat in the presence of his accusers. The Moors, who abominate pork to such an extent that they cannot bear even to look at it, declared that the Armenian had amply refuted their charge,[24] and left him in peace.

The Brother and Isaac set out with their servants, and after travelling for three months reached Paquim, the royal city of China. Here they were received by Father Mattheus Ricio, who rejoiced at their safe return, while deeply lamenting the death of Brother Bento de Goes. Isaac was sent well provided to Amacao [Macao] where the Fathers raised a good sum for him, which they helped him to invest in goods that are esteemed in India. On his way to Malaca the ship in which he sailed was seized by the Olandeses [the Dutch], whose Captain questioned him, and learning from him of the journey which Brother Bento de Goes had made to discover Catayo, and all for the sake of the Christians who were said to be living there, he marvelled at the Brother's great courage; and when he heard of the countries he had traversed, and the kingdoms he had discovered, travelling by land through the heart of that vast Eastern interior which stretches from Goa to China (for indeed this must be accounted one of the most daring journeys of discovery, perhaps the most daring, that any man has ever made), he ordered Isaac to set down all the details in writing, saying that there were Jesuit Fathers in his country to whom he would show the account, that they might know how much those of their Company were doing to spread throughout the East the law of God which they followed. From the kind manner in which the Captain treated the Portuguese, Isaac concluded that he must be either a Catholic or a man of exceptional intelligence and good feeling.[25] He took them safely to Malaca, where the Fathers received Isaac very kindly, and made provision for his journey to India. After touching at Cochim, he reached Goa. Here, at the *casa professa*, he found Father Manoel Pinheiro who had come from Mogor, and in his company he set out for Cambaya.[26] The Father Provincial ordered him to be given a hundred *pardaos*[27] for the expenses of his journey.

NOTES

NOTES TO CHAPTER I

Introductory

[1] Akbar moved from Lahore to Agra in the latter part of 1598, prior to joining his armies in the Deccan. See *Akbar and the Jesuits*, p. 88.

[2] This word originally denoted only Northern China, which, at an early period, was in the possession of a Manchurian tribe known as the Khitai, a name which was subsequently applied by the peoples of Central Asia to the whole of China. Cambalu (*Khan-baligh*, "the city of the Khans") was the Turki name for the capital of China. The name Pe-king, or "North Court," dates from the early part of the fifteenth century when the royal residence, which in the middle of the previous century had been transferred to Nan-king, or "South Court," was moved back to its ancient seat. It was this double set of names which gave rise to the belief, so deeply rooted in mediæval Europe, that Cathay and China were separate countries, and Cambaluc and Peking their respective capitals. On the map of Tartary in the *Theatrum Orbis Terrarum* of Ortelius, Cathay is shown as a country lying to the north-west of China, and in the description accompanying the map, which du Jarric evidently had in mind, we read: "Eſt his quoque Cataia Regio, cuius Metropolis eſt Cambalu, quæ vt Nicolaus de Comitibus tradit, duo detrigenta Italica milliaria in ambitu habet, aut, vt M. Paulus Venetus scribit, trigenta duo. Quadrata eſt forma, in singulis angulis arces conſtructæ videntur, quatuor milliariorum circuitum habentes, in quibus continuè Imperatoris præsidia sunt."

Father Ricci's explanation of the name 'Cambalù,' if untenable, is, at any rate, intereſting. In all the Chinese books, he says, the Tartars are called *Lu*. *Pa* means 'the north,' and *cam*, both in the language of the Tartars and the Chinese, means 'great.' Hence, when the Tartar subdued China, he called the city where he eſtablished his court, Campalù, which name the Saracens of Persia, who found a difficulty in pronouncing the letter 'p,' changed to Cambalù. Marco Polo, Ricci adds, who was with the Tartars when they conquered China, was the firſt to bring to Europe news of this great kingdom, which he spoke of as 'Cataio,' and its capital as 'Cambalu'; and hence, when the Portuguese who went there by sea, brought back news of a kingdom called 'Cina,' with its capital 'Pacchino,' the cosmographers of Europe at once jumped to the conclusion that 'Cina' and 'Cataio' were different countries; "per esser già mutato, vennero i noſtri cosmographi a fare di un regno doi, l' uno appresso all' altro, senza potersi sino al giorno di hoggi la verità di questo" (*Op. Stor.*, I, 297).

[3] The *Historia Orientalis* of Haython the Armenian (Hetoum, Prince of Gorigos) was written at the beginning of the fourteenth century. His account of Cathay occurs in the first chapter. I take the following from the Latin edition published in 1529: "Secta vero illius regni gentium vix posset aliquo modo enarrari. Quoniam aliqui sunt qui colunt idola de metallo, alij vero boues adorant, qa terra laborant, ex qua crescunt frumenta & alia nutritiua. Alij colunt magnas arbores, alij naturalia, alij astronomia, alij Solem colunt, alij Luna, alij vero nullam habent fidem vel legem, sed sicut bruta animalia, ducunt bestialiter vitam suam."

[4] As will be seen, the merchant's experiences were very similar to those of Brother Goes on his arrival at Suchou (see p. 154).

[5] Ghoraghat, in the Dinajpur district of Bengal, is about 120 miles north of Calcutta. As Yule points out, the 'kingdom' must mean that of Kuch Bihar, concerning which, and the route through it to Tibet, see Wessels's *Early Jesuit Travellers*, p. 124 *et seq.*

[6] We see from Father Xavier's letters that it was originally intended to dispatch a company of Fathers to Cathay with a view to establishing a permanent settlement. The change of plan was no doubt due to the uncertainty which prevailed regarding not only the whereabouts, but the very existence of the Christians of Cathay. In 1596, Father Ricci had written to the General of the Society at Rome stating his firm conviction, based on his own careful enquiries, that the names 'Cathay' and 'China' denoted one and the same country: "Il Cataio, al mio parere, non è di altro regno che della Cina; e quel grande re che lui dice non è altro che il re della Cina; e così la Cina, se bene per altro nome, è conosciuta tra Tartari e Persiani" (*Op. Stor.*, II, 228). Ricci's letter was not regarded as conclusive at Goa; but it must have carried great weight; and it was evidently in view of his very definite assurances that the Jesuit authorities decided to defer the dispatch of a fully equipped mission until Cathay and its reputed Christian inhabitants had been actually discovered. This is confirmed by Father Pimenta's letter to the General of the Society dated 1st December, 1601, in which, in reference to the Cathay Mission, the Father stated that Brother Bento de Goes was to go first "to explore this important affair."

In the same report Pimenta stated that the King of Portugal had written to him expressing strong approval of the proposed mission, and he enclosed in his report a copy of the King's letter. In reference to Cathay His Majesty wrote, "I was pleased to hear of the discovery of that so ancient Christianity in Catayo of which you give me an account, of which there was no knowledge before. . . . I greatly recommend to you that on your part you should find the necessary labourers for maintaining the Christianity of Catayo, and I trust that the Viceroy will give you all the favour and help necessary . . . with him and the Archbishop of Goa you will discuss this matter, particularly since it tends so much to the service of God and mine. . . ." I have here quoted from the Rev. H. Hosten's translation of Father Pimenta's letter (*J. and Proc. A.S.B.*, XXIII, 1927).

[7] These were the three sons of Mirza Shahrukh, who had taken refuge at Akbar's court after having been driven out of Badakshan by Abdulla Khan, the Usbeg ruler of Bokhara. The children attended the school opened at Lahore by the Fathers who conducted the third Mission to Akbar's court (see *Akbar and the Jesuits*, pp. 69 and 239). Goes himself served with this Mission, which reached Lahore in May, 1595, and was doubtless a teacher in the school. Abdulla Khan died in 1598, having previously lost most of his possessions. Soon after his death the people of Badakshan contrived to throw off the Usbeg yoke, and gave their allegiance to Mirza Husain, who was, or was declared to be, the eldest son of Shahrukh. The latter died in Malwa in 1607, leaving to Jahangir seven more children (four sons and three daughters), "of whom," remarks that Emperor, evidently not over-pleased with the legacy, "he had made no mention to my father." The boys, he adds, were placed amongst his confidential servants, and the girls were put under the care of the attendants of the zenana.

NOTES TO CHAPTER II

LAHORE TO YARKAND

[1] This chapter is taken from Part II of the *Relations* (fols. 61b-65a).

[2] Guerreiro refers to the two travellers Antonio de Payva and Pedro de Covilham, who, in the year 1487, were sent by King John II of Portugal to search for the kingdom of Prester John in India. It should be remembered that the word 'India' had, at this period, a very wide, and a very vague, signification. It was often used to denote the East generally, including even the eastern parts of Africa. On hearing at Aden of a Christian king in Ethiopia, the travellers separated, Payva crossing to Africa to investigate the report, whilst Covilham continued his journey to India. In 1490, Covilham also made his way to Ethiopia, and the reports which he sent to Portugal furnished conclusive evidence that the kingdom of Abyssinia was the kingdom of Prester John (see Sir Denison Ross's valuable monograph on Prester John in *Travel and Travellers of the Middle Ages* [Kegan Paul, 1926], pp. 172-194). No one, however, appears to have paid much attention to Covilham's reports, and for many years the erroneous belief, founded on the statements of Marco Polo, that the kingdom of Prester John was to be looked for in Central Asia, continued to hold its ground in Europe. "It was not," says Sir Denison Ross, "until the visit of the British traveller Bruce in the eighteenth century that the curtain was fully lifted from Prester John's Ethiopian kingdom."

[3] Goes was a member of the third Mission to the court of Akbar, which arrived at Lahore in May, 1595. The embassy here referred to is that which Akbar dispatched to Goa in May, 1601. Goes accompanied the embassy at Akbar's special request, taking with him a number of Portuguese and half-caste children who had fallen into the Emperor's hands after the capture of the fortress of Asirgarh (see *Akbar and the Jesuits*, p. 115).

[4] For an account of Leon Grimon, see *Akbar and the Jesuits*, pp. 45-49, 229. Ricci calls Leon Grimon a priest, but du Jarric, in his account of the second Mission to the court of Akbar, refers to him as a subdeacon. This designation is doubtless the correct one, as du Jarric took his account from the report, dated November, 1591, of the Provincial at Goa.

Father Xavier was the leader of the third Mission, of which Father Pinheiro was also one of the original members. Father François Corsi joined the Mission in 1600 and Father Machado in 1602. The latter travelled from Goa to Agra in company with Goes.

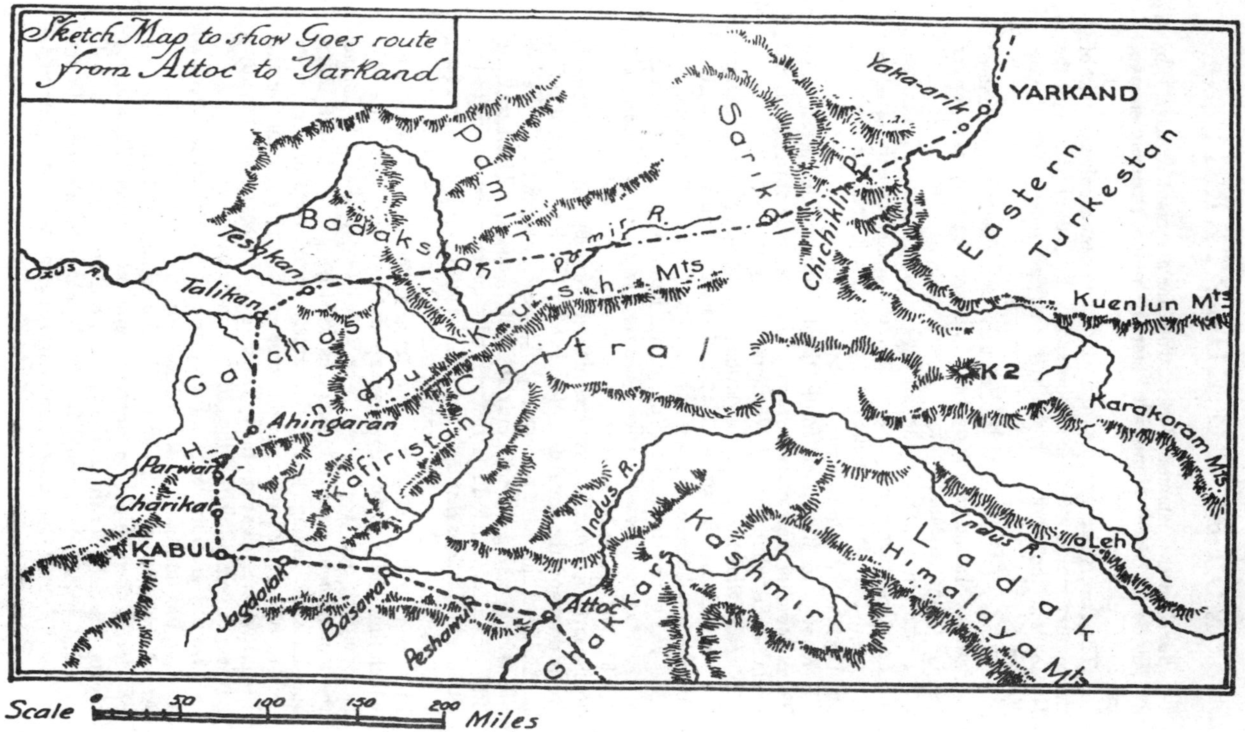

Sketch Map to show Goes route from Attoc to Yarkand

NOTES TO CHAPTER II

[5] *Banda* is the common Persian word for a servant or slave. In du Jarric's *Histoire* it is misspelt 'branda,' which, strangely enough, puzzled Yule.

[6] The Portuguese used the word 'India' to denote only that part of the country which was in their possession. Both the English and the Dutch used the word in a similarly restricted sense. See *Hobson-Jobson*, p. 434.

[7] This is a mistake for '14th February' (see the date at the end of the letter). In the year 1603 Lent began on February 12th, Easter Sunday falling on March 30th.

[8] i.e. the river Ravi, on the left bank of which Lahore is situated. Though Goes carried his goods across the river on February 14th, the caravan did not start for some days, probably not until the beginning of March. See note 10 *infra*.

[9] Known to Europeans in Southern India as 'hoppers.' The Tamil name for these cakes is *apam*. They are made of rice flour, and resemble the 'chupatties' of Northern India.

[10] Yule, who used the Latin version of du Jarric's *Histoire*, in which the name Gaçar appears as 'Gazaria,' assumed that this distance of 102 *coss* is to be measured, not from Lahore, but from Kabul, and that Goes was at this time crossing the Hindu Kush in the neighbourhood of the Hazara (Kezareh) tribes (*Cathay and the Way Thither*, IV, p. 183). I think, however, there is no doubt that the distance is to be measured from Lahore as Goes himself definitely states; for though we do not know the actual date of his letter, he evidently wrote it before he could possibly have reached Kabul, or even Peshawar. "We are still fasting, taking our food only at night," he says. This important little sentence, which du Jarric, who only quotes a few words of the letter, omits, tells us that the season of Lent was not yet past. In 1603, Easter Sunday fell on the 30th March. The letter must, therefore, have been written before that date, let us say on the 25th March, by which time the caravan might be expected to have covered 102 *coss*, or something over 200 miles. The word 'Gaçar' I take to denote the mountainous country of the Ghakkars, lying between the Indus and Kashmir, through which the caravan would have to pass on its way to Attock, and which at this time constituted a province of the Mogul empire. I admit the softened 'c' of 'Gaçar' is a difficulty; but it is quite possible that the cedilla is an error.

Tavernier gives the length of the journey from Lahore to Attock as 125 *coss*; so that Goes must have been within two or three marches of Attock when he wrote his letter. In this region, even in the middle of March, there might be plenty of snow left on the hills, and the nights, especially for those who had to spend them in the open and ill provided with shelter, would be bitterly cold. Goes's words do not necessarily imply that snow was actually lying on the route. The cold, he wrote, was very severe—" porque imos correndo as serras que estão cubertas de neve."

The fact that a letter written at Lahore on the 4th March reached Goes on the 7th (these dates are not given by du Jarric), indicates that though the Brother carried his goods across the river on the 14th February, some days, perhaps a fortnight or more, must have elapsed before the caravan started. If it had started on the 14th February, Pinheiro would hardly have attempted to write to Goes on the 4th March; and had he done so, the letter would not have overtaken him in three days.

NOTES TO CHAPTER III

At Yarkand

[1] This chapter is from Part IV of the *Relations* (fols. 164a-166b).

[2] Goes reached Yarkand in November, 1603 (*vide* p. 152). We have no reason to doubt the correctness of this date, which must have been taken from Goes's notes. Ricci, it is true, mentions it, as Wessels observes, "very cautiously": "Pare che questa arrivata fu l' istesso anno di 1603 in novembre" (*Op. Stor.*, I, 536). Ricci's caution, however, is not surprising, since, by his own misreckoning, Goes was still at Kabul in November, 1603 (see note 6, p. 174).

[3] Ricci says the present included a silver watch: "Il fratello Benedetto fu a visitare il re di Cascàr per nome *Mahamethàn*, il gli diede un bello presente di un horiuolo di ferro per portare al collo, specchi di vitrio et altri cose di Europa, con che stette molto contento e fu sempre suo amico e fautore" (*Opere Storiche*, I, 539).

The identification of 'Mahamethan' with Muhammad Sultan, the son of Abdul Rashid Khan of Kashgar (*Cathay and the Way Thither*, IV, 191), is doubtless correct. Muhammad Sultan had been Governor of Yarkand whilst his brother, Abdul Karim, was reigning at Kashgar. After his accession, he assumed the title 'Khan,' and appears to have transferred the seat of government to Yarkand. He was, says Mirza Muhammad Haidar, "a wealthy prince and a good Musulman. He persisted in following the road of justice and equity, and was so unremitting in his exertions, that during his blessed reign most of the tribes of the Moghuls became Musulmans. It is well known what severe measures he had recourse to in bringing the Moghuls to be believers in Islam. If, for instance, a Moghul did not wear a turban, a horse-shoe nail was driven into his head; and treatment of this kind was common (may God recompense him with good)" (*Tarikh-i-Rashidi*, tr. Sir D. Ross, p. 58). Goes's description of the manner in which the people of Yarkand were driven to their prayers (pp. 142-3), is all in accord with what the author of the *Tarikh-i-Rashidi* tells us of Muhammad Khan. Of the Khan's nephew, the Prince of Khotan, I can find no mention, either in the *Tarikh-i-Rashidi*, or elsewhere.

[4] This occurred whilst the Brother was at Kabul (*vide* p. 150). Ricci says that Goes advanced the Queen 600 gold pieces, which he raised by selling some of his goods, and that the Queen subsequently repaid him in pieces of jade, "pietra di iaspe, molto fina, che e la migliore mercantia che di Casar portano alla Cina." Khotan has

always been famous for its jade, which was, and is still regarded as finer than that found in any other locality. The Queen was at this time on her way back to her country after having performed the *hajj*, or pilgrimage to Mecca. It was on this account that she was styled *Hajji Khanum*, "the Lady of the Pilgrimage." The best that Guerreiro can make of this title is 'Acchanam.' Du Jarric follows Guerreiro's spelling; but in the Latin version of the *Histoire*, Mattia Martinez, to make the disguise more complete, gives us 'Ahe-haxam.' Ricci gets a little nearer the mark with 'Age Hanem': "Chiamavasi questa signora *Age Hanem*; *Age* e soprannomo de' Saraceni che sono andati alla Mecca, come sarebbe tra noi beato, e veniva allora dalla Mecca." The lady, we are told later, was sister to the King of Kashgar (whose capital was at this time at Yarkand), and mother of the ruler of the subsidiary kingdom of Khotan, who appears to have been regarded as heir-apparent to the throne of Kashgar. Khotan, which Goes visited before he left Yarkand, lies about 180 miles south-east of the latter city. The Brother went there, Ricci tells us, to get his loan repaid by the Queen. The trip occupied him a month.

It appears from Father Xavier's letter of September 6th, 1604, that the Queen, after reaching Badakshan, attached herself to, and completed her journey with the caravan with which Goes was travelling. Xavier wrote that the only news he had received from the Brother was that he had passed safely through the kingdom of Badakshan, which was much disturbed with wars. He had been sick with fever, as had also the Armenian Isaac; but at the time of writing he was sufficiently recovered to continue his journey. The passage in Xavier's letter is as follows: "Do Irmão Bento de Gois tenho pouco q̃ escreuer, a ultima noua q̃ delle temos he que nos chegou hua carta delle do reyno de Badaciao que he fora dos reynos deste Rey Acabar, quando chegou aquelle reyno adoeceo de febre elle e hũ moço armenio q̃ leuaua, mas ja q̃ estaua sao quando escreueo e para partir e yr auante, estaua aquella terra desenquieta com guerros mas passarão, e despois nos chegou noua de auer chegado aquella S^ora^ que hia em aquella cafila (em a qual o Irmão hia como encostado) ao reyno de Casgar donde ella era e governa seu Irmão. Confiamos em D^s^ que chegaria o Irmão com saude com ella, e daly não he muito longe o ? ? do Catayo. Os trabalhos que leua D^s^ n. S^or^ guarde e traga com saude e bom despacho."

[5] The manner of enforcing the practices of Islam had not greatly changed when Robert Shaw visited Yarkand in 1869. "The Kazee," he wrote, "or religious magistrate, always perambulates the streets with his satellites, like a Cambridge proctor with his bull-dogs. They are armed with a peculiar kind of broad leather strap, attached to a short wooden handle, and with this strap they castigate all men who are found without turbans, and all women without veils. When they are seen coming everybody scuttles out of the way, lest some fault

should be found with them" (*High Tartary, Yarkand, and Kashgar*, p. 466).

[6] In Portuguese dictionaries the meaning given to 'Caciz' (Arabic *Kashish*) is a Muhammadan priest, or *mulla*, and in this sense it is used by the Jesuit writers, though the proper signification of the Arabic word is a "Christian presbyter." The word is to be met with in numerous guises, *casis*, *caxis*, *cashish*, etc. See *Hobson-Jobson*, p. 169, and *Cathay and the Way Thither*, IV, p. 223.

[7] A very optimistic estimate, as Goes found out ere he recommenced his journey. We learn from Father Xavier's letter of September, 1606, that on the day before his departure from Yarkand Goes again wrote to his friends in India. In this letter he said that another eight months must elapse before he could reach Cathay. He was well, he wrote, and though known to be a Christian, he had on the whole met with friendly treatment. In the same letter he expressed his grief at losing the companionship of Demetrius, who, being unable to take his merchandise into Cathay, had returned to India. On many occasions he had been a friend in need to Goes, and they had parted with mutual regret. Xavier adds that Demetrius reached Lahore just after the death of Akbar [i.e. at the end of October, 1605]. Insurrections, following on the King's death, had made travelling a dangerous business, and before reaching Lahore, the caravan to which Demetrius had attached himself was obliged to take refuge in a fortress to which a body of insurgents laid siege. After rendering valuable assistance to the Captain of the place, Demetrius managed to escape, and found his way to Lahore and thence to Agra, where he took up his abode with a Greek friend who lived near the Fathers. Not many days later he fell sick, and, after a lingering illness, died peacefully in his friend's house, having made his will, and with the Fathers at hand to administer the last rites, and speed his parting soul. The passage in Xavier's letter runs as follows:

"Ja tenho escritto os anos atras da yda do Fr. Bento de Gois por o Catayo, ouvera oito dez meses que nos vierão cartas delle da cidade de Yarcand corte de reino de Casgar que esta ja perto de Catayo [a word, or words, missing here] alguns meses, e quando escreuia estaua para partir o dia seguinte daly e dizem que ainda ha de esperar oito meses antes que chega ao Catayo porque se esperaua que tornasse hua caffila do Catayo por essa outra poder passar. Elle vai com saude conhecido por Xtão e não mal quisto. Alguns mouros vierão a Agra que o deixerão la e nos dauão muitos certos sinais delle e muito boas nouas. Agora esta o bom peregrino mais so 'o que nunca onde mais auia mester companhia, mas Deos lhe fara como costuma aos que por seu amor se priuão de humana consolação. Digo que esta mais so'o por que hum Grego mercador que daqui foi com elle e o acompanhou ate a dita cidade de Yarcand e o ajudou muito bem com emprestimos e outras ajudas final[te] como ja não lhe armaua por sua mercancia passar ao Catayo se despedio delle ficando ambos com bem de saudades mutuas, e como o bem ditto S[or] dixe *qui recipit justum in nomine justi mercedem justi accipiet* pagolhe muito misericordios[te] esta boa comp[a] que ao ditto Fr. fizera, por que no caminho à vinda o livrou de graves perigos, hum delles foi que ja quando estaua perto de Lahor ouvindose a noua da morte do Rey Aqbar muitos se aleuantarão em muitas partes, e entre elles o fiqerão huns de junto do porto onde hauia de vir esta cafila com quem elle vinha, ouverãose de recolher a hua fortaleza onde os poserão de cerqo e elle com seu gente ajudou muito bem ao Capitão della e quando todos cuidauamos ser aly tomado e morto, escapou e veo a saluamento com seu fato deixando boa parte do seu outros que vinhão com elle, veo a Lahor e daly ate Agra onde estando ja como em sua casa descansando na de hum Grego grande seu amigo casado pegado a nos adoecea de hũa doença vagarosa ordena sua alma a fazenda, e morra com todos los sacr[os] recebidos com o p[re] a cabeceira e com testamento feito em casa de hum tanto seu amigo que não auia mais, de tudo isso carecera em qualquer outra parte que morrera, mas não quis o Sor Deos que morresse entre mouros desconolado quem tanto boa comp[a] fizera em tam trabalhossos caminhos a seu seruo."

In his letter of August 8th, 1607, Xavier stated that Goes had written from Yarkand giving an account of his reception and treatment by the King, and of the good arrangements that had been made for the continuation of his journey. In the same letter Father Xavier says that further news had been brought to him by some merchants who had met the Brother at Yarkand : "Alguns mercadores vierão aqui que o conhecerão là e por amor delle nos vinhão buscar, e nos dezião delle muitos louvores." A letter had also been received from a Christian servant of the King at Kabul, who wrote that he had learnt from a Moorish merchant of Goes's safe departure from Yarkand. The same merchant, he said, was bringing letters from the Brother for the Padres at Lahore. That numerous letters, of which we have no knowledge, must have been sent to India by Goes during the earlier part of his pilgrimage is evident from the following passage in Xavier's letter : "As cartas que delle temos são quasi de dous annos, ja mandai a V.R. os que lhe vinhão ; com esta mando alguns que vierão para mim por ellas saberão os trabalhos que passou e os perigos em que se viu. D n. S[or] o guarde e traja com bem." What has become of these letters ? Have they all perished, or is there a chance that some of them may yet be brought to light ? What, again, has become of Goes's mutilated diary, which Ricci must surely have preserved ?

[8] This personage I take to have been a brother, and probably the successor, of king Tsewang Namgyal, who ruled over Ladakh in Western Tibet, from 1530 to 1560. Tsewang Namgyal died childless ; but he left two brothers, the elder named Gonpo Namgyal, and the younger

NOTES TO CHAPTER III

Jamyang Namgyal (see Dr. A. H. Francke's *History of Western Tibet*, p. 91). From the dates given in the 'records,' it would seem that Tsewang Namgyal was succeeded by Jamyang Namgyal, who is said to have reigned from 1660 to 1690. Why Gonpo did not succeed is not stated. Gonpo's name is, however, to be found in what is known as the *Domkhar* inscription (see Dr. Francke's *Ladvags rGyalrabs*, or *Chronicles of Ladakh*, published in the *Journal and Proceedings of Asiatic Society of Bengal*, Vol. VI, 1910), and according to this inscription it appears that Gonpo Namgyal actually did come to the throne in 1660, and reigned for a short time. How he lost his kingdom, or what subsequently befell him, we are not told; in fact, the only other information we possess about him is that which is here provided by Guerreiro, assuming, that is to say, that he was the 'Gombuna Miguel' whom Goes met at Yarkand, and there does not seem to be anyone else who meets the case. The title *namgyal*, "the altogether victorious," was borne by a long line of kings of Ladakh. The first to hold it was Lhachen Bhagan (1470–1500), who is called the founder of the *namgyal* dynasty. In 1603 Ladakh was ruled by Senge Namgyal, the son of Jamyang Namgyal, and nephew of Gonpo. He reigned, we are told, from 1590 to 1630; but, as Dr. Francke observes, little reliance is to be placed on the dates given in the Chronicles.

[9] 'Angil' is perhaps for *kanjur*, the name of one of the two collections of the Buddhist Canon in Tibetan.

[10] In his *Notes on Bro. Bento de Goes*, published in the *Journal and Proceedings, Asiatic Society of Bengal*, Vol. XXIII, 1927, the Rev. H. Hosten gives the translation of a letter written by Father Nicholas Trigault on December 24th, 1607, in which reference is made to one of the letters sent to India by Goes whilst on his way to 'Cathay.' According to Trigault, Goes says that "he has reliable information that in that great Empire of Cathay there are great vestiges of Christianity; for they have mitred Bishops, confer baptism, keep Lent, and the priests observe celibacy, and other such proofs of our Christianity. He learned all these things from a physician, who was a captive in the hands of the Turks, and said that he would write to us soon more certain and reliable news about it." There cannot, I think, be any doubt that the captive physician here referred to is to be identified with the Tibetan doctor, Lunrique, mentioned in the text, and that Trigault was mistaken in supposing that the information which he gave Goes related to Cathay.

[11] 'Botelhana' is apparently a corruption of *but-khana*, the Persian word for an idol-temple, or pagoda. I can offer no explanation of the word 'ito-lama.'

[12] This is probably the Tibetan word *kon-chog*, signifying 'the Most High,' or 'God.'

NOTES TO CHAPTER IV

Yarkand to Suchou

[1] This chapter, taken from Part V of the *Relations* (fols. 23a-27b), is based on Father Ricci's letter to the General at Rome written at the end of the year 1607 (see Introduction, p. xxv).

[2] This date, evidently taken from Ricci's letter, is incorrect; the same mistake occurs in the *Commentarj* (*Op. Stor.*, I, 529). We know from Goes's letter of the 30th December, 1602, which Guerreiro has himself quoted, that he left Agra on the 29th of October of that year.

[3] Guerreiro is following Ricci, who makes the journey from Lahore to Attock occupy three and three-quarter months, made up as follows:

From Lahore to Attock	1 month.
Halt at Attock	2 weeks.
Halt after crossing the Indus	5 days.
Remainder of journey to Peshawar	2 months.

The time given for the journey to Attock may be accepted as approximately correct; for we know that before the end of March the caravan was passing through the province of Ghakkar, on the western border of which Attock is situated. But the two months allotted to the journey from the Indus to Peshawar is an obvious error, the distance being about thirty miles. Yule suggests that "it may have been entered in Goes's notes as 'II *mensil*' (Persian *manzil*, a stage or march), and that this was understood by the Italians as 'II *menses*'" (*Cathay and the Way Thither*, IV, 181). Whatever the explanation, the distance must have been covered in two or three days. We may, therefore, safely assume that Goes reached Peshawar in less than two months after his departure from Lahore.

[4] The country of Kafiristan, for an account of which see *Cathay and the Way Thither*, IV, 204, lies to the north of the Kabul valley, stretching to the southern slopes of the Hindu Kush, and to the borders of Kashmir. The statement in the text that the caravan with which Goes travelled entered Kafiristan is doubtless incorrect. In the *Commentarj* we read that, after leaving Peshawar, "they proceeded to another small town where they fell in with a certain pilgrim and devotee, from whom they learned that at a distance of thirty days' journey there was a city called Capperstam, &c." The exact spot where this halt was made cannot be determined. Yule supposed it to be at Jalalabad (*Cathay*, IV, 206). Ricci's narrative, however, suggests that the caravan had not traversed more than a third of the distance between

Peshawar and Kabul (about 180 miles); whereas Jalalabad is 80 miles from Peshawar. We are told also that the caravan had reached a "small town" (luogo piccolo), which hardly seems to indicate Jalalabad. I should, therefore, be inclined to place the halt nearer to Peshawar, possibly at Basawal. Jahangir halted at Basawal when on his way to Kabul in 1607, and also at Jagdalak.

[5] Jagdalak is about sixty miles by road from Kabul. Shahamat Ali, who passed through the place in 1839, says: "A grove of mulberry trees denotes this place. Formerly there was a fort, and the Afghan monarchs on their way from and to Kabul used to camp here" (*Sikhs and Afghans*, p. 460). Ricci spells the name 'Ghideli.' For the identification with Jagdalak, see *Cathay*, IV, 206.

[6] Ricci's figures are again impossible. Indeed, our main difficulty in connection with the travels of Goes is to reconcile the known dates with the 'times' given in the itinerary as presented in the *Commentarj*. We know, for example, that the Brother left Lahore at the beginning of March, 1603, and that he reached Yarkand in November of the same year. His journey to that city, therefore, occupied between eight and nine months. And yet, as Yule has pointed out, if we add up the times of the marches and halts given in Ricci's itinerary, we reach a total of close on two years. Ricci had to rely for his information on the salvaged portions of Goes's diary, and the memory of his servant Isaac. Now it is impossible to suppose that Isaac could have kept in his head the times of all the halts and all the marches in a journey of nearly two years, with a gap of another two years before he was cross-examined on the subject. We must therefore conclude that the actual figures given by Ricci were the figures of Bento de Goes; for if not, whose were they? And being the figures of Goes himself, we are justified in assuming that they are approximately accurate. But if the dates on Goes's letters are correct, which we cannot doubt, and if the figures taken from his diary are also correct, we can only conclude that in many cases these latter figures do not denote what Ricci supposed them to denote. Let us look at his time-table of the journey between Peshawar and Kabul. The time spent in actual travel was as follows:

Peshawar to the first halt	... ...	20 days.
First halt to Jagdalak	... ...	25 „
Jagdalak to Kabul	... ...	20 „
Total	... ...	65 days.

Peshawar is 180 miles from Kabul, so that the rate of travelling averaged well under three miles a day, which is absurd. It is manifest, therefore, that the above numbers do not denote days. I would go a step further, and suggest that they do not denote time at all, but distance. Assuming this to be the case, and assuming that Goes calculated his distances in *legoas*, or leagues, our table would mean that the journey from Peshawar to Kabul was one, not of sixty-five days, but of sixty-five leagues, which is near enough to 180 miles to be classed as approximately correct. And this is not the only section of Goes's journey where the substitution of leagues for days supplies what is at any rate a reasonable solution of Ricci's inexplicable figures. After leaving Kabul, the caravan proceeded, via Charikar and the Parwan pass, to Talikhan, a town on the river Ak-sarai, a branch of the Oxus. The distance in a direct line from Parwan to Talikhan is 112 miles; but, owing to the nature of the country, the route traversed was probably a good deal nearer two hundred miles than one. We do not know the actual line followed by the caravan; but in any case the journey can hardly have taken sixty days (not counting halts), as Ricci would have us believe (Parwan to Aingharan, 20 days; Aingharan to Calcia, 15 days; Calcia to Gialalabath, 10 days; Gialalabath to Talhan, 15 days: total, 60 days). On the other hand, it may very well have been a journey of sixty leagues. Again, we are told that from Iakonich (Yaka-arik), where the last halt was made before reaching Yarkand, Goes went on in advance of the caravan and, according to Ricci, reached Yarkand in five days. The distance in this case was fifteen miles, or—five leagues.

It may of course be mere coincidence that in the instances I have given the word 'league' suits the context better than 'days.' I do not, therefore, claim to have established my theory, which I put forward only as a possible explanation of some of the difficulties which Ricci's itinerary presents. In many cases Goes did give the length of marches in days, more particularly during the last half of his pilgrimage. Ricci's mistake lay in supposing that his figures represented days in every case.

The time specified for the halt at a particular place is often quite as puzzling as the time said to have been taken in reaching it. On the journey from Peshawar to Kabul, for example, we are told that twenty days were spent at the first halt mentioned, and no less than eight months at Kabul. A way-side halt of twenty days, a similar period having already been spent at Peshawar "for needful repose," seems very unlikely; while eight months at Kabul would take us well into the year 1604, by which time Goes was comfortably writing letters in Yarkand. One is tempted to suggest 'hours' for 'days,' and 'weeks' for 'months.' In fact, as the Brother was not equipped with an aeroplane, it is only by some assumption of this kind that we can make head or tail of his wanderings.

[7] Cf. *Op. Stor.*, I, 532: "Di quisto loro ritorno a Lahor il prete Leone Grimano, non potendo sopportare i disagi di sì lungo cammino e l' altro compagno Demetrio ne restò in quella cità." Demetrius

subsequently rejoined Goes at Yarkand, but did not accompany him beyond that city.

8 Charikar is 40 miles due north of Kabul on the southern slopes of the Hindu Kush. In his letter of September 6th, 1604, Father Xavier, referring to a letter from Goes written from the kingdom of Badakshan, which lies on the north of the Hindu Kush, says that it was after reaching this kingdom that the Brother fell sick (*adoeceo de fevre*).

9 *Chegarao a Calca terra de homes ruiuos & louros.* It will be noticed that Calca is referred to as a *terra*, a 'land.' The passage must, therefore, mean, not that the caravan halted at a place called Calca, but that it had entered the Calca (Galcha) country. The Galchas are the inhabitants of the mountainous parts of Badakshan and the more easterly districts of Shignan, Wakhan and Sarikol (*vide* Sir D. Ross's translation of the *Tarikh-i-Rashidi*, p. 220). The fair hair and complexions of the Galchas have been remarked on by other travellers, including Sir Aurel Stein, who compares them in this respect to the Chitralis (*Ruins of Desert Cathay*, I, 33). After Talikhan, the next halting place mentioned is Chescan (Teshkan), about 50 miles further east. The caravan must, therefore, have passed through the heart of the Galcha country. Trigault wrote 'Cheman' for Chescan in his Latin version of the *Commentarj*, and it is only since the discovery and publication of the latter work that the direction taken by the caravan after leaving Talikhan has been known. From Chescan onwards our traveller's route is a matter of conjecture, until we pick up his tracks again in the Sarikol district on the eastern side of the Pamir plateau. According to the *Commentarj*, his route across the plateau lay through Tenghi Badascian (the Badakshan defile) to Ciarciunar, and thence over a steep mountain called Sacrithima to Serpanil, after which Sarikol was reached in twenty days. But, with the exception of Serpanil which, as Yule states, is probably for Sir-i-Pamir, "The head or top of Pamir," none of these places has been satisfactorily identified.

10 "Tomou hua touca de preço, & metendo lhe hua pedra a lançou mais longe que pode." In his memoirs Ricci says it was the turban which he was wearing that Goes threw away: "Il fratello, pigliando il turbante che portava nella testa a guisa degli armenij di tela della India, lo lanciò quanto longi potette" (*Op. Stor.*, I, 534). Du Jarric transfers the epithet 'precious' from the turban to the stone, and makes the passage run, "il jette sa toque avec une pierre de grand prix qu'il y auoit." Wessels follows du Jarric and writes, "He took his Armenian cap, in which a precious stone glittered, flinging it, etc." The text account seems to me the most probable. I picture Brother Benedict trudging manfully along beside his lagging beast, the latter laden with his wares. From these, as the robbers come in sight, he snatches a "costly turban," and folding a pebble in it to give it weight, flings it far behind him, in the hope of staying his pursuers. The

robbers pounce on the prize, and whilst they wrangle over its possession, the Brother scrambles up behind his pack, and urging his reluctant Pegasus into an unaccustomed gallop succeeds in rejoining his fellow-travellers.

[11] This looks like another of Ricci's blunders. We know that by the beginning of August, 1605, Goes had reached Turfan, some two hundred miles beyond Chalis (Kara-shahr); for we are told (*Op. Stor.*, I, 547) that he left Turfan on the 4th September, having stayed there a month. That being so, he cannot have left Chalis much later than the middle of July. He must, therefore, have reached that city, where he spent three months, before the middle of April, or within five months of his departure from Yarkand.

Chalis was reached after a twenty-five days' journey from Cucia (Kuchar), where a halt of a month had taken place. Kuchar must, therefore, have been reached by about the middle of February. Between this city and Yarkand we are sure of only one halting-place, namely Aksu, which was reached twenty-five days after leaving Yarkand (i.e. on December 9th, 1604). Of the journey from Aksu to Kuchar we have no details beyond a string of unrecognisable names.

From Turfan Goes went on to Camul (Kumul or Hami), where he arrived on the 17th October. After resting for a month, he again set forth, and eventually reached Suchou at the end of the month of December.

Thus, taking into consideration only the halting-places that have been definitely located, the time-table of Goes's journey between Yarkand and Su-chou works out approximately as follows:

Yarkand ...	dep. November 14.	1604
Aksu	arr. December 9. Halt of 15 days. dep. December 24.	
Kuchar (Cucia) ...	arr. mid-February. Halt of 1 month. dep. mid-March.	1605
Kara-shahr (Chalis)	arr. mid-April. Halt of 3 months. dep. mid-July.	
Turfan	arr. August 4 (*circ.*). Halt of 1 month. dep. September 4.	
Hami (Camul) ...	arr. October 17. Halt of 1 month. dep. November 17.	
Su-chou	arr. end of December.	

Regarding the identification of Chalis with Kara-shahr, the reader is referred to Yule's convincing note on the subject (*Cathay and the Way Thither*, IV, 234), and to the *Tarikh-i-Rashidi* (Introd., p. 99). According to the latter work, Kara-shahr, the ancient Chinese name of which was Yen-ki, was, in the days of Mirza Haidar, known as

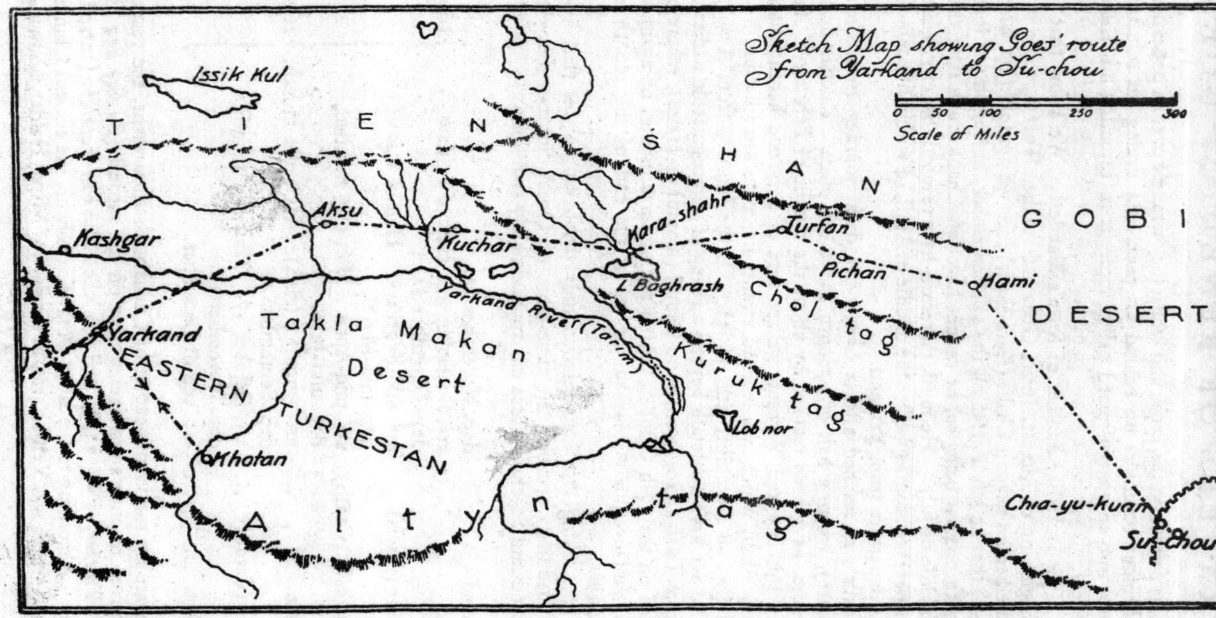
Sketch Map showing Goes' route
from Yarkand to Su-chou
0 50 100 250 300
Scale of Miles
Issik Kul
T I E N S H A N
GOBI
DESERT
Kashgar
Aksu
Kuchar
Kara-shahr
Turfan
Pichan
Hami
L. Baghrash
Chol tag
Kuruk tag
Lob nor
Yarkand River (Tarim)
Takla Makan Desert
Yarkand
EASTERN TURKESTAN
Khotan
Altyn tag
Chia-yu-kuan
Su-chou

MAP II

Chalis. This would seem to put the identification beyond doubt. Chalis is shown on the map of Tartary in the *Theatrum Orbis Terrarum* and also on Ogilby's map of Asia (1672), where it is spelt 'Chialis'; but for purposes of identification these early maps are of little assistance.

[12] In his letter of March 8th, 1608, to the General of the Society, Ricci refers to this incident as follows: "Nel mezzo del viaggio s' incontrò con certi Mori, che erano venuti dal Cataio, e stettero con noi quell' anno che arrivassimo a Pachino et il seguente 1601 dentro d'un palazzo dove stanno tutti i forastieri che vengono col nome de imbasciatori alla Cina. Questi gli diedero nova di noi, e per più certezza gli mostrorno in una carta scritto non so che in nostra lettera, che avevano raccolto avanti la nostra porta, e per questo venne da lì a cominciare ad intendere che potevamo esser noi e che il Cataio era l' istessa Cina" (*Op. Stor.*, II, 348).

[13] Cf. *Commentarj*, I, p. 547: "Allo spedire di questa patente, stando presenti suoi letterati e *cazissi*, gli domandò il signore della terra se aveva da scrivere in essa il nome di christiano, cioè della legge di Giesù. Repose il fratello Benedetto che sì, e che scrivesse *Abdullà Isai*, cioè *Abdullà della legge di Giesù*, perchè come christiano era passato per tutto quello cammino e come tale lo voleve finire." Ricci mentions this 'patent' in the list he gives of the possessions of Goes which eventually came into his hands. These included, he says, "le tre patenti che portava con gli sigilli del re di Cascàr, del Signor di Cotàn, e del Signore di Cialis" (*Op. Stor.*, I, 557).

[14] The Great Wall was reached at 'Chiaicuon' (Chiayu-Kuan, or the "Barrier of the Pleasant Valley"), about 25 miles from Suchou. The time stated to have been occupied in travelling from Hami to Chiayu-Kuan is clearly incorrect. The distance between the two places is 535 kilometres, or roughly 335 miles, a journey which must have taken at least three weeks, and probably more, for we are told that as the road was infested with brigands the caravan travelled only at night. Chiayu-Kuan cannot, therefore, have been reached much before the middle of December. In the next paragraph we are told that the caravan was kept waiting for twenty-five days before being allowed to pass the 'barrier.' This must likewise be a mistake, since we know that Goes arrived at Suchou before the end of December. In both cases the figures are Ricci's. The sentence in the *Commentarj* is, "Di Camùl [Hami] in nove giorni arrivorno ai muri settentrionale del regno della Cina, in un luogo detto Chiaicuon, dove stettero aspettando vinticinque giorni, sino che si diede nuova di loro al vicerè o *tutano*." It almost looks as though, by some error, the words *nove* and *vinticinque* had been interchanged, and that it was the journey which occupied twenty-five days, and the halt at Chiayu-Kuan nine. It will be remembered that Goes's diary reached Ricci in fragments.

To fit these together must have been an extremely difficult task, and one in which a mistake, such as I have here suggested, might very easily have occurred.

[15] It was doubtless with this letter that Ricci sent the Provincial his first account of Goes's travels, written, as he states in his letter quoted on p. xxv, after Brother Fernandez had come back from Su-chou. The Brother, accompanied by Isaac, reached Peking on the 28th of October, 1607 (*Op. Stor.*, I, 556).

[16] i.e. the *Tao-tai*, or provincial governor. Ricci gives his title as 'tutan,' which he says is equivalent to 'viceroy': "E, per quanto tuttu il governo delle provincie fuora della corte è subordinato alla corte di Pacchino, per questa causa sopra tutti questi mandarini in ogni provincia, vi sono altri doi magistrati supremi della corte, uno che sempre resiede nella provincia, che si chiama *tutan*, l' altro che ogn' anno vieni di Pacchino e si chiama *ciaiuen*.

Il *tutan*, per avere grande potere sopra i magistrati e sudditi e intendere ne' soldati e cose principali dello statto risponde al nostro offitio di vicerè. Il *ciaiuen* è come un commissario" (*Op. Stor.*, I, 42).

[17] The town of Su-chou is in the province of Kansu, and is distant about 25 miles from Chiayu-Kuan, and 120 miles from Kan-chou, the head-quarters of the province, where the viceroy resided. If Ricci is to be trusted, both Su-chou and Kan-chou belonged, in his day, to the province of Shen-si.

[18] This letter, being insufficiently addressed, was never delivered. In March, 1606, Goes wrote another, which reached its destination eight months later, *vide* Ricci's letter of March 8th, 1608: "Come nè sapeva il luogo della nostra casa, nè il nome in lingua cina, non ci seppe fare il soprascritto che era necessario; pure scrisse doi o tre lettere al meglio che potette e, volsi Iddio, che una doppo di otto mesi mi venisse alli mani, e fu nel principio del mese di novembre dell' anno 1606 (*Op. Stor.*, II, 348).

In a letter to the General of the Society dated 18th October, 1607, Ricci had already mentioned the receipt of Goes's letter, and the dispatch of a Brother to his assistance; but at that time he had had no tidings of the Brother, though nearly a year had elapsed since his departure, and he evidently wrote in some anxiety. The passage in the letter runs: "Il fratello Benedetto Goes, che i superiori dell' India mandarono sei anni sono [as Father Venturi points out in a foot-note, it was actually less than five years ago] per la via di Mogor a scoprire il Cataio, sta già alle porte della Cina nella provincia di Xanti, d' onde la Quaresima del 606 scrisse alli padri di Pachino di non aver trovato altro Cataio che questo regno, e che gli mandassero istruttione per potere andare a trovarli, perchè la compagnia, con la quale era venuto, dovea al solito trattenersi là due anni, avanti che la lasciassero passare a Pachino. Gli mandarono i padri subito un fratello col necessario per il viaggio di quattro mesi tra l' andare e il ritornare; già è quasi l' anno che parti per quelle parti il fratello di qua, e fin' ora non ne abbiamo nuova alcuna. La lettera di Benedetto si manda per via dell' India, d' onde quei padri informeranno V.P. più particolarmente di questo negotio proprio di quella provincia (*Op. Stor.*, II, 327). Fernandez and Isaac arrived at Peking ten days after the dispatch of this letter.

[19] This is a mistake. Demetrius managed to get as far as Yarkand; but Grimon, as we know, fell out at Kabul.

[20] Fernandez reached Su-chou on the 31st March, having set out from Peking on the 12th December of the preceding year. In his letter of March 8th, 1608, to the General at Rome, Ricci wrote: "Dessimo al fratello Giovanni l' ordine di quello che aveva da fare e danari sufficienti per menar seco a questa corte il fratel Benedetto. Partì a 12 decembre, ma quando là arrivò, che fu l' ultimo giorno di marzo dell' anno 1607, stava il fratello molto infermo di più di un mese de infirmita, causata da travagli che i Mori gli davano in questa terra, sopra quei che aveva patito in sì lungo viaggio e da lì a dieci giorno moritte" (*Op. Stor.*, II, 349). The death of Goes is placed on the same date, i.e. April 10th, in Ricci's letter of August 22nd, 1608; but in the *Memoirs* it is stated to have occurred eleven days after Fernandes' arrival at Su-chou (*ibid.*, I, 533), which accords with the date given in the text.

[21] Yule (*Cathay and the Way Thither*, IV, p. 172) has the following note on this place: "*Kolechi*, a small port of Travancore, which Fra Paolino will have to be the Colchi of the Periplus. It has dropped out of our modern maps."

[22] This miracle is described, with additional details, in the *Oriente Conquistado* of Francisco de Sousa (Vol. II, pp. 258-259), and the story also appears in the *Annuæ Litteræ Soc. Jesu* of the year 1583 (*vide* the Rev. H. Hosten's *Notes on Bro. Bento de Goes*, referred to on p. 172).

This paragraph contains practically all that we know of Benedict Goes prior to his joining the Society. In his *Early Jesuit Travellers* (p. 7), the Rev. C. Wessels states, on the authority of the *Annua Litera Provinciæ Goanæ* for the year 1609, that Goes entered the noviciate of Goa in February, 1584, being then twenty-three years of age; but that before completing his two years' noviceship "he quitted and went to Ormuz. Regret soon followed, and on applying he was again admitted, and by the end of March or the beginning of April, 1588, being twenty-six years old, he was a novice once more." In the list of members of the mission-province of Goa, dated 31st December, 1588, his name is entered as follows: "Benito de Goes, Portugues de la Isla de Sant' Miguel, de la Villa Franca, Obispado de Angra; de 26 años; robusto; de nueve meses de la Companhia" (*ibid.*, p. 7 note). The question whether 'Goes' was a real or an assumed name is fully discussed in the same work (pp. 8-10).

[23] This evidently means Ricci's letter of the 12th November, 1607, which Guerreiro has already mentioned (p. 155), and which constituted his chief authority for this chapter (see Introduction, p. xxv).

[24] The collapse of the prosecution is thus described by Ricci in his letter of August 22nd, 1608 : " Quello che dette il tratto alla bilancia fu che, allegando i Mori che Isaac era Moro, e che il cataio l' aveva ingannato, forno [i.e. Fernandes] un giorno al governatore con più di trenta Mori, e portò il fratello carne di porco, e, avanti a tutti i Mori cominciorno a mangiarla, e l' istesso fece Isaac ; con il qual spettacolo cominciorno tutti i Mori a sputare et anatemattizzargli et si uscirno tutti dalla audientia uno dietro all' altro, et il governatore restò chiarito di non essere Isaac Moro " (*Op. Stor.*, II, 351).

[25] These particulars about the captain of the Dutch ship are not given by Ricci, who merely states that Isaac's ship was captured by Dutch pirates in the straits of Singapore, and that he was ransomed by the Portuguese of Malacca : " Et, essendosi Isac imbarcato per passare all' India e da lì ritornare al Mogore, dove stava sua moglie e figliuoli, fu presa la barca da' corsari olandesi nello stretto di Sincapure e, riscattato da quei di Malacca, arrivò pure al fine all' India doppo si gravi travagli " (*Op. Stor.*, I, 557). According to Trigault's version, Isaac, on reaching the west coast of India, heard that his wife was dead, so, instead of returning to Mogor, he settled at Chaul.

[26] This was probably in July, 1609, when, as we know, Pinheiro was sent from Goa to Cambay to negotiate with Jahangir's ambassador, Muqarrab Khan (see note 15, p. 111).

[27] At the beginning of the seventeenth century the *pardao* was equivalent to about 2s. 6d. For a full account of this coin and its value see *Hobson-Jobson*, pp. 672-678.

PART III

THE MISSION TO PEGU

CHAPTER I[1]

The Ruin of Pegu

Chatigam [Chittagong] is one of the principal cities and ports of Bengala.[2] It is in what is known as the kingdom of the Mogos,[3] and is under the sway of the King of Arracão, the most powerful of the rulers in all Bengala,[4] who has made a fortress here, and has set up a king under his hand. Almost all the port has been given over to the Portuguese who live there, and to whom the King is very well inclined, as they have assisted him in his wars, and have been of service to him in many other ways. To some of them he has given stipends amounting to thirty thousand *crusados*, and he has declared his intention of making one of them a king under his hand in Bengala, which he could very well do, being the lord of many kingdoms, and possessing more than two hundred leagues of coast-line. His word is, however, but the word of a Gentile. He shows the Portuguese these favours now, because, being in need of their services, he is anxious to content them; but it is greatly to be feared that when he has no further use for them, his behaviour will be very different.

This King is the possessor of the celebrated white elephant, the fame of which is spread throughout the East, and to which both he and his people pay reverence and make obeisance. This elephant is a mighty beast. Every time he is taken out there is great rejoicing, and bands of musicians accompany him wherever he goes. Seeing what has befallen the various kings in whose possession he has been, one can hardly help believing that this animal possesses the powers of the Evil One; for five or six of the powerful kings to whom it has belonged have sooner or later been destroyed, both they and their kingdoms. The last of them, the King of Pegu,[5] who was once the lord of twelve or fifteen kingdoms, whose power was once so great that he could, whenever he chose, put a million men in the field, whose subjects were without number and whose riches no man could compute, lived to see himself stripped of all the lands he had conquered, and his kingdom desolated and deserted, except by a few miserable beings who roamed like savages in its jungles.

Before his final downfall, this King was besieged in his capital, then all that was left to him of his kingdom, by the King of Tangu, who was formerly his vassal, and he of Arracam, of whom we have just spoken. Seeing himself at the end of his resourses, the King of Pegu made terms with his assailants. To the King of Tangu he surrendered his person, his wife, and his children, and all the countless treasure he possessed. To the King of Arracam he gave five out of the sixty-seven immense statues of his gods, which his father had made, all of gold and glittering with precious stones, and in addition, five *alqueires*[6] of precious stones, amongst which were some of the most priceless gems in the world. He also gave him his daughter to wife, and two of his sons as hostages. Finally, and transcending all, he surrendered to him the white elephant, the pride and the glory of his kingdom.[7]

At the end of the year 1599, the King of Arracam, ladened with his spoils, left Pegu for his own kingdom.[8] He entered his capital in triumph, preceded by the white elephant splendidly harnessed, and attended by the brother and the two sons of the King of Pegu. The daughter of the latter, who had been given to him as wife, had expected to be on the King's right hand when he entered the city; and when she found that she was put on his left side, whilst the old queen was put on his right, and that the latter was decked out in the finery and jewels that had been brought from Pegu, she refused to regard the occasion as a triumph, and wept bitterly as she entered the city, saying to those near her, "Look how that old woman is dressed up! Everything that she has on her is mine!" But far more tragic was the fate of her father; for, after the departure of the King of Arracam, the King of Tangu, in whose hands he was left, not only took possession of his wealth, but put him to death. So vast were the treasures of Pegu that, to remove them to his capital, the King of Tangu employed seventeen caravans, each consisting of eight thousand beasts, horses, bullocks, buffaloes, and elephants; and these were loaded only with gold and precious stones; for everything that was made of silver or of other metals the King left behind as of no account. His leavings, which were afterwards taken by the King of Arracam, were estimated to be worth three million gold pieces.

When the King of Arracam returned victorious to

his capital city (which has the same name,[9] and is of great size and more populous than Lisbon in its most prosperous days), the Fathers Belchior da Fonseca and Francisco Fernandes[10] set out from Chatigam to visit him. They were accompanied by a Portuguese gentleman named Hieronymo Monteyro, for whom the King had a special regard. On learning of their arrival, the King at once sent for them, and when they entered his presence he greeted them very cordially, and invited them to sit near the princes of Pegu who were with him on this occasion. They had scarcely taken their seats when news was brought that the King of Tangu had, in violation of his covenant, slain the King of Pegu and his wife and his children. This announcement of the fate of his father-in-law so perturbed the King that he asked the fathers to withdraw, saying that he was unable to talk with them just then, but that he would be glad to see them at another and more convenient hour.

The next morning the Fathers received a message to say that he was ready to receive them. On their way to him, they fell in with the Coramgarim,[11] who is uncle to the King, and the most powerful lord in these kingdoms. They exchanged greetings, and after many compliments on both sides, the Coramgarim invited them to enter his boat, and they conversed with him during the remainder of their journey. They found the King on the river. He was on a splendid barge, built of wood, and so large that it seemed like a house. The interior, which was very spacious, was all painted and gilded, and none of the conveniences of a house were wanting. The King, who now wore a smiling countenance, commenced the conversation by asking the Fathers what they desired most in this life. They replied that there were many things that they desired, but that more than all they prayed to God for forgiveness for their sins, for grace to serve Him and exalt His glory, and for the conversion of the whole world, and especially of His Majesty's subjects, to their holy faith. He then asked them if a Christian could kill any animal without committing a sin. They told him that they could do this without sin, since God had created animals for the service of man, and man for His own service. They added, however, that they would be committing a sin if they killed animals that did not belong to them, for by so doing they would bring misfortune on the owners. But it was evident that the King, like Pilate, when he asked, *quid est veritas?* considered the answering of his questions a matter of no importance. At the close of the interview he said that he would be glad to have some Fathers at Chatigam, and also at Arracam, where he resides, and that he would arrange for their maintenance and make them an allowance, which he would double the next year. Having been thus kindly dismissed by this Gentile King, the Fathers took their leave of him.[12] Father Francisco returned to Chatigam, and Father Belchior da Fonseca to his residence at Chandecam.[13]

The King of Arracam, having been informed of the fate of the King of Pegu, and that after putting him to death the King of Tangu had seized and carried off all his great store of treasure, as we have narrated above, set out without delay for Machao [Macao][14], which was the King of Pegu's fortress, and at the same time summoned thither all the Portuguese whom he maintained in his lands of Bengala, that they might assist him, should the necessity arise, against the King of Tangu.

As the Portuguese were very anxious to take a priest with them, and as the King had himself called for some members of the Company, it was decided by the two Fathers at Chatigam that one of them, Father Francisco Fernandes, should remain in that place, and that the other, Father Ioam Andre, should accompany the Portuguese to Pegu, a decision which they came to the more willingly because of their anxiety to find out how far the state of affairs in Pegu was favourable to the introduction of Christianity into that kingdom.

When the party reached Siriam,[15] which is the chief port of Pegu, word was sent to the King, who was then at Mauio [Macao], which is distant six or seven leagues from Siriam, where he was collecting the silver and other remnants of the treasure left in the fortress, in which he also found more than three thousand two hundred pieces of artillery of various sizes. He sent word to the Father and the Portuguese to come and see him, and he received and dismissed them with much kindness.

As long as the Father remained at Siriam, he laboured zealously in the service of our Lord, confessing and administering the sacraments to the Christians who were there, and exhorting them to be earnest in their prayers and in their observance of the season of Lent, which was then in progress. During Holy Week he made, with much devotion, a representation of the holy Sepulchre, which both the King and his son came to see. As to the opportunities for introducing Christianity, he found that there were none. For the kingdom of Pegu was now a kingdom of jungles, haunted by tigers and other wild beasts, and destitute of human habitation, save for a few villages of Sapuns, who are wild people belonging to these parts.

As the plight of this kingdom was the most terrible and pitiful that the world has ever known, and as it shows in a wonderful manner how the justice of heaven overtook these Gentile peoples, on account of their abominable sins and idolatries, and the evil deeds of their King, a brief account must be given, though it would be possible to tell a long story, of the evils which led to it.

The desolation and ruin of this rich, populous, and fertile country was brought about by the greed, the cruelty, and the evil administration of the last king who possessed it. So great were the sufferings which this tyrant inflicted, both on his own vassals and on the people of the twelve large kingdoms which conquest had brought under his sway, that at last, unable to endure their miseries, his subjects, now in one part and now in another, rose in revolt against him. At the same time other countries made continuous war upon him, killing thousands of his soldiers, until his armies were completely destroyed, and the wretched King, powerless and destitute of resources, was driven to make terms with, and surrender himself to his former vassal, the King of Tangu, who, as we have narrated above, seized everything that he possessed, and put him, and his wife and his children, to death.

The warfare which the King of Pegu made against his own subjects could not have been more ruthless had it been waged by their worst enemy, or the most inhuman tyrant that has ever been known. Seeing that, on all sides, he was regarded with ill-will, and that in consequence of the defeat of his armies many refused to go to war, while others fled from the enemy, or took up arms against him, his rage and ferocity knew no limits. To punish the Pegus, he ordered their right hands to be cut off with a sword; others he sent to the kingdoms of the Bramas, to be sold or exchanged for horses. In the case of those who had rebelled against him, he punished with death not only the culprits themselves and their leaders, but all who were dependent on them. Thus, on one occasion, he caused to be apprehended forty of the chief nobles of his court, men who had aided his father in the conquest of many lands; and though they had never before committed any offence against him, he caused them with their wives, their children, and all their dependents, who were innumerable, to be placed in the midst of a great circle of wood and faggots, which was then set on fire, and they were burnt to death. Those who tried to escape from the fire were killed by the soldiers who had been placed round it. Many times he destroyed in this manner the families and dependents, men, women, and children, old and young, of those who fled from his enemies. Others he ordered to be drowned in the rivers, which became so blocked with corpses that even small boats could not pass along them.

But even these unheard-of cruelties failed to appease his fury, which increased to such a pitch that, to complete his vengeance on his rebellious subjects, he prohibited them from sowing their fields, so that they died in thousands from sheer hunger. By this infamous decree, unparalleled in the history of human tyranny, the Pegus were reduced to the direst extremity of misery and want. Driven by the fear of death in its most agonising form, they took to devouring one another. Mothers devoured their children, and children their parents. The stronger preyed on the weaker. Human flesh was publicly sold in shambles. . . .[16] In this manner were the countless inhabitants of Pegu destroyed, as well as those of Aua, Prum, Martabam, Murmulam,[17] and other adjacent kingdoms, so that there are now no people left in all this region, which is in a state of utter desolation, its cities in ruins, and its fields strewn with human bones.

Seeing the condition to which Pegu was reduced, and that it was useless to think of introducing Christianity into the country until it had been re-peopled, which could not be for some time to come, Father Ioam Andre left Siriam and returned to Chatigam.

CHAPTER II[1]

PHILIP DE BRITO ESTABLISHES HIMSELF AT SYRIAM

THERE was at this time in the service of the King of Arracam a Portuguese named Felippe de Brito Nicote,[2] a rich and honourable man, and the Captain of many Portuguese, whom he had brought with him to Pegu. He had already rendered the King valuable service, having twice restored him to his throne, when he had been driven from it by his rebellious subjects, and in all his wars had proved himself the ablest of his Captains. As a reward for all that he had done, the King made him Governor and lord of the kingdom of Pegu,[3] such as it was, with permission to build at Syrião (which is a port on the shores of the same kingdom, where its rivers, including that which flows from Tangu, empty themselves into the gulf which is called Machario[4]) a fortress and stockades as a defence against his enemies, and to gather around him all the Pegus who came to him from the jungles or elsewhere to live under his protection and rule. Felippe de Brito made the most of his opportunities. He began by erecting that year, 1599,[5] a stockade of wood, and before the end of the year 1602 he had completed the building of a stone fortress, well equipped with guns and munitions, and very favourably situated for defensive purposes. At the same time he laid out a town and built houses for the people of the kingdom of Pegu, who began to come from divers parts to live in peace and security under his rule. In October, 1603, the town contained fourteen or fifteen thousand inhabitants, all engaged in cultivating the land. Their numbers are increasing, and there is good hope that the town will become a populous city, and that this will lead to the re-peopling of the whole kingdom.

Seeing the rapid growth of the fortress and city of Siriam, the King of Arracam began to be alarmed at the power which Felippe de Brito was acquiring. His fears were fostered by a certain Rume who was then much in his favour, and also by the ambassadors of the King of Massulapatam, and by other Moors who came to his court, all of whom told him that it was unwise to place so much trust in the Portuguese; for they were a people whom it was very difficult to dislodge from a place where they had once taken root. They also told him that they would undertake in less than two years' time to place twenty thousand Moors in Pegu who would pay him a yearly tribute of two *bares*[6] of gold. The country, they said, had lost its population, but not its mines of gold and silver and precious stones, and the rivers which enriched its soil still ran to the sea. His Majesty should, therefore, consider well into whose hands he delivered this port. The Moors, he knew, would always be *garibos*,[7] that is very submissive, with no other desire but to live under his protection; and furthermore, by taking the port from the Portuguese and giving it to them, he would make the King of Massulapatam his friend for ever. The latter, it should be mentioned, had, through his ambassadors, promised large presents to the nobles of

Arracam if they should persuade their King to this course.

About this time, Felippe de Brito visited Arracam, and learning what the Moors had been contriving against him, he went to the King and told him that if he cast aside the friendship of the Portuguese his overthrow would be certain. He could not hope to uproot the Portuguese since they were lords of the sea, and if he killed fifty of them, a thousand would come to take their place; so that there would be perpetual warfare until he was destroyed. He added that the support of the Portuguese had never been more necessary to him than at that time; for the Moors, who were conquering everything in Bengal, were already at his gates,[8] and their general, Manasingua, had promised Achebar [Akbar], the great Mogor, that he should be lord of the white elephant, which was then in His Majesty's possession.

By this the King was to some extent disillusioned; and when Gaspar da Silva, who came at this time as ambassador from the Viceroy of India, reached his court, he gave him a very friendly reception, and granted all his requests. He also expressed his willingness that Felippe de Brito should go to India to obtain ships to help him against the Great Mogor. But when the ambassador and Felippe de Brito had departed, the former to Bengala on his way to India, and the latter to Pegu to proceed with his fortifications, the King again gave ear to his counsellors, and at their instigation, sent a message to Felippe de Brito to say that it had been brought to his notice that he was building a stone fortress in Pegu, and that it was his will that he should proceed no further with the same, but that he should pull down all that he had built, otherwise he would send his armies to do it, and that he, de Brito, was at once to come and see him.

To this message de Brito sent a cautious but courteous reply. At the same time he bribed the messengers that they might tell the King that he would certainly lose his kingdom if he broke with the Portuguese. He also sent large presents to his counsellors that they might be well disposed towards him; while he sought to appease the King himself by a present worth seventeen thousand *crusados*, which included a girdle of gold worth fifteen thousand. Meanwhile, however, he was procuring from Bengala munitions and other supplies for his fortress.

The King had left behind in Pegu a *Banha*,[9] which corresponds to a duke, with an armed force, for the purpose of making a display, and keeping a check on the power of Felippe de Brito. The *Banha* was a native of the country, and a regular brigand to boot. That he might be treated with respect, the King had many times commended him by letter to Felippe de Brito. However, many quarrels took place between him and the Portuguese, who resented the presence of his troops. On this account, and to prevent the Pegus from forming a connection with their countryman, de Brito determined to rid himself of his troublesome neighbour by making war on him. Accordingly, on the 27th of February, with a large force of Portuguese and people of the country, he attacked the *Banha's* stockade, which was very strong, and having forced an entry, slew thirty of his men and took ninety prisoners. Seeing that he had gained the victory, the rest of the defenders came over to his side. In the meantime the Portuguese captured twelve of his vessels, twenty of his horses, and a quantity of provisions. They were also left in possession of all the fields he had sown. The *Banha*, whose wife had been killed, escaped with only fifteen followers.

After this the fortress and city enjoyed a time of prosperity; for the natives were able to cultivate the land in peace, which they did so extensively that there was soon no need to import rice from outside; and it was hoped that rice would soon be so abundant that more of it would be exported to India from Pegu than from Bengala. As the people enjoy peace and are well treated, there is no doubt that all the Pegus who are at present living in Tangu, Prum [Prome], Iangoma [Jancoma],[10] Auaa [Ava], Syam [Siam], and Arracam, and they are very many, will come to us, not only because of their love for their country, but because they will no longer have to fear the oppression they endured under their late King, and which they are now enduring in other lands. All are disposed to receive baptism, so that by God's grace this land will become a stronghold of the Christian faith.

Having provided for the security of his fortress and city, Felippe de Brito sent ambassadors to the neighbouring kings to make treaties of peace and friendship with them, and to dissuade them from alliances with the King of Arracam, the common enemy of all. In his message, which was sent to Tangu, Prum, Iangoma, Syam, and other minor states, he asked the kings to accept his friendship, to promise, in times of necessity, to assist him with supplies for his fortress, and to send their ambassadors with him to the State of India. All sent favourable replies, except the King of Syam, who was advised by a certain Portuguese named Martim de Torres, who was at his court when the ambassador arrived, to have nothing to do with Felippe de Brito. The latter, de Torres told the King, would surely deceive him, for he was nothing more than the King of Arracam's slave, while the dispatch of an ambassador in his company was out of the question, since the State of India did not recognise him. Nevertheless, though the King of Syam did not send an ambassador like the other Kings, he replied very courteously, as to a prince, and sent back forty Portuguese who had been captives in his hands.

Accompanied by the ambassadors of these kings and princes, Felippe de Brito went to India, to make over the fortress and the kingdom of Pegu to the State, and to tender his submission and devotion to His Majesty. He saw to it that the fortress was well supplied with men, guns, and provisions, and all else that was likely to be needed during his absence, and left ships for its protection. He returned from Goa in the month of December, 1602,[11] having been very honourably dispatched by the Viceroy, bringing with him sixteen rowing vessels manned by three hundred Portuguese. This fleet, with the ships that are already in these parts, namely a hundred and seventy at Sundiua [Sandip I.], thirty in Arracam, ten at Chatigam, and others elsewhere, will, God willing, make the Portuguese undisputed maſters of all the ports of Bengala and Pegu.

CHAPTER III[1]

Ten Reasons for Holding the Ports of Bengala

(1) More than two thousand five hundred persons, pure Portuguese and half-castes [mesticos], who are living in these parts as outlaws or refugees, serving various Gentile and Moorish kings, can be reclaimed to the service of God and His Majesty. They will be able to live together in our cities and fortresses, where also can be sheltered many orphan girls with whom they will be able to marry, the King granting them lands for their maintenance.

(2) By the establishment of custom-houses in these ports and fortresses the revenue of the State will be increased, and His Majesty will have the wherewithal to stock his magazines, and supply his fleets, both here and in India.

(3) From Pegu, as from Bengala, can be obtained all the timber required for the armadas of India, for it grows very abundantly in these parts. Formerly it was much used by the Turks for building their *gales*. They used to transport it to Suez, whither it could be conveyed more easily than timber from Alexandra. Here, too, can be built very cheaply as many vessels as are required for all parts of the State of India, both in the North and in the South.

(4) From these ports of Pegu and Bengala supplies and munitions can be sent to Malaca, and other places in the South, very easily and at all seasons. This is a

very important consideration; for from India they can only be sent with difficulty, and that but once a year, on account of the monsoons.

(5) From Pegu it would be an easy matter with our fleet to subdue Martabam, Reytauai [Tavoy], Tanacari [Tenasserim], Iunsalam [Junk-Ceylon],[2] and Queda, all of which are now in the hands of the King of Syam, who wrongfully took possession of them, they being all in a deserted state; for twice the King of Syam attacked Pegu, each time compelling the people of these kingdoms to accompany him by sea with supplies that could not be brought by land, and in these journeyings the greater part of them perished; so that these kingdoms are now so destitute of people that there is not in all of them as much cultivated land as there is round our port and city of Siriam.

(6) Our possession of Pegu puts an end to the pretensions which the King of Syam has to this kingdom and to Tangu, which latter country he covets on account of the treasures of Pegu which the King of Tangu seized and took there, after capturing and slaying the King of Pegu, his father-in-law. So greatly does the King of Syam desire this conquest that, since his failure to take the city of Tangu in 1599, when seventy thousand of his men perished from hunger, and when he lost many elephants and horses and all the guns he had taken with him, he has refused to enter his capital, and declares that he will not do so until he has conquered both Tangu and Pegu; and with this object in view he is busily collecting supplies and munitions of war. He has asked the Olandeses [the

Dutch] whose ships are at Patane,[3] to supply him with ten or twelve artillerymen. They have already sent him two, who came to him when Felippe de Brito was about to set out from Pegu for India, in 1603.

(7) By being masters of this port, the Portuguese will be able to perform another valuable service for His Majesty; for, with their fleet they can intercept the many ships which come yearly from Surrate [Surat] to Martabam, Reytauai [Tavoy], Iunssalao, Tanacri [Tenasserim], and Queda, to load cargoes of pepper and other goods for Meca, and can make them come to our fortress and pay duty at the custom-house which is to be established there, both on the goods they bring from India, and on those they take back from these parts. This also is a very important consideration, as it will add much to His Majesty's revenues; for there is no way of escape for these ships, except by sea; so that if the Portuguese are masters of the sea they will have complete control over them, for they can patrol all this coast with their fleets, just as they patrol the coast of Malabar in India, and none will have power to resist or molest them.

(8) One of the most important of the worldly advantages belonging to our occupation of this fortress of Siriam is the opportunity which it presents for laying hands on the treasures of Pegu, which, as we have said, are in the possession of the King of Tangu, whose kingdom is distant but six days' journey by land, and nine by water. Felippe de Brito, when he was sent there by the King of Arracam,[4] saw all that there was to be seen in it, and carefully observed its situation,

and the site and disposition of the royal city, of which he took the measurements, and made notes of everything within its walls. He says that it is 1,450 fathoms [*bracas*] in length, and 1,400 in breadth. It has twenty gates. From gate to gate there are five watch-towers [*guaritas*], and between each pair of these, forty embrasures [*ameas*]. There is a good-sized moat, measuring about twenty-five fathoms across. The walls are not very high, and are about twenty-five spans in thickness. There are no gun-platforms [*bataria*], the walls being nothing but rubble with a brick facing; the latter is not more than six spans thick, and often crumbles away in the winter season. The houses are made of straw, and the population is scanty. At the time Felippe de Brito was there, the King had twenty thousand Pegus; but today he has not more than three thousand, large numbers of them having come to our fortress under contract with Felippe de Brito; for the land there is barren, and the people cannot get any silver; whilst here they can get abundance of everything. These were the pick of his people, for though they had been conquered by him, hardship had made them strong and courageous. The King has some fifteen thousand Burmese soldiers [*Bramas*]; but they are a weak and poor-spirited lot. He has eight hundred horses of the country, and a large number of guns, including even camelets, which he took from the kingdom of Pegu; but he has no powder beyond a small quantity given to him by the King of Arracam. His chief constable is a lascar, or common seaman, who was once in our pay. In the account which he sent to the

Viceroy, Felippe de Brito wrote that, in two years' time, with the troops already available in Bengala, and others which he could raise there, and with the people of the country, of whom he had twice as many in his service as the King of Tangu, and of better quality, he would be ready, if His Majesty gave his approval, to attack this country; for the king who ruled it was a despot. Without incurring any great risk it would be possible to gain possession of his vast treasure, and, once the Portuguese were masters of Tangu, they would be able to subdue other kingdoms bordering on that coast and the gulf of Machareo, which has a coast-line of eighty leagues. He wrote also that, outside the royal city of Tangu, the King has no forces; and, as far as the King of Arracam is concerned, even the Pegus in our fortress go out and seize his cattle, there being none to protect them.

(9) By means of this conquest, the Portuguese will be able to hold in check the Olandeses, and prevent them from setting foot in Pegu and in many other kingdoms, from which they are not far away. The governor of the King of Syam, who is at Martabam, sent two ships to Achem[5] with an ambassador who took presents to the Olandeses, and offered them these ports, telling them of the commodities they could obtain in them. They replied that though at that time they were unable to accept his offer, they hoped to be able to do so in the near future. In March of this year, 1603, he sent another ship; but when Felippe de Brito arrived,[6] he gave orders that the vessel, with the message it brings, was to be captured on its return, which was likely to

be in September. The journey by sea from our fortress to Martabam takes twenty-four hours; but by land, on account of the bay, it takes five days.

(10) Of far more account than temporal gains or wealth, or aught that can be done to serve His Majesty, is the work that can here be accomplished for the glory of God, by the winning of countless souls for the kingdom of heaven, for the people are by nature docile and easy to convert. This can only be done with the help of God, and if those who govern here and in those parts are zealous for His honour, and hold His glory, and the welfare of souls, as of more concern than worldly success and prosperity. If He grants us the latter, it is that we may make His service, and the care of souls in these lands, our first duty.

CHAPTER IV[1]

Defeat of the Arakanese Armada

In the previous chapters we have told of the fortress which the Portuguese noble, Phelipe de Brito of Nicote, built at his own cost, at the entrance to the port of Siriam, which is the chief port of the kingdom of Pegu. This kingdom, which was now so wasted and deserted that it contained little but jungles and wild beasts, had been conquered by the King of Aracao, who had given it to Phelipe de Brito as a recompense for his many and great services.

This Portuguese noble was induced to take charge of this kingdom, and to build in it this fortress, by the hope that he might be able to restore, at least in some measure, its former greatness and beauty, and lay in it the foundations of a great Christian stronghold, so that it should become a source of strength to the State of India, and a crown of these realms. He hoped also to revive its commerce, which, indeed, began steadily to develop from that time. Another strong reason which he had for building this fortress was that it would enable him to prevent the landing of the Turks of Mecha, who always desired to come there on account of the timber which grew abundantly in those parts; This they required for the building of their ships and *gales*; and in former days they used to take it to Sues, whither it could be carried more cheaply than wood from any other country. If the Portuguese had not prevented them in time, and if God had not inspired Phelipe de Brito to undertake this enterprise and carry it through at his own cost, there is no doubt that the Moors and Turks would have stepped in and possessed themselves of this region, to the lasting detriment of the whole State of India.[2]

To render his position secure, Phelipe de Brito, in the year 1603, went to Goa to make over the fortress, and declare his fealty to His Majesty, and to consult the Viceroy in regard to its management. The same year, having settled all these matters, he returned to Pegù. On his way, he stopped at Cochim, where he spoke with the Father Provincial, and begged his permission to take back with him some Fathers of the Company; for though at first they would, he said, find it difficult to clear the soil, they would in the end gather much sweet fruit. Encouraged by such hopes, the Father Provincial wrote at once to the four Fathers[3] who were in Bengala, directing that two of them should proceed to Pegù; for in the kingdoms of Bengala the gates were being closed more and more resolutely against the holy Gospel. It seemed as though our Lord had inspired the Provincial to take this course; for the Fathers of Bengala, owing to the unsatisfactory state of affairs in those kingdoms, had already determined to return to India; and after receiving this letter, two of them came back to Cochim, whilst the other two went to Pegù, where they arrived in February, 1604, to the great contentment and consolation of the Portuguese who were in the fortress. As soon as the latter had news of their arrival, which was at night, they showed their joy by dancing and playing musical instruments. They said that God had come amongst them, and that now they knew that their fortress was secure, since the Fathers had entered it. As soon as it was dawn the Captain-General, Phelipe de Brito, and all the Portuguese, sought the sea-shore, where, with unbounded pleasure, they feasted and made holiday. A house had already been prepared for the Fathers, in which they were now hospitably entertained. They commenced without delay to perform the duties proper to their calling, preaching, hearing confession, expounding the doctrines of their faith and seeking for converts, doing all with gladness and to the comfort and benefit of those amongst whom they laboured. All the Portuguese, as well as the Christians of the country, made confession, and were thus strengthened to resist the temptations to sin which abound in these lands. Not only the soldiers of the fortress, but the merchants of the country, as well as many others, came to seek the Fathers' help and advice, and all alike came to regard them as their sole comforters.

Our Captain-General, Phelipe de Brito, greatly desired to see all the needs of the Fathers abundantly supplied; but on account of the heavy expenses he had been obliged to incur in connection with the fortress, and because of the losses he had sustained, he was unable to do for them as much as he wished. Nevertheless the Fathers wanted for nothing; for they had a house to live in, though it was only of wood, and also a little church which, pending the erection of a larger building, had been provided for them. The latter had cost only four hundred *pardaos*; but a thousand would not suffice for such a building in Portugal, so abundant is timber in these parts.

The marvellous favours which heaven has bestowed on this enterprise have encouraged all to hope that in this kingdom the gate will be opened wide to the holy Gospel. On many occasions when the fortress has been reduced to the direst straits by hunger, God has miraculously succoured it with supplies from many quarters; but above all He has given us a victory over the Moors of Arracam, the completeness of which can scarcely be realised, except by those who actually witnessed it. The story of it is as follows. The Moors who were at the court of the King of Arracam, seeing the increasing strength of the fortress which Phelipe de Brito had built, and resenting his possession of this portion of the kingdom of Pegu, in which they so greatly desired to set foot, promised to pay the King a yearly tribute of many *bares* of gold if he would expel the Portuguese, and give the fortress to them. They urged him so persistently, and put such fear into his mind of the evils that were to be expected if the Portuguese were left undisturbed, that they completely destroyed his friendly feelings for Phelipe de Brito, and the trust he had formerly placed in him. Thus worked upon, the King at first tried to lure our Captain-General to his court with persuasive messages, and when these proved ineffectual, he sent word to him with many threats that the fortifications he had erected were to be razed to the ground. Finally he determined to send all his forces to capture the fortress, and wipe out the Portuguese name in those parts.

And so, not content with what he had done to us in Ratiguam,[4] a great port of Bengala, in November, 1602, and the many other injuries he had inflicted on us, destroying many Christian places, burning churches, and slaying and taking captive many people, including Father Francisco Fernando of our Company, and after having taken from us in March, 1603, the island of Sunduia,[5] he now determined to remove that other thorn which was still left in his flesh, and which was beginning to cause him such discomfiture, namely the fortress of Pegu.

Accordingly, at the end of the year 1604, he put on the sea an armada of nearly five hundred and fifty ships, carrying a force of fifteen thousand men. He placed his eldest son in command of it, and sent with him his Captain-General and all the chief captains of his kingdom. The Prince was not only to destroy the Portuguese in Pegu, but to subdue other kingdoms and fortresses in those parts of which the King desired to have possession. Before the fleet set sail, the King caused it to be made known in Pegu that it was being sent against other Gentile kingdoms; but its real object was to destroy our fortress and afterwards to capture the ports and cities of Martauam, Teua [Tavoy] and Tanaçari. This was learnt subsequently from the orders which the fleet carried. But our Captain-General, Phelipe de Brito, was not deceived. He knew the treacherous nature of the King, and was fully alive to his designs. Nevertheless, remembering his obligations to him, for it was from the King that he had received this kingdom, he sent a message begging him not to send his fleet to Pegu, since, if it came there, he would be obliged to resist it.

The King ignored this message, and his armada put to sea. It consisted of five hundred *jaleas* and forty *catures*[6] with many guns. Very small in comparison was the fleet which the Portuguese made ready; for it comprised only eight ships, but all very well equipped, and a hundred and eighty Portuguese soldiers. They put to sea as soon as it was known that the enemy's armada was on its way. The two fleets met off a point of the land which is called Negrais,[7] and a desperate battle took place. Three times the enemy retired and three times returned to renew the struggle. With God's help the Portuguese gained the advantage in each of these encounters, in the course of which they sank many of the enemy's *jaleas* and *catures*, killing more than a thousand men, and capturing five hundred. Of their own men, not one was killed, and only three or four were wounded.

Seeing how ill it had fared with him in this sea fight, and as it was his intention to disembark his forces and attack our fortress by land, the Prince now kept his fleet close in to the shore. Accordingly, the Portuguese ships, which were larger and of deeper draught than those of the enemy, and which now stood in need of repairs, were taken back to the harbour, and the men returned to the fortress.

When it was seen that the enemy's armada had entered the river, and with such precipitancy that several of their vessels which were near the shore had become stranded on shallows or sandbanks, the Portuguese immediately manned their ships, and took up a position at a point which they knew the enemy must pass if he came to attack us. A few days later, the Prince likewise having repaired his damaged ships, the armada advanced up the river; and on the 28th January, 1605, the two fleets met, and a fourth engagement took place in front of the fortress.[8] For a time neither side gained any advantage, so stubborn was the contest; but at last, by the grace of God, the tide of battle turned in our favour, and the enemy's ships were driven into a narrow channel from which there was no outlet to the sea, and on that and the following day, the Portuguese captured all that great and numerous armada, of which not a single ship escaped to carry the news of the disaster to the King.

When the ships entered this channel, the Prince, who was heir to the throne of Arracam, and his captains, who were the greatest in the kingdom, and all his soldiers, seeing that escape by water was impossible, abandoned everything, and leaping ashore sought refuge in the jungles, hoping to save their lives and to find their way by land back to Arracam. But the Prince's followers, driven by hunger and the many other hardships which they had to suffer, soon began to desert him. Some came over to us, others made their way to Tangu or Param [Prome]; till at last, out of fifteen thousand men, only three thousand remained with their Prince. Aware of this, Phelipe de Brito made his way with all speed to a spot where he knew that the Prince's force could be intercepted, and there he fell on it with fifty Portuguese soldiers and two hundred Pegus who were in his service. The fugitives at first offered some resistance, thinking that they had to deal only with Pegus. But on seeing the Portuguese, the greater portion of them surrendered, while the remainder took to flight. Amongst the former were the Prince, his Captain-General and other captains, and a bastard son of the former King of Pegu. All were conducted to the fortress as prisoners, to be dealt with, more especially in the case of the Prince, as the Viceroy should direct. The King offered a great sum of money as ransom for his son, as he could well afford to do, seeing that he was the richest and most powerful king in all those parts and in Bengala.[9]

It would be difficult to estimate the great importance of this victory. As far as temporal affairs were concerned it did much to strengthen the hold which the Portuguese had already secured on this kingdom, and laid the foundations of a great estate in these parts, which may one day be the crown of our realm. But more than this it paved the way for the establishment of a great Church, which may lead to the conversion of the infidels in all these kingdoms, where up till now only the devil is worshipped.

The booty obtained on this occasion was enormous; for, leaving out of account the ships and prisoners, the Portuguese captured more than a thousand pieces of artillery, large and small, as well as great quantities of munitions and supplies, all of which they used to furnish and equip their fortress.

The Jesuit Father Ṅatal Salerno, one of the two who had been sent from Bengala, was present in all these battles. He was always to be found in the thick of the fight, animating the soldiers, hearing their confessions, and aiding them with his prayers. It was to the Father that the soldiers attributed their victory, so great was their belief in the power of his virtues and prayers. Our Captain-General commended him no less to the Father Provincial; for he took no credit to himself for the victory, but gave all the glory and honour to God, from whom all blessings come.

CHAPTER V[1]

In which a Treaty is Made and Broken

As has been said in previous relations, our occupation of Pegu is one of the most important of our eastern enterprises, not only on account of the material advantages which our kingdom derives from it, but because of the opportunity it offers for the extension of our holy faith by the preaching of the Gospel. For although the country of Pegu itself is almost devoid of inhabitants, there are in the neighbouring regions, and along all the coast of the bay of Bengala, vast numbers of Gentiles, who are able to find refuge from oppression under the shadow of the Portuguese fortresses, where it is possible to convert them to our faith, and thus greatly to extend the Church of God in these parts.

As to things temporal, there is not in all the East a country so rich, or which produces the necessities of life in greater abundance. Apart from mines of gold, and silver, and precious stones, which are to be found in all these lands, so fertile is the soil of Pegu that, if it is well irrigated, it will produce three rich crops of rice every year; and it will yield equally good crops of wheat, vegetables, and indeed of anything that is sown in it.

Not far away is the kingdom of Tangu, where are now the immense stores of gold and precious stones which it took the kings of Pegu centuries to amass, and amongst which are the richest gems in the world. The Fathers, and other Portuguese, declare that this kingdom could be taken with a force of a thousand men. Then there is the kingdom of Pru [Prome], very rich in timber, elephants, lac, and pepper, both the long and the short kinds, of which His Majesty could easily become the lord, as he could also of the kingdom by the *gangas*,[2] or upper river, which is the kingdom of Vua [Ava], where is abundance of precious stones, such as rubies, sapphires, and spinels, as well as benzoin, lead, copper, lac, silk, and amber. These three kingdoms are all on the river, and can be reached by our ships which go from Siriam. Only the city of Tangu is to be reached by land, being distant from the water's edge about the range of a falconet. On the coast of the lower portion of the gulf, which extends to the south, are the cities of Tauay [Tavoy], Tanassarim, Martabam, and Luncalam[3] [Junk-Ceylon]. These are on the outskirts of the kingdoms of Iangoma, Siam, and Langam [Luang Praban], and in all of these are to be found many valuable commodities, including gold and other metals, both those which the land produces, and those which come from outside. They are not far away, and could be conquered, as could all Bengala, from this fortress of Siriam; so that when those who are in the South have need of assistance, it would no longer be necessary to send it from India, whence it goes with so much risk and difficulty; for it would be able to go from Bengala and Pegu, where are all the necessary facilities, and the voyage along the coast is very easy. In addition, His Majesty will have many rich lands for distribution amongst his poor subjects, for whom in

India there is not a span. Also a ship can come from the Kingdom direct to Pegu which will help to render our conquest secure and permanent. Nor is there any fear that it would have to return without a cargo, as many wrongly suppose; for every year it could take back the pepper which comes from Queda and Dachem [Achim], as is done at Cochim, and here could be done very easily. There will also be for cargo the commodities of the country and of Bengala which can come here every year more easily than they go from Bengala to Cochim, there being only eighty leagues of coast between Bengala and Siriam, and the voyage can be made both in the winter and summer seasons. At Negrais there is a very splendid harbour, as large as the city of Goa.

Formerly, in the time of the last King of Pegu and his predecessors, all those commodities which I have said are obtainable in Martauam, Tauay, Tanasarim, Lunculam, and other neighbouring parts and kingdoms, used to come to this port of Siriam. And the reason of their coming was that the cotton goods of Choromandel were brought only to this port; and hither came many ships from Meca to load the goods which, on account of this cotton, were brought here. The Portuguese also took many freights, so that the trade of the kingdom of Pegu was very lucrative and extensive. But today these goods no longer come to Siriam; and this is because the cottons of Choromandel are now taken to Tauay, Tanasarim, and Martauam, from whence they go to Siam, Langiao [Luang Praban], Camboja, and other neighbouring kingdoms, and even to Tangu. These same cotton goods reach the kingdom of Vua [Ava] by way of Arracam, and precious stones are sent the same way, which formerly were brought to Pegu. Hence the trade of our port is much diminished, and His Majesty is losing the profit which he ought to be getting from it; all of which could be remedied by observing the usage which the State of India formerly established with the barbarous King of Pegu, by which it was ordained that the cottons of Choromandel should be brought to Siriam, and to no other port, and that the Portuguese on their part should take it only to the port of Goa, and that no other voyages should afterwards be made with it. By the consequent advent of our ships to this port, our trade and His Majesty's profits would steadily increase, and the arrival here of many Portuguese would render our fortress more and more secure, and our fleet powerful enough to control all these seas, and to overawe the Kings who are our neighbours, so that none of them would dare to raise a hand against us.[4]

Although our fortress is not at present in a strong or prosperous state, yet God has so marvellously helped our Captain-General, Felippe de Brito, the founder of it, in all the difficulties which from the beginning he has had to encounter, that it is manifestly His purpose to use it for the advancement of His holy faith.

We must now resume the thread of our narrative. After the great and marvellous victory described in the previous chapter, our Captain-General asked Father Natal Salerno of our Company to go to Arracam to negotiate terms of peace, and, having accomplished this, to remain there as a hostage, until the Prince had been restored to his father, as he soon was.[5] Then, trusting in the promises which this faithless King swore by his Pagodas that he would fulfil, Felippe de Brito sent his son, Marcos de Brito, with a party of Portuguese, to take possession of the island of Sundiua which, according to the treaty, belonged to him. But the King, by treacherous means, slew Marcos de Brito and nearly all who were with him. He also seized more than five thousand Christians who were in his territories, treating them with barbarous cruelty, and subjecting the women to the grossest insults. Amongst others, he captured three priests, in addition to which he profaned their sacred vessels, and desecrated and tore down a crucifix. He also tried to seize by treachery a number of Portuguese who were then in his ports, whither they had come, as was their custom, for purposes of trade; but having been warned of his hostile intentions, they were able to withdraw to a place of safety, with the exception of one galliot, which had proceeded some distance up a river, where it was attacked by a hundred and fifty vessels of the enemy. The thirty Portuguese who were on the galliot resisted the attack with great determination, and after killing many of their assailants, succeeded in saving both themselves and their ship.[6]

Not content with these outrages and insults, the King determined to destroy the fortress of Siriam, and all the Portuguese who were within it; and for this purpose he began to muster all the forces he possessed. While he was in the midst of his preparations, a great storm burst over his capital, and the lightning struck not only his royal residence, but the stall of the white elephant, and the chief temples of his idols. This so terrified his *talapojos*,[7] who are his priests, that they besought him to look to his actions, for these things were a sign that destruction was to overtake him, on account of the injuries he had done to the Gods of the Christians, and to the Christians themselves and the Portuguese, by breaking the treaty of peace he had made with them. The blinded King replied that if he had to perish, he would see to it that they perished first, so that they should have no chance of glorying in his death. And without more ado, he had thirty of his chief priests put to death. Meanwhile, Felippe de Brito, greatly as he felt the loss of his son and the other Portuguese, turned his thoughts from grief to vengeance; and as soon as he heard of the great force which his enemy was making ready to bring against him, he commenced his preparations for meeting the attack. Having good reason to fear that when the King of Arracam came to attack him by sea, other kings, who were his neighbours and confederates, would lay siege to his fortress by land, he dispatched Father Natal Salerno to Malaca to obtain assistance from the Viceroy, who was there at that time. The State of Malaca was not what the Father had expected to find it; nevertheless, the Viceroy was able to send Felippe de Brito two *gales* and six sailing vessels [*nauios*], with which, and those he already possessed, he felt that he could face the whole of Bengala.

Up to this point our information is from letters that

have come to us by sea from Moncao[8] [Macao]; but news, which is regarded as trustworthy, has since reached us by land that the King of the Mogos set forth with a very powerful fleet, said to have consisted of more than a thousand ships; and that on his way to our fortress he had three encounters with our ships, in all of which he was worsted, and especially in the last, in which the Prince, his son, was again captured with many of his people. It is reported that the Prince, though severely wounded, managed to escape in one of their boats; but that our vessels were gone in pursuit, with good hopes of taking him. It is also said that our Captain-General, encouraged by this victory, is purposing to go on to Arracam. But of these events we shall, God willing, be able to write more fully and clearly in our next relation.

There are at present two Fathers of the Company at Siriam, where they are labouring with much zeal. One of them stays there continuously, attending to the church and the duties connected therewith, confessing, preaching, teaching the doctrines of our faith, and fulfilling the various other duties belonging to his office. The other is almost always at sea, for the men of our fleet are never willing to go forth to battle unless he is with them, so confident are they that his virtues and prayers will bring them victory. Little is at present being done towards the conversion of the infidels. This is not because there are not many who desire to be baptised, but because the people are still in a very unsettled state owing to the continual wars which are taking place, and the Fathers think it best to postpone this important work until the country is in a more tranquil state, which will only be after their chief enemy, the King of Arracam, has been destroyed; for it is he, and his desire, to expel the Portuguese from all these parts, that disturbs the peace of our fortress and city. Nevertheless, a certain number of persons have received baptism. These have been for the most part sick children, of whom the Lord has taken many to himself. Amongst the conversions made at this time, the most important was that of a wealthy Jew, who was a dealer in precious stones, and who was also a man of much learning, and well versed in the holy Scriptures and in the Hebrew tongue. After wandering over the greater part of the world, he had found his way to Syam, and being told that there were Fathers of the Company in Pegu, he came to the fortress of Siriam to see them. He said that he had been led by the Scriptures to see the truth of our holy faith, but that he desired enlightenment on certain points which still troubled him. The answers which the Fathers gave to his questions completely satisfied him, and he begged so earnestly to be baptised that it was evident that he had been illumined by the Holy Spirit, and had heard the voice of God. He was baptised with great solemnity, the service being witnessed by all the Portuguese, many of whom had known him before, and who marvelled to see him thus changed from what he had been, like Saul who became Paul and a preacher of Jesus Christ and his holy law. He died a few days after his baptism, from a disease which he had contracted before he left Syam.

CHAPTER VI[1]

The Battle of Negrais

In the kingdom of Pegu, and in the city and fortress of Siriam, which is the seat of Philippe de Brito, the General of that kingdom, there were residing two Fathers of our Company; but, by the will of God, one of them, namely the Father Natal Salerno, lost his life in a desperate naval engagement between the infidels and the Portuguese. And because this was one of the most memorable encounters which have taken place in India between the Portuguese and these Gentios, and because it was entered upon for the sake of the Faith, and brought so great glory to God, it seems fitting, for the consolation of the faithful, and to give them cause to praise our Lord, that some account of it should here be set down. For it is not out of place in an ecclesiastical history to refer, when it seems appropriate to the matters of which we are treating, to the wars which the Christians waged in the defence, or for the propagation of the Christian religion.

It was through the King of Prù [Prome] that Philippe de Brito received intelligence of the treachery of the King of Arracam, and how the barbarian had, with great energy, prepared a vast armada, on which he had embarked all his power, with the intention of coming, as soon as the winter season was ended, to besiege the fortress of Siriam: how, in short, he was bringing with him a fleet which in ships, men, guns, and munitions of war, was the most powerful that had ever appeared on the Indian seas. His ships were 1,200 in number, and each one was propelled by oars, because of the inlets and lagoons which break up all the coast of the Gangetic gulf, and which are only to be navigated by vessels of shallow draft. Of these ships, seventy-five were galliots[2] of very large size, each carrying a dozen pieces of heavy artillery, such as esperas, camelets,[3] and falcons. They were also well equipped with screens [*paueses*] and network [*xareta*][4] and were fully manned. The other vessels were *jaleas*, which are smaller than galliots and very light, with fifteen oars on each side. The fleet carried 3,500 pieces of artillery, big and little; and the soldiers, amongst whom were Moors, Patans, Persians, and Malabars, numbered about thirty thousand, including eight thousand musketeers. The King himself came with the fleet, accompanied by the Prince, his son and heir, the flower of the nobility of his kingdom, and all his fighting men. The King of Chocoria[5] with his men also joined him.

Before this armada set sail from Arracam, news of its coming reached our Captain-General, who, with great determination and energy made preparations for intercepting it on the high seas. Though greatly inferior to the enemy both in ships and men, our little force was rendered strong by the cause for which it was to fight, which was the defence of the Faith, and by the spirit and courage of our soldiers. It consisted of but eight galliots and four sanguicels,[6] which are boats of a much smaller size and very light. Our soldiers numbered two hundred and forty. The chief command of this tiny armada was given to Paulo do Rego, who was one of the bravest soldiers in India, and who had served in the same capacity in previous battles.

This gallant Captain set out with his armada in search of the enemy, being determined to give battle. As he coasted along, he made descents on the enemy's shores, destroying with fire every maritime town which he entered, and putting the inhabitants to the sword. After a time, having received information of the course which the enemy's fleet was taking on its way to our fortress of Siriam, he awaited its approach in what is called the channel of Negais [Negrais]. Here he offered battle; but the King declined the challenge, and taking shelter under the land, placed himself amongst rocks and sandbanks, a position which gave him security whilst it was full of danger for our ships.

Seeing that the enemy did not intend to come out, our Captain cast anchor in front of his position, at the distance of a falcon-shot. Presently, a number of the King's provision ships arrived; and when our Captain fell upon these to destroy them, the lighter vessels of the armada came to their assistance. A close fight ensued, in which we captured the *jalea* of the Captain who was leading the attack. The Captain himself, whose name was Maruja, was killed. He was a person of high rank, and much thought of by the King. Finally, after other skirmishes had taken place, our Captain, on the last day of March, 1607, decided to give battle at two o'clock in the afternoon. But at that hour there came on a violent storm of rain, which lasted for one and a half hours, so that he was unable to commence the attack before four o'clock.

Although the very sea seemed to be hidden by the multitude of the King's ships, for, for each one of ours he could count 120, whilst his men outnumbered ours almost to the same extent, nevertheless, this spectacle, so far from daunting our soldiers, served only to inspire them with new courage; and calling on the name of the Lord, and of our Lady the Virgin, and trusting in the arm of God which had been their support in the past in the battles they had fought against the infidels both in India and in Europe, they assailed the enemy with the utmost impetuosity. Flinging themselves on that forest of ships, they penetrated it from van to rear, dealing destruction as they went. There was nothing which came in their way that they did not destroy, and many of the King's galliots were left burning, or stranded, or sinking. Panic seized his soldiers, and the barbarian King, overcome with fear, quitted his royal ship, and embarknig on a lighter vessel which had been kept in readiness for such an emergency, took to flight. Finding they had reached the rear of the enemy's fleet, our ships turned about and renewed the attack with the same vigour as before, passing through the midst of the King's ships and destroying all that lay in their path, which they continued to do until night fell, when our Captain judged it would be unwise to prolong the encounter. At ten o'clock in the evening he withdrew his ships, greatly regretting that there were not left a few hours of daylight to enable him to secure the victory which was already in his grasp, and which, could he have made it complete, would have been one of the most glorious the world has ever seen. So great was the confusion amongst the enemy's ships, that for two hours after we had retired they continued fighting amongst themselves, mistaking in the darkness of the night their own vessels for ours.

In this battle the enemy's losses amounted to one thousand eight hundred persons killed, and two thousand wounded. Amongst the former were many of the King's relations, his chief Sea-Captain [Capitam mor do mar], the chief Captain of all the Moors, and many other captains of note. Besides the havoc which was wrought amongst his *jaleas* and light vessels, five of his great galliots were sunk, three were set on fire, and fourteen were driven ashore.

Six days later, that is on the 4th April, there was a second battle. For the King, having repaired the losses his armada had suffered in the previous engagement, came to search for our ships, which in good order, and divided into two squadrons, went boldly to meet him. The armada advanced in four squadrons, and our Captain-in-chief, Paulo do Rego, immediately engaged the leading squadron, and such was the fury of his attack that he speedily gained the upper hand, dispersing both galliots and smaller vessels. But as he turned to engage some of the enemy who still resisted him, it happened that his ship ran upon some piles which were below the surface of the water, and could not be dislodged. Seeing his plight, the enemy attacked him on all sides, and there was a desperate conflict. Our men defended themselves with the utmost courage; but as they could not move their ship, they could only fight and die where they were. One of our Captains went to the assistance of our Captain-in-chief, and with many entreaties urged him at least to save his life and the lives of those who were with him, which he could have done by abandoning his ship for the other. But he would not be prevailed upon, answering, like the brave Machabeus of old, "God forbid that we should behave in such a manner, and make the enemy think we fly from them. Since it is His will, let us die like Christians and faithful cavaliers." And so he continued to fight with marvellous heroism, surrounded by great numbers of the enemy, who from every side bombarded our ship with grenades and canisters of gunpowder. These at last set fire to our own powder, of which the Captain's ship carried a large quantity, being the magazine of the fleet. This completed the destruction of our ship,[7] and with it perished our Captain-in-chief and all his company, without the escape of a single man. The Captain of the ship who went to his succour also perished.

When it was seen what had befallen our Captain, the rest of our fleet, which in another quarter was engaging and had almost overcome the enemy, withdrew fighting and in good order to the fortress, where the ships arrived all badly damaged by bombards, and full of water. In this battle there fell on the enemy's side the chief Captain of the King of Chocoria, and many other Captains and men, whose number is not known. On our side, besides the Captain-in-chief and his company, there fell, as has been said, the Captain of the ship that went to his aid, with whom also fell four soldiers, whilst others were wounded.

Our losses also included Father Natal Salerno of our Company, who was on the Captain-General's ship. This good Father was a Sicilian by birth, and of a very noble disposition. By his piety, his gentleness, and the sweetness of his discourse, combined with a child-like simplicity such as is very rarely met with, he captivated the hearts of all with whom he came in contact. He was so beloved by the soldiers, and so great was their faith in his virtue, that they would not embark unless they took him with them, believing that with him, and through his merits, they were sure of victory; for such had been their experience in their past battles, in which the good Father had always accompanied them. At this time, he had only just returned from Malaca, whither he had been sent by the Captain-General on business pertaining to the safety of the fortress. Without allowing him a moment's rest, the Captains and soldiers had insisted that he should accompany them, though he needed little pressing, so great was his zeal for the Faith, and so earnest his desire to aid them in their glorious enterprise. His death was sincerely mourned by all, and particularly by our Captain-General, Philippe de Brito, by whom the Father had been greatly respected and loved.

CHAPTER VII

The Siege of Syriam

The King of Arracam thought that the Portuguese, having loſt their chief Captain, Paulo do Rego, would no longer have the courage to defend themselves, especially as there had now come to his assiſtance, the Prince of Tangu and his two brothers, and also a brother of the King, who, with sixteen thousand fighting men, six hundred horses, and eighteen elephants were ready to lay siege to the fortress by land, whilſt he himself with his armada attacked it from the sea. Accordingly, both he and the Prince his son sent messages to our Captain-General, Philippe de Brito. The Prince in his message said that the General would do wisely, seeing that Paulo do Rego was dead, to come and speak privately with his father, and that he himself would intercede for him, in return for the kind treatment he had received whilſt a prisoner in his hands in the fortress of Siriam. The King's message was to the effect that, as he had been joined by a large force from Tangu, our General could no longer escape defeat, and that if he would come and throw himself at his feet he would pardon him, and would give him the fortress and make peace. In response to the Prince, Philippe de Brito said that he appreciated his desire to oblige him, but that he would reserve it for greater things; and that if he thought that the loss of one Captain would prevent him from holding the fortress, the issue of the war would very soon undeceive him. To the King he replied that his promises of peace were only made to be broken; that it was unnecessary for him to receive the fortress at his hands, since he held it for His Majesty the King of Portugal, to whom, as his vassal and Captain, he had given his allegiance; that of the coming of the Princes of Tangu he made no account, for experience had taught him that their forces, like those of the King himself, were of little worth; that he would be only too pleased if he would summon other friendly kings to his aid, so that there might be some credit in holding the fortress, within which, he said, he had every expectation of entertaining His Majesty, as on a previous occasion he had entertained his son.

This answer roused the King to such indignation that he called his soldiers together and made them an oration, in which he told them in plain words that if they did not avenge the insult he had received, not one of them should ever return to Arracam; for if they escaped the swords of the Portuguese, his own was ready to fall on their necks. And they had good need of such warning; for so great was the fear with which our soldiers had inspired them, that if he had not displayed this resolution, nothing would have induced them to stand their ground and fight. And, in fact, in all the engagements which followed, it was only the threats and presence of the King, and the naked sword which was always in his hand, that made them go into battle or turn back when flying. After this there were three more naval fights, in all of which God aided our soldiers, so that they came out victorious, having destroyed the armada of Magua, and having slain many of the enemy, as in the first two battles.

As we, too, had lost a number of men, chiefly captains, as well as three ships, and as it seemed to be the enemy's intention to destroy our force little by little, though with great loss to themselves, our General, to prevent this, and to ensure the safety of the fortress, had all our ships drawn up on the shore, and having disembarked the men, made preparations to meet the enemy henceforward in the field. The King also landed his soldiers, but kept his fleet manned, after which his forces on the one side, and those of Tangu on the other, besieged the fortress by land, whilst he with the remainder of his armada bombarded it from the sea; and for thirty days so continuous and fierce was their attack that there was not a day or a night during which the defenders had any respite from the unceasing fire of their guns. Many times our little garrison, though so greatly outnumbered, sallied forth to fight in the open with sword and lance; and, by the will of God, not once did the enemy get the better of the encounter, but was always defeated with great slaughter, and with the loss of his stockades and shelters, which our men destroyed. It would be impossible to describe in detail the various incidents of this siege, and the feats of arms which our soldiers performed, recalling those early days in India when God so miraculously helped his servants, and fought for them against the enemies of his faith. It was a marvellous spectacle, and one that was often witnessed during these days, to see a large body of troops so completely routed by a handful of men that, despite the dreadful threats of the King, and though the Prince his son slew many with his own hand, nothing could stay their flight.

On one occasion our General sent two Captains with sixty Portuguese soldiers and two hundred Pegus to attack a stockade which the enemy had erected less than half a league from the fortress, and which played an important part in their operations. It was manned by a strong force of musketeers under a great Captain named Mauia. At great risk, and passing by many dangerous places, our men reached the stockade at daybreak, and falling on the enemy with great courage and vehemence, put seventy of their best men to the sword, including four Captains. They then went in pursuit of the others who had fled as they entered the stockade, and coming up with them on the bank of the river, drove them into the mud, many including their chief Captain being wounded, the latter very severely. Whilst the Portuguese soldiers were following ing up their victory, the Pegus, with none to hinder them, set fire to the stockade, killing or capturing any whom they found concealed within it. Then, having collected a large quantity of arms, the whole party, in full view of the armada and of another stockade which was occupied by the enemy, withdrew to the fortress, without a single person being either killed or wounded.

After other battles, in which the enemy greatly outnumbered us with his elephants, horses, musketeers, and light artillery, the King one day decided to make an attack both by sea and by land with the whole of his power. A number of vessels loaded with straw and fuel were sent to set fire to our ships, which had been drawn up on the shore, but were well barricaded and all in readiness for battle. These vessels were closely followed by the rest of the armada. The King was on his royal ship, and, standing where he could be seen by all, urged and encouraged his men to fight. He had given orders that, at the same time, all the land forces, both his own and those of Tangu, were to make an assault on the fortress, believing that, with our small numbers, it would be impossible for us to defend our ships from an attack by sea, and at the same time hold the fortress against his land forces.

By sea, then, came the whole of the enemy's naval power, the ships making straight for the shore and the quay where our General with thirty men had taken his stand, in order to defend the quay itself, and our ships which were near it. They were received with artillery and musketry fire which caused terrible destruction, shattering their galliots and other vessels, and killing many of their bravest Captains and soldiers, who fought with such determination that it seemed as if they chose to be vanquished and killed, rather than be seen alive by their King. The latter was himself in great danger; for those in the fortifications, recognising his ship, turned a piece of artillery on to it, and the shot so nearly reached its mark that the ship was obliged to retire. It was only the person and presence of the King that had maintained the fight; and the moment his ship withdrew, the entire armada followed suit.

Nor were our men less successful by land where,

during the same hours, that is from midday till night, they engaged in the field the combined armies of the King of Tangu, and of the Mogos. In this battle the enemy's forces were completely defeated, and driven back with heavy losses to their encampment. After the events of this day, the King, realising at last how little chance he had of overcoming the Portuguese, decided to abandon the siege. So, on the 9th of May, the Prince of Tangu sent some three hundred of the best men he had with him towards our stockades to keep our troops engaged, so that he might be able to leave his camp, and march away unmolested. But a party of our men moved out and fell upon them, driving them back to their camp with great loss. The state of panic in which they returned quickly infected the other troops, who, believing their camp was no longer secure, leapt over the pallisades and took to flight. Our troops were unable to pursue them owing to the lateness of the hour. The same night the King of Arracam embarked all his land forces, and the next day, which was the 10th of May, departed for his own country, leaving our men so worn out by all that they had been through that they were unable, to their great disappointment, to go in pursuit of him.[1]

During the siege much damage was done to the fortress and in the city by the enemy's guns. Numbers of houses were destroyed, and churches, and many were wounded. But very different were the losses of the enemy. For of that vast armada which the barbarian King brought against us, consisting as we have said above of one thousand and two hundred sail, he took back to his country only two hundred and sixty-two vessels (twelve galliots and two hundred and fifty *jaleas*); of the remainder, some were burnt or sunk by us; others he set fire to and sank himself, or ran them ashore, not having sufficient people to man them and take them away. Of his artillery the greater part was left behind buried on the sea-shore; and from information which afterwards reached our General from Arracam, it was learnt that he lost as many as ten thousand of his men, amongst whom were many of his chief Captains, mostly Moors, for it was these who exposed themselves where the danger was great. The King of Tangu lost six elephants, forty horses, and fifteen hundred men including his chief Captains. On our side eighty-six men were killed, including ten Captains and our Captain-in-chief, Paulo do Rego.

When the enemy had departed, our General repaired the fortress as well as he could, and when the men had enjoyed some rest after their past exertions, he ordered the fleet to put to sea, partly to show that the strength of the Portuguese was not exhausted, and also to go in search of provisions and plunder. The Lord delivered into their hands some Moorish ships very richly ladened; and though one of these resisted in a very determined manner, they boarded it and slew those who defended it. Our soldiers were well satisfied with the booty they secured.

On the 12th of the following January, the Portuguese suffered a calamity as heavy as any they had experienced in the past; for a fire broke out in their fortress and burnt with such fury that the entire structure, which was mainly composed of wood, was destroyed. By the mercy of God, the General escaped from the flames but with one leg half burnt. His wife also had a very narrow escape. All the goods and the treasure which were in the fortress perished. Houses, churches and their ornaments, provision stores, munition stores—all were destroyed. Apart from these losses, the seriousness of which it would be impossible to exaggerate, the fortress was now rendered completely untenable. But the General, Philippe de Brito, being a man of dauntless spirit, set to work with great energy to rebuild it, but in a higher and more defensible place, anticipating that the King of Arracam, on learning what had happened, would soon be returning to attack it. This the King soon determined to do; but while he was preparing an armada for the purpose, God confounded his designs; for at this very time news reached him that a Portuguese Captain, by name Belchior Godinho, having come from India with four ships, and having been joined by another bold Captain named Bastiam Gonçaluez,[2] who with some *jaleas* and a few Portuguese had made himself greatly feared in those parts, had descended upon Dianga, a port of this same Mogo King, completely destroying it and capturing sixty pieces of artillery, and that he intended to do likewise to the fortress at Chatigam, which is a very rich and busy city. Godinho had already destroyed the adjacent villages and suburbs, but had not yet attacked the fortress, because his men, knowing that the assault would be a very perilous affair, and being unwilling to risk their lives without first having made confession, which, there being no priest with them, they were unable to do, had begged him to postpone the enterprise until a priest to whom they could confess had been obtained, so that they might die, if die they must, like Christians and like the good Catholics they were.

These tidings greatly alarmed the King, and having to defend his own kingdom he abandoned his intention of going to Siriam, and recalled his ships which were already on the rivers. Belchior Godinho with all the supplies he could get went to the assistance of the fortress; and having seen that it was in a position to defend itself, sailed for India in search of further assistance, doing all at his own expense. After this our General learnt that when the Mogo was in the midst of his preparations for bringing an armada to Siriam, by the will of Providence, and as a just judgment on him, his royal palace was completely destroyed by fire. Three hundred of his concubines were in the building, as well as a large store of munitions of war; and the fire spread to some of the ships which he had intended to send against the Portuguese. Besides this, a ship which was bringing him six hundred Moorish mercenaries from Masulapatam was struck by lightning and sunk. All who were on board were drowned except ten, who escaped in a small boat. This news made our General all the more eager to dispatch the armada which he had made ready to send against this tyrant. As our Captains and soldiers were reluctant to embark unless accompanied by a Father of the Company to whom they could confess, and who would encourage them in times of peril, their wishes were granted, and the Father, Manoel Pirez, the Superior of that Mission, who was much beloved and respected by all, was sent with them. Father Ioam Maria, who had come from India to be his companion, remained in the fortress.[3]

CHAPTER VIII[1]

The Fortress Captured

This victory, gained at so little cost over two such powerful kings, added greatly to the reputation of the Portuguese amongst the surrounding peoples, to whom it seemed that the little fortress of Serião, under its captain, Philippe de Brito, was able to hold its own against the forces of any king whatsoever. But Philippe de Brito, whose energy and determination seemed to triumph over everything, attempted to build beyond the strength of his foundations.

It happened at this time that the King of Ova, having collected a force of a hundred and fifty thousand men, which included thirty thousand cavalry, three thousand fighting elephants, and two thousand vessels great and small, attacked and easily subdued the kingdom of Porao [Prome]. He left a small force in the principal city, and carried away as captives the King and the Queen and the chief nobles of the kingdom. He then went to attack the kingdom of Tangu. After he had besieged it for two months, the King of Tangu accepted his terms, which were, that he should become his vassal, and give up to him all his elephants, and the famous rubies and other precious stones which he had taken from the Emperor of Pegu. When everything had been handed over, the King of Ova, carried on a high throne, made the circuit of the walls of the city, the King of Tangu mounted on an *alia,*[2] which is a female elephant, riding on his left side. At the conclusion of his triumph, he handed his vassal the keys of the city, after which, leaving him a few elephants of little worth, some pieces of light artillery such as *berços* and *roqueiras*,[3] and a small body of horsemen under a Captain whom he could trust, he returned to Ova, taking with him all the Captains and other persons of consequence in the kingdom of Tangu, which he thus left an easy prey for anyone who might come to seize it.

The opportunity presented by the defenceless state of this kingdom, and that of Porao, was not lost on Philippe de Brito; and in the year 1610 he attacked Porao with his armada, and meeting with little resistance, entered the city and plundered it of the little that remained in it. Then, bringing some Pegus with him, he returned to the fortress at Serião; for the King of Ova had already sent much people, with cavalry, to relieve Porao.

At this time, Philippe de Brito allied himself with the King of Martavão, which is ten leagues from Serião, marrying his son Simão de Brito with the daughter of this King, under the directions of the Father Frei Francisco da Annunciação, of the order of the Dominicans, whom we have mentioned before. After the lady had been catechised and baptised, the betrothal took place before Philippe de Brito, who was embarked with all his soldiers on a big fleet which he had near to the walls of Marmulão[4] (a kingdom contiguous to Martavão). It was arranged between Philippe de Brito and the Banhadelá, who was the King of Martavão and father of the bride, that the Banhanoy, the King's son, should go with Philippe de Brito to live at Syriam, and that Simão de Brito should remain with the king his father-in-law. As soon as the Banhanoy had come on board the fleet, Philippe de Brito and the Banhadelá exchanged pledges of friendship, vowing that they would be brothers in arms, that the friends and enemies of the one should be the friends and enemies of the other, and that if either should be in danger or in need, the other should come to his assistance with all the means at his disposal. Philippe de Brito sent the Father Francisco to administer the oath to the King, and he himself took the same in the name of His Majesty. The King was in the presence of his people when the Father arrived with an interpreter. The Father asked His Majesty to order something higher to be brought to hold the image of our Lady, on which he was to swear. The Banha, without a word, had a golden stool brought; seeing which, those present began to say to one another, " Either the Banha is mad, or he is in great fear of the Portuguese." Hearing their murmurs, and looking on the beautiful image of our Lady, which was that which the Viceroy, Aires de Saldanha, had given to his niece, the wife of Philippe de Brito, the Banha said, " I know what I am doing; for so beautiful a lady cannot be any other than the mother or the daughter of God." He then laid before the image an offering of betel and areca nut, which greatly amazed all who were with him.

Having made their vows, Philippe de Brito and the Banha arranged to make a combined attack on the King of Tangu, vassal of the King of Ova, Philippe de

Brito saying that his vow of friendship to the King of Tangu (which he had actually sworn)[6] had been taken before that King became the vassal of Ova, and that he was not, therefore, under any obligation to comply with it, and that, moreover, it was not the King of Tangu that he was going to make war upon on this occasion, but the vassal of the King of Ova. Accordingly, at the end of the year 1610, Philippe de Brito and the Captains and people of the Banhadelá set out for Tangu with a great fleet of more than a hundred vessels, of which the Portuguese supplied twenty with two hundred men, the remainder of the force consisting of Christian and Gentile Pegus, and the people of the said King of Martavão. When Philippe de Brito appeared with his fleet before the city of Tangu, the King sent word to him that he would become the vassal of His Majesty, if nothing more was demanded of him. But Philippe de Brito looked for much more than this, and paying no attention to the message, laid siege to the city. After five days, seeing how few the defenders were, he ordered seventy of the best soldiers he had brought with him to scale the walls. These men, and others who followed them, bravely attacked the King of Tangu, who met them with two hundred mounted soldiers which the King of Ova had left in the city, and who were led by Mareco Joab, the King's brother, and general of the kingdom. Mareco Joab, who was mounted on a huge elephant, fell upon our men with such vigour that he almost succeeded in driving them out of the city. But Francisco Martins, a captain of great spirit, discharged his musket at him, and killed him. The elephant thereon turned and took to flight, followed by the horsemen of the King of Ova, and all on account of this lucky shot. The King of Tangu straightway sounded his trumpets, and sent word to Philippe de Brito that he was the vassal of the great King of Portugal, and that he was ready to surrender his person and all that he possessed. A truce of three hours followed the receipt of this message, during which the Queen of Tangu and the wife of Mareco Joab, taking with them the most valuable of the jewels in the King's treasury, made their escape from the city by a postern gate which our men had left unguarded; for the city was so great that they had not enough men to surround it. Although these ladies took away with them the most precious of the King's possessions, the treasure found by Philippe de Brito and his soldiers amounted in value to nine hundred thousand *crusados*. It included, besides silver and gold, two *martavanas*[6] filled with precious stones, but not of very fine quality, two rubies which adorned the door of the King's oratory, each, it is said, the size of a bullet, as well as many stones of immense value which the King of Tangu and his sons wore on their persons. With these princes, and the riches aforesaid, Philippe de Brito entered Serião in triumph, having the King of Tangu on his right hand. He provided a residence for the King in some fine houses near to his own, where formerly the captive prince of Arracão had been lodged. Thus again the treasures of Pegu brought disaster on their possessor. And there was yet to be another victim, as we shall see.

The King of Tangu, besides being related to the King of Ova, was his vassal, and under his protection. The latter, puffed up with pride on account of his recent victories, thought that none could venture to oppose him. When, therefore, he heard what Philippe de Brito had done at Tangu, he was filled with rage; and, casting aside his *cabaia* and throwing his turban on the ground, which amongst these people are the highest manifestations of displeasure, he left his city and took a solemn oath before his idol, Biay de Degú, that he would not again enter it until he had avenged the death of his cousin Mareco Joab, and the insult he had received from Philippe de Brito. Accordingly, he sent peremptory orders to all parts of his kingdom summoning every man of twenty years of age and over to join him; and in a short time he had collected an army such as we have described above, consisting of a hundred and twenty thousand men, and four hundred ships, on which he embarked, besides his own fighting men, six thousand Moors *de carapuça*.[7] With this great force he came to attack the fortress of Syriam.

The King of Ova with the above-mentioned force reached Syriam on the 19th February, 1613. On the next day his men set fire to everything that was outside the fortress. The following night they placed many ladders against the bastion of Francisco Mendes, which was held by a captain named Agostinho de Sousa; but those who made the attempt met with so hot a reception that they withdrew, and did not repeat the experiment, preferring to wage war in some other fashion.

The fortress was at this time in a very weak state; for Philippe de Brito had allowed most of his people to go to India. Nor was there any gunpowder, except what was made each day, which scarcely sufficed for loading the muskets; so that not a single bombard was fired on the enemy, who, in consequence, did not hesitate to come near to the walls. So little foresight had been used, that when large quantities of gunpowder came into their hands at Tangu, the Portuguese regarded it as of no value and set fire to it; and afterwards, when it would have been possible to send a married resident of the fortress to procure powder in Bengala, a soldier was sent instead, who not only did not procure any, but made off with the money that had been entrusted to him for the purpose, giving no thought to the needs of the fortress, nor to the sufferings which his treachery might cause. A galliot belonging to a resident of Serioã was sent to San-Thomé for the same purpose; but it was the will of God that no succour should reach the besieged from any quarter. Within the fortress itself insubordination was rife, and justice and reason were banished. Murders were committed on the smallest provocation; and such outrages Philippe de Brito had not the courage to punish, for in their growing unruliness the Portuguese trampled upon all authority. At the commencement of the siege, Philippe de Brito had at his disposal ninety-seven Portuguese and more than three thousand Pegus. Though they had nothing to fight with but boiling oil, tar, and water, they placed themselves on the walls to make a show of strength. On the first night our men themselves slew Gomes da Costa, who had been appointed Captain-in-chief of the troops; for, by their contrivance, a soldier discharged a musket at him from behind, and he fell dead. In the morning they chose as Captain-in-chief one Agostinho Fernandes, who had come from Banguela, and besides him another, nicknamed "Dominus-tecum," who with a portion of the defenders was to render assistance wherever it should be most necessary. All else they did was to strengthen the walls on the inside with a lining of earth, the women assisting them.

During the third night, the enemy surrounded the fortress with a stockade. Whilst they were engaged on this work, not a single piece of artillery was discharged against them, and thus our shortage of gunpowder was disclosed. From the stockade on the eastern side they made tunnels up to the walls, which they undermined with a work of forty mines. They then began to bombard the bastion of São Domingos. During this attack a cannon-ball pierced the bastion of the Captain-General, and fell on the oratory, causing great panic amongst the women. This gun was one which the enemy, who had no heavy artillery, had taken from a ship which had arrived from Bengala, and which, unable to defend itself against the large number of vessels by which it was attacked, was captured.

Seeing that the fortress was undermined, and that its walls were already breached, our men held a council of war, and decided to send three ships to attack the enemy's fleet, believing that all their men were on shore.

They had scarcely set out when one of the three was attacked by many vessels of the enemy, who boarded it, and passing ropes to the land, dragged it up on to the shore, and there every man on board was killed. The other two were similarly attacked as they came back; but though those on board were all wounded, they succeeded in returning to the fortress, and took their places on the walls.

At the end of the third week of the siege our men, who had not ceased fighting day or night, were almost worn out. The Pegus cried out to them, "Fight on, Portuguese: for you do not know what it means to fall into the hands of the Bramas." But, as has been said above, they had nothing to fight with but boiling oil and tar, so that the enemy grew more and more daring in their attempts to reach the walls. The Portuguese did not now number more than fifty; for seventeen of them had been burnt to death in a stockade which had been made to protect a shattered bastion; while the Pegus were beginning to show signs of disaffection.

On the thirty-fourth day, our men took counsel together as to whether they should surrender themselves to the Bramas, if the Pegus surrendered; for they daily expected that they would do so. They decided to ask the King if he would grant them their lives, and allow them to depart in a ship. Accordingly, they sent him an *ola*,[8] which is the same as a letter, begging him, with all the eloquence at their command, to grant them these terms. The letter was taken by a Portuguese named Sebastião Rodrigues Panchina; but the enemy refused to receive it, and would not permit our envoy to enter their stockade. His arrival was made known to the King, who sent word to him that he had best get back whence he had come, for he was determined to spare no one; and with this answer Sebastião Rodrigues returned sadly to the fortress.

At this juncture, the Mogo king of Arracão, who was now on friendly terms with Philippe de Brito, taking alarm at the near approach of his powerful enemy the King of Ova, who, he knew, was not likely to leave him unmolested, sent a fleet of fifty *jaleas* to the assistance of our fortress, hoping thereby to avert the danger which threatened him. But this only added fuel to the fire; for the King of Ova's fleet speedily overcame and captured all the vessels of the Mogo king, and the few who escaped from them sought refuge in the fortress.

For three days more our men continued to fight. On the evening of the thirty-sixth day of the siege, the enemy attacked them on all sides, both by sea and by land. By daybreak most of ours had been killed, and all were wounded. At eight o'clock in the morning, seeing that the grenades thrown by our men contained nothing but lime, which did little harm, the whole of the King's guard advanced in a body. At the same instant the captain of the Pegus, who was called Banhalao, leapt from the walls and joined the besiegers, who thereupon rushed into the fortress, where there was now none to resist them. By the King's orders no quarter was given either to men or women. At the well of Francisco Mendes, and in other parts of the fortress, they slew more than seven hundred persons, including Pegus, Canarins,[9] and Portuguese. At four o'clock in the afternoon the Prince, who is now the King, entered the fortress with his younger brother, and ordered the slaughter to cease. Philippe de Brito and his wife were made prisoners and at midnight the former was tied up and strangled to death. A stake was then fixed in the ground on which his body was impaled.[10]

Such was the end of Philippe de Brito and the fortress of Syriam. The King of Ova took away as captives five thousand Christians of the country (who did not renounce their faith in captivity),[11] and a hundred and sixty Portuguese, including twenty-two white women, which shows how populous and prosperous this settlement had become. Indeed, had Philippe de Brito been content to extend his power little by little, instead of embarking on such difficult enterprises and making such powerful enemies, the fortress of Syriam might have become the greatest of His Majesty's possessions in the East, both for the acquirement of riches and for the conversion of souls.

NOTES TO CHAPTER I

The Ruin of Pegu

[1] From Part I of the *Relations*, pp. 62-71.

[2] The name 'Bengala' was loosely used by the Jesuits, and other Portuguese writers of the sixteenth and seventeenth centuries, to denote the Gangetic delta and the surrounding districts, including Orissa on the western side of the Bay of Bengal, and the kingdom of Arakan on the eastern side. At the end of the reign of Akbar, the river Meghna may be said to have marked the eastern limit of the Mogul province of Bengal; for though Akbar appears at times to have exercised, or at any rate to have claimed, some sort of jurisdiction over Chittagong, this port remained in the possession of the Kings of Arakan until the reign of Aurangzib. It was finally conquered and annexed to the Mogul empire in 1665. The Bengal province was always a trouble to Akbar, and for many years his control over the lower portion, that is to say, the tract between the estuaries of the Hooghly and the Meghna, was little more than nominal. Ralph Fitch, who went to Siripur in 1586, wrote, "They be all hereabout rebels against their king Zelabdim Echebar"; and it is plain from Father Pimenta's letters of the years 1599 and 1600 that at that time the various 'kings' of this tract were, to all intents and purposes, independent.

The name Chittagong (to be derived, according to Yule, from the Sanskrit *Chaturgrama*, 'the four villages') is to be met with in numerous disguises. In the *Voyages* of Ibn Batuta it appears as 'Sudkawan.' De Barros, and most of the Portuguese writers, spell it 'Chatigam.' Linschoten has 'Chatigan,' and Orme 'Chittigan.' The town is also frequently referred to as Porto Grande, the Portuguese name for the estuary of the Meghna, of which Chittagong is the principal port. In the same way, town of the Satigam is frequently referred to as Porto Pequeno, the name given to the estuary of the Hooghly (see Mr. W. H. Moreland's note on the seaports of Bengal on pp. 307-9 of his *India at the Death of Akbar*). That the word *porto* in each of these cases is used to denote, not a town, but an estuary (including both the tidal portion of the river and the gulf into which it flows) is shown, as Mr. Moreland points out, by such expressions as, "Siripur, qui est une demeure des Portugais des appartenances du grand port" (Du Jarric, *Histoire*, I, 610); "De Siripur ils passerent a Chatigam, qui est le nom de la ville, située au grand port" (*ibid.*, I, 611); "Fomos a Chatigao bandel do porto grande" (Pimenta, Letter of November 26th, 1599). The Portuguese not infrequently named cities after the

NOTES TO CHAPTER I

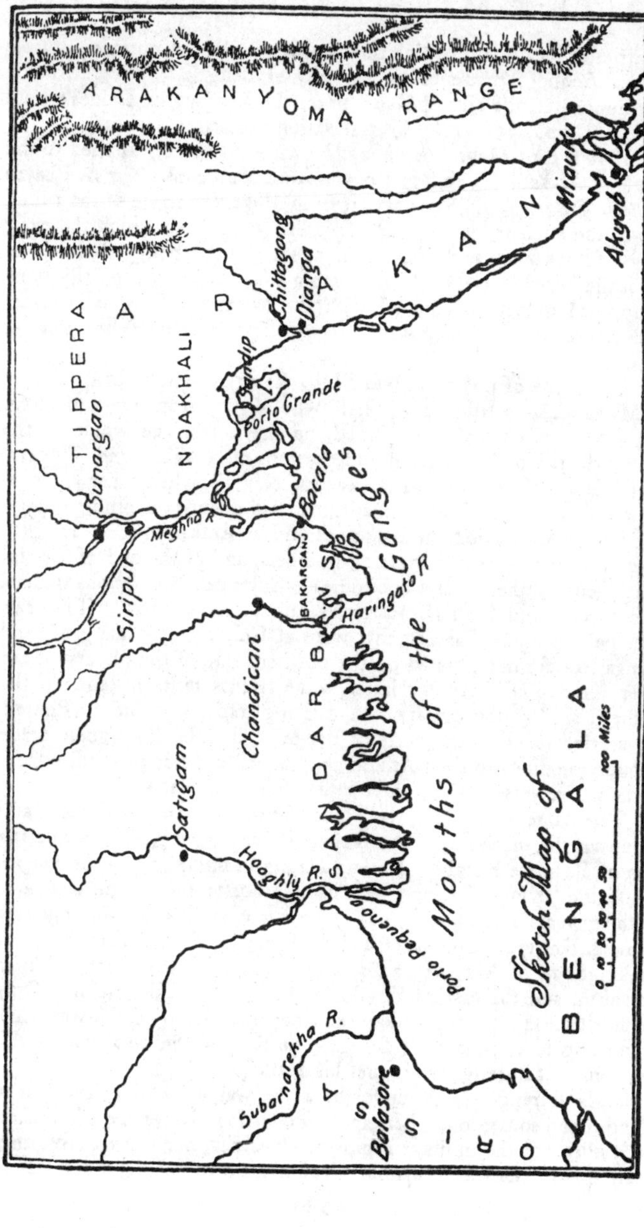

MAP III.—BENGALA

countries or localities in which they were situated. A notable example is their frequent reference to the 'city of Bengala,' by which name they designated the city of Gaur (*vide* Mr. Longworth Dames's note in Vol. II, pp. 135-144, of his translation of Duarte Barbosa).

[3] *Mogo* is for 'Magh' or 'Mugg,' a name commonly applied to the people of Arakan. The origin of the word is obscure. Sir A. Phayre (*History of Burma*, p. 48) derives it from *Maga*, the name of the ruling race of the ancient kingdom of Magadha (Behar), to which the early Kings of Arakan are said to have belonged. Another suggested derivation is the Persian word *magh*, meaning a fire-worshipper, and the name is supposed to have originated with the Muhammadans, who sometimes confused Buddhists with fire-worshippers (see *Hobson-Jobson*, p. 594).

[4] The name of this King was Meng Rajagyi, sometimes known by his Muhammadan title, Salim Shah, who reigned from 1593 to 1612. Meng Rajagyi's kingdom included, on the north, the whole of the present district of Chittagong, and portions of Noakhali and Tippera. To the south it extended as far as cape Negrais, while what are now known as the Arakan Yomas constituted its ill-defined eastern boundary. The Portuguese made their first appearance in Arakan in the year 1517. After this they came in increasing numbers, and at the end of the sixteenth century there was a considerable European population, traders, adventurers, and scamps, scattered about the country. The two principal Portuguese settlements were at Chittagong [Chatigam] and Dianga, the former situated on the northern side of the estuary of the River Kurnaphuli, and the latter, some twenty miles distant, on the southern side of the estuary. A thriving trade, says Sir A. Phayre, was carried on with the ports of Bengal, "but the Portuguese made themselves odious to their Asiatic neighbours by their piratical attacks on the native vessels which their galleys fell in with at sea."

[5] The name of this king was Nanda Bureng. He was the son, and the unworthy successor, of the famous Bureng Naung, the conquering hero of Burmese history. Bureng Naung's assumption of the magnificent title 'King of Kings' was no idle boast; for in the course of his thirty years' reign (1551–1581), he extended his sway not only over the neighbouring kingdoms of Tangu, Prome, and Martaban, but over the kingdoms of Ava, Mogaung, and Monyin, in the north, Siam in the south, and the eastern kingdoms of Laos and Chieng-mai. Only the maritime kingdom of Arakan remained unsubdued; and it was while attempting to complete his Burmese empire by the conquest of this kingdom that Bureng Naung met his death.

Nanda Bureng was as unworthy as he was unfit to succeed to so splendid and so perilous a heritage. Possessing neither the administrative ability nor the military genius of his father, nor indeed any other kingly quality, he was incapable of ruling his own people, much less an empire. One by one the tributary kingdoms recovered their independence, and before he had been eight years on the throne his territories were bounded by the walls of his capital city. The remainder of his miserable story is told in the text. "Thus," to quote the words of Sir Arthur Phayre, "the great empire of united Pegu and Burma, which a generation before had excited the wonder of European travellers, was utterly broken up; and the wide delta of the Irawadi, with a soil fertile as Egypt, and in a geographical position commanding the outlet of a great natural highway, was abandoned by those who might claim to represent the ancient rulers, and left to be parcelled out by petty local chiefs and European adventurers."

[6] The Portuguese *alquier* is equal to about two English gallons.

[7] Ralph Fitch, who was at Pegu in 1586, says that the King then had four white elephants. "This King," he says, "in his title is called the King of the White Elephants. If any other king have one, and will not send it him, he will make warre with him for it; for he had rather lose a great part of his kingdome then not to conquere him. They do very great service unto these white elephants; every one of them standeth in an house gilded with golde, and they doe feede in vessels of silver gilt. One of them when he doth go to the river to be washed, as every day they do, goeth under a canopy of golde or of silke carried over him by six or eight men, and eight or ten men goe before him playing on drummes, shawmes, or other instruments; and when he is washed and commeth out of the river, there is a gentleman which doth wash his feet in a silver basin; which is his office given him by the King. There is no such account made of any black elephant, be he never so great."

[8] This is not in accordance with Bocarro's account (see note 1, p. 273).

[9] The capital of Arakan at this time was Mrauku or Myohaung, situated on the river Lemro, some sixty miles to the north-east of Akyab. The city, as is evident from the statement in the text, and from the King's letter quoted in note 12, was also known as Arakan, a name which is often given to it today.

[10] At the end of the year 1599 the Jesuit Mission to Bengala was in charge of the Fathers Francisco Fernandez, John Andrew Boves (Ioam Andre Boues), and Melchior Fonseca. The two former resided at Chatigam, and the last named at Chandican. In 1601 Melchior Fonseca went to Goa to ask for further assistance. This request Father Pimenta, the visitor in India, was against complying with, as the Mission to Japan had greatly exhausted his supply of workers. But the Viceroy, Ayres de Saldanha, peremptorily set aside his objections, and ordered him, under pain of his severe displeasure, to send at least four additional Fathers to Bengala. In his Annual Letter to the General of the Society, dated 1st December, 1601, Pimenta wrote: "Let your

Paternity know that the Viceroy of India went so far as to tell me before the Archbishop and the Bishop of Angamale and others that he would request me with chains (*que de grilhos mo pediria*). I was surprised and said that the Company was his, but that His Lordship could order, dispose, etc. The Father was not satisfied with fewer than four companions. He left Goa with three, quite picked subjects: Fathers Andre de Nabais, Bras Nunez and Natal Salerno, and the order was sent to S. Thome that Fr. Simão de Sà should start from there; however he did not go, because the galliot of Pegu had left the very day when the order arrived." The Viceroy had evidently been greatly impressed by an optimistic account he had received from Philip de Brito of the prospects of the Portuguese in those parts. In his letter to Pimenta ordering the dispatch of the Fathers he wrote, "By letters and informations which I had from the kingdoms of Bengala and Pegu, I learned of the great fruit and notable service to Our Lord which the few Fathers of the Company residing in those parts obtain and render by teaching, and instructing, and the example they give to the Portuguese, and by the conversion of the Infidels, and that they are earnestly invited by the infidel Kings and Lords, who promise to give them leave to preach the holy Gospel and build churches among them, even offering the needful for their expenses. . . . I therefore request and charge your Paternity (thus discharging my own conscience in the matter) to send to those parts many Religious of the Company that they may satisfy the desires of those Kings and Lords, and by preaching the holy Gospel may spread Holy Church throughout all those Provinces, chiefly throughout Aracão, Pegu and Martavão."

Of the Fathers mentioned above, Francisco Fernandez died at Chatigam in 1602, and the following year Melchior Fonseca died at Chandican. Andrew Boves and Andreas de Nabais returned to India in 1604. Blassius Nunes and Natal Salerno resided in Arakan till 1604, when they joined Philip de Brito at Syriam. Further details regarding these Fathers are to be found in the Rev. H. Hosten's notes to his translation of Pimenta's Annual Letter (see note 2, p. 259). It is from this translation that the extracts I have quoted are taken.

[11] According to Manrique (*vide* Colonel Luard's translation, Vol. I, p. 90) this was "a title corresponding to that of Captain-General of sea and land forces." Bocarro says the King's 'corangary' was "capitao geral de mar" (vide *Decada* 13, p. 126). In a subsequent passage he speaks of "O principe de Arracão com o seu general ou corangarim." The correct word is *Korangri* or Koyangyi, the letters 'r' and 'y' being interchangable in Burmese. It is made up of the three words *ko* = 'body,' *ran* or *yan* = 'to surround,' and *gri* or *gyi* = 'chief' or 'head (as in *thu-gyi*, 'a village headman'). The title, therefore, means literally "the chief of the *koyan* or body-guard."

[12] The circumstances which led to this visit may be gathered from

NOTES TO CHAPTER I

Father Pimenta's letter to the General of the Society, dated December 1st, 1600. We learn that before the visit took place a letter had already been received from the King saying that he would welcome the residence of Fathers of the Company in his kingdom, that he would make provision for their maintenance, and that they would be free to build churches, and to baptize any who desired to become Christians. This was in reply to a letter which Father Fernandez, who was then at Chittagong, had sent to him. It had been the Father's intention to take the letter himself, but illness prevented him from doing so, and it was entrusted to Ieronimo Monteiro (que he homem muito honrado & amigo da Companhia & cabe muito com el Rey de Arracão). On the receipt of the King's reply, the Fathers decided to go and pay their respects to him, and thank him in person for the favours he had shown them. Pimenta's letter contains nothing further on the subject; but it was evidently this visit of thanks which Guerreiro here describes. The King's letter, which Pimenta quotes, was as follows: "O muito alto & poderoso Rey de Arracão, Tiparas, Chacomas, & Bengala, Senhor dos reinos de Pegu &c. a vos Padres da Companhia de IESV. Folguey muito com a vossa carta, por vir chea de palauras encaminhadas ao seruico de Deus, alem da informacao que Manoel de Matos & Ieronimo Monteiro me derao de vossa virtude & partes boas. Folgarey muito de virdes a mim pera assentarmos os negocios dos Portugueses, & aonde podereis fazer Igreja & Christãos aquelles que de sua vontade se quiserem fazer, pera isso vos darey comedias, & a gente de seruico que for necessaria. Dada & feita nesta cidade de Arracão com meu selo real."

[13] Chandican was at this time one of the most important of the miniature kingdoms of Bengala. It is frequently mentioned by writers of the sixteenth and seventeenth centuries, and is marked on many early maps, often as an island, as on John Ogilby's map of the Mogul Empire, where it is called "Insula Chandacan." There appears to be no modern town with which the capital of the kingdom can be identified. In all probability the site of Chandican, like that of Siripur and other once populous towns of the Gangetic delta, has vanished in consequence of the changes that have taken place in the courses of the delta rivers. We are, however, told enough about Chandican to enable us to determine approximately its position. Father Pimenta refers to it in his letter to the General of the Society dated November 26th, 1599, as being midway between Porto Pequeno and Porto Grande, and conveniently situated for visiting all parts of Bengala (Está este Chandecão no meio do caminho do porto pequeno pera o grande. Estancia acomodada pera acudir della a todas as partes de Bengala). In his letter of December, 1600, Pimenta states that when Father Fernandez arrived at Siripur, which was about eighteen miles south of Sonargaon (Fitch calls it six leagues), he was informed that the Raya, or King,

of Chandican was seriously annoyed with him for not visiting him. This suggests that Chandican and Siripur were not a great distance apart. Again, Father Melchior Fonseca, writing on January 20th, 1600, tells us that, on his way from Chatigam (Chittagong) to Chandican, he visited Bacala, a town in the district of Bakarganj, of which 'Bacala' or 'Bakla' was the old name. Mr. H. Beveridge, in his *Manual* of the Bakarganj district, suggests the present village of Kachua, on the river Tetulia, as the site of the town of Bacala. Father Fonseca says that the remainder of his journey was through cultivated fields and rich pasture lands, watered by many streams. He reached Chandican on the 20th November, having left Chatigam the previous month. He does not mention the length of his stay at Bacala. Taken collectively, these statements indicate some spot in a direction north-west from Kachua as the site of Chandican. In the sketch map on page 253 I have shown it on the River Haringhata; but this is merely a suggestion. There is nothing to indicate the extent of the kingdom of Chandican. Colonel Luard (*Travels of Manrique*, I, p. 8) says that "the tract of country lying east of the Hūgli river was known as Chandekhan in the fifteenth century and after." In his sketch map (*ibid.*, Introduction, p. xxiv) he shows the town of Chandekhan to the south-east of Siripur. But neither of these towns is correctly placed on this map, which Colonel Luard evidently had no opportunity of revising (*vide* his list of corrections at the end of his book).

[14] Macao was the name of a town on the Pegu river, situated, according to the Venetian traveller, Cesare Federeci, about twelve miles from Pegu city, of which it was the port (see *Hobson-Jobson*, p. 527). It was visited by Ralph Fitch, who says, "From Cirion [Syriam] we went to Macao, which is a pretie town; where we left our boats, and in the morning taking delingeges [dhoolies] . . . came to Pegu the same day." Guerreiro is of course wrong in describing Macao as the King of Pegu's fortress.

[15] In a letter written from Syriam on March 23rd, 1600, Father Andre wrote that he set out in company with Philip de Brito on the 25th February, and reached Syriam in fifteen days: "Pareceo ao padre Francisco Fernandez que fosse eu pelo seruico que se faria a Deus nosso Senhor. E assi aos 25 de Feuereiro me parti em hua galeota com o mesmo Felipe de Brito, & favorecendomos Deus muito na viagem, chegamos em quinze dias a esta barra de Sirião."

[16] Here follow a number of gruesome and revolting details which I have taken the liberty of omitting.

[17] See note 4, p. 275.

NOTES TO CHAPTER II

PHILIP DE BRITO ESTABLISHES HIMSELF AT SYRIAM

[1] From Part II of the *Relations*, fols. 45a-47b.

[2] There are various accounts of the origin of Felippe de Brito de Nicote. According to Sir A. Phayre, he was "a young Portuguese, originally a shipboy who had served as a menial in the King of Arakan's palace." Faria y Sousa says that the King "had raised him from a vile collier to his favour and esteem." The Fathers, on the other hand, lead us to suppose that he was, as his name implies, a person of some rank; and this view is supported by the *Grand Diccionaire Universel*, in which it is stated that he was born about 1550, and was the nephew of Jean Nicot, a distinguished diplomatist, and the introducer of tobacco into France. In a footnote on page 159, of his edition of *Bocarro*, Sr. J. de Lima Felner remarks on "the similarity of names and coincidence in dates," and asks, "Was Philippe de Brito, who was born in Lisbon, related to Jão Nicot who was French ambassador in Portugal till the year 1560, and became celebrated by giving his name to the tobacco plant introduced [into Portugal] by a nephew of our historian Damião de Goes?" Sr. de Lima Felner commends his question to the attention of "the genealogical expert," and the reader will doubtless be content to do likewise.

If de Brito had no claim to noble birth, he was evidently, at this time at any rate, a person of considerable means. Father Pimenta, in his Annual Letter to the General of the Society written on the 1st December, 1601, quotes a letter he had received in January of that year from de Brito containing an offer to endow the College at Quilon, and asking what sum would suffice to provide for the maintenance of that institution. "This man," the Father wrote, "is very rich and can found many colleges; and to our residence of Negapatao he has given big alms." The major portion of Pimenta's letter, with an English translation and notes by the Rev. H. Hosten, S.J., was recently published in the *Journal and Proceedings* of the Asiatic Society of Bengal (Vol. XXIII, 1927, No. 1).

[3] See note 2, p. 264.

[4] The name Macareo, which is here given to the Gulf of Martaban, was the term applied by early navigators to the bore, or tidal-wave, which is a prominent feature of the estuary of the Sittang river, and also of the Gulf of Cambay. The origin of the word has not been satisfactorily determined. It has been derived from the Sanskrit word *makara*, meaning 'a sea-monster'; but the suggestion appears to have

little to support it beyond its plausibility. It has also been suggested that the French word *macrée* (later *mascaret*), meaning 'a bore,' and especially the bore of the river Garonne, may have given rise to 'macareo'; but Mgr. Dalgado, in his *Glossario-Luso-Asiatico*, says that he has little doubt that the French borrowed the word 'macareo,' changing it first into *macrée*, and afterwards into the more polished *mascaret*. For a full discussion of the subject the reader is referred to the work mentioned above, and to *Hobson-Jobson* (p. 527).

[5] This is a mistake on Guerreiro's part. De Brito joined the King in Pegu in the early part of 1600 (see note 4, p. 263); it must, therefore, have been in that year that he commenced to fortify himself at Syriam.

[6] 'Bare' is for the Sanskrit *bahar*, the name of an Indian measure of weight. According to Barbosa (1516), *bahar* was equivalent to 4 *quintals*, or roughly 400 lbs. But the *bahar* varied in different localities, and at different periods, and also according to the nature of the article weighed (*vide Hobson-Jobson*, p. 48).

[7] The Persian word *gharib* means 'humble,' 'lowly.' The expression *gharib-parwar*, 'Cherisher of the poor,' is much used in addressing superiors.

[8] Man Singh was appointed Governor of the province of Bengal in 1585, and he held the appointment almost without intermission until Akbar's death twenty years later. The danger to which de Brito pointed was far from being an imaginary one. At this very time Man Singh was at Dacca, where he had already reduced 'Canderray,' the powerful Raja of Siripur, to submission. In his account of this year (1602), the author of the supplement to the *Akbarnama* says: "Various items of news from Bengal brought joy. In the first place, Rajah Man Singh came to Dhaka [Dacca] and by means of hopes and fears brought the ruler Kedar Rai on the right road of service" (*Akbarnama*, tr. Beveridge, p. 1213).

Early in the following year (1603) the King of Arakan himself took the offensive by attacking Sonargaon; but the attempt was a costly failure (*ibid.*, p. 1231). He then proceeded with a fleet and a large army, in which were many Portuguese, to attack Srinagar (about twenty miles south-east of Dacca). This time he was joined by Kedar Rai; but their combined forces were heavily defeated. Kedar Rai was killed and the 'Magh' retreated to his own country. "One of the occurrences," says the author of the supplement, "was the success of the royal arms in Bengal, the downfall of Kedar Zamindar, and the retreat of the Magh Rajah. News came that Kedar—who was a noted proprietor in Bengal—had joined the Magh zamindar with a large fleet, and used force against the *thana* of Srinagar. On hearing of this, Rajah Man Singh sent an army provided with artillery against that presumptuous man. Near Nagar Sur (?) the latter appeared with a large force and a great battle took place. The enemy was defeated, and many were slain. Kedar was wounded with bullets and was flying half-dead. The brave troops followed him and captured him. There was a little life in him when he was brought before the Rajah, but he soon died. With his death the flames of disturbance in Bengal were extinguished" (*ibid.*, p. 1235).

[9] 'Banha' appears to be for *binnya*, signifying 'lord of the land.' The title was borne by many of the kings and princes of Pegu. The complete designation of this particular 'duke' was, according to Bocarro, 'Bannadala,' i.e. *Binnya-Dala*, the Lord of Dala. Dala was the name of a town and district of the Irrawaddy delta. The town was close to where the city of Rangoon now stands, but on the opposite side of the river. A further reference to the 'Banha' will be found in note 2, p. 264.

[10] Jancoma [Jangomay, Jamahey, Zangomay, etc.] was the Portuguese name for Chiengmai (called by the Burmese 'Zimme'), at this time the largest of the numerous Lao, or Shan, kingdoms lying between the Burmese and Chinese frontiers, and to the north of Siam. The English traveller Ralph Fitch visited 'Jamahey,' which he describes as "a very faire and great towne, with faire houses of stone, well peopled. . . . Hither come many marchants out of China, and bring great store of muske, golde, silver, and many other things of China worke. Here is great store of victuals; they have such plenty that they will not milk the buffles, as they do in other places. Here is great store of copper and benjamin [benzoin]."

[11] This is clearly a mistake for 1603, for it was in that year, not in 1602, that de Brito went to India. Whilst at Goa the enterprising 'King of Syriam' married Dona Luiza de Saldanha, a niece of the Viceroy, Ayres de Saldanha. According to Faria y Sousa, the lady was afterwards unfaithful to him, and responsible, to a large extent, for his ultimate crash. Bocarro says nothing of this.

NOTES TO CHAPTER III

TEN REASONS FOR HOLDING THE PORTS OF BENGALA

[1] This chapter (belonging to Part II of the *Relations*, fols. 47b-49b) contains the substance of a report written by Philip de Brito whilst at Goa in 1603. The report was forwarded by the Viceroy, Ayres de Saldanha, to the King of Portugal, together with a petition from de Brito praying that he might be appointed Commander for life of the fortress of Syriam, that a portion of the revenue from the custom-house should be assigned to him for his support, and for the support of his wife, Dona Luiza da Saldanha, after his death, and that his son, assuming that he left one of an age for service, should succeed him as Commander of the fortress. The King received the report in 1604, and on March 2nd, 1605, he sent a letter to Don Alfonso de Castro, who had in the mean time succeeded Saldanha as Viceroy, asking for fuller information in regard to the various matters dealt with in the report. He had, His Majesty states, already rewarded de Brito's conspicuous services by making him a Knight of the Order of Christ, and a Gentleman of his Household, and he asks the Viceroy's opinion as to what further should be done for him. In a second letter, dated January 23rd, 1607, the King acknowledged the Viceroy's reply, which he received on December 24th, 1605, and informed him that the command of the fortress was to be given to Philip de Brito for life, and afterwards to his son, supposing him to leave one fit to succeed him. De Brito was to receive a third part of the revenue of the custom-house during his life-time; but this was not to be continued to his son, who would receive only so much as should subsequently be deemed expedient. No allowance would be made to de Brito's widow.

The letters of King Philip III, from which the above particulars are taken, can be read in Antonio de Bulhao Pato's *Documentos Remettidos da India*. The letter of March 2nd, 1605, is on pp. 23-26, and that of January 23rd, 1607, on pp. 173-178 of Vol. I.

To receive the *habito de Christo* was a high honour. The Knights of Christ were originally a purely religious company, admission to which could only be granted by the Pope, and ranked as the highest of papal honours. Gradually, however, the monastic character of the Order disappeared, and by the end of the fifteenth century the power to create knights passed from the Pope to the King. Every subsequent King of Portugal has been a Grand Master of the Order.

[2] Junk-Ceylon is an island off the west coast of the Malay Peninsula, about 8 degrees above the equator. For suggested derivations of the

name, see *Hobson-Jobson*, p. 473. Queddah (probably from the Hindi word *Kedah*, meaning a stockade for entrapping elephants), the place next mentioned, is a port also on the west of the Malay Peninsula, and situated about 6 degrees above the equator. Barbosa describes 'Quedaa' as a very flourishing seaport. "This is," he says, "a place of wholesale trade, and Moorish ships come hither yearly from divers regions. Here grows abundance of fine pepper which they carry to Malaca and China" (*Barbosa*, tr. Longworth Dames, II, p. 165). The port, says Mr. Longworth Dames, was tributary to Siam until 1909, when the suzerain rights were transferred to the British Government.

[3] The Siamese port of Patani was situated on the east coast of the Malay Peninsula. It had been an important Dutch trading centre since 1602, by which year Dutch merchants were established at Bantam, Achin, and also in the Spice Islands (see Moreland's *From Akbar to Aurangzeb*, p. 16).

[4] This was at the end of the year 1599, after the siege of Pegu. Bocarro states (*Decada*, p. 126) that the King of Arakan, owing to disturbances in his own country, withdrew from the siege before it was ended, and that after the fall of the fortress he sent de Brito, accompanied by his 'corangary,' to Tangu, to claim his share of the spoils and to conduct the princess and the two princes of Pegu to Arakan. It was, says Bocarro, when passing Syriam on his way to Tangu that de Brito observed the suitability of the former place as a site for a fortress and custom-house. The date of de Brito's return to Arakan is not stated; but, according to Guerreiro, the triumphal entry took place before the end of the year. Nor do we know the actual date of the King's subsequent departure for Pegu; but it must have been before the 25th February, 1600, for de Brito and Father Andre, who had been ordered to follow him, commenced their journey on that date (see note 15, p. 258).

[5] The State of Achin, famous for its pepper and spices, is in the north-west of Sumatra. The Portuguese frequently called it Dachem (d'Achem). The Dutch established a trading settlement there in 1602. At that time the 'king' of Achin was the chief power in the island, and an inveterate enemy of the Portuguese.

[6] This evidently means, when de Brito returned to the fortress after his visit to the King of Arakan, recorded in the previous chapter. Soon after his return he set out for India. He remained at Goa during the monsoon months, and came back to Syriam at the end of the year (1603).

NOTES TO CHAPTER IV

Defeat of the Arakanese Armada

[1] From Part III of the *Relations*, fols. 102a-104b.

[2] The text account of the circumstances which enabled the Portuguese to establish themselves in Pegu is throughout a glorification of Philip de Brito, who, though he was doubtless a fine fellow in many ways, does not seem to have been a suitable subject for a halo. The rights which the King of Arakan conferred at this time on his Portuguese favourite are nowhere very clearly stated; but we may safely take it that he did not, as Guerreiro would have us believe, make him a present of the entire kingdom of Pegu. We gather from Faria y Sousa and Bocarro that the King's grant included nothing more than the port of Syriam, and that in the means he adopted to secure his supremacy and enlarge his possessions, de Brito was thoroughly unscrupulous. Faria y Sousa's account, showing de Brito *minus* his halo, runs as follows (I quote the translation by Captain J. Stevens, 1695): "Xilimixa [Salim Shah], King of Arracam, to express his gratitude to the Portuguese who had served him, gave them the port of Siriam at the mouth of the river of the same name. This grant was obtained of the King by Philip de Brito and Nicote, who most ungratefully proved false to that Prince, that had lifted him from a vile collier to his favour and esteem. The manner of it was thus.

"Xilimixa, confiding in Nicote, was by him persuaded to erect a custom-house at the mouth of that river for the increase of his revenue, and his [de Brito's] design was to seize upon it, and build a fort there to give footing to the Portuguese for the conquest of that kingdom. The King, who suspected not the design, having finished the work, put it into the hands of one Bannadala, who fortified himself, and suffered no Portuguese to enter there except F. Belchior de la Luz, a Dominican. Nicote seeing that design fail, resolved to carry it out by other means before the works were too far advanced. He had with him three Portuguese officers, viz., John de Oliva, Paul del Rego, and Salvador Rebeyro, with fifty men; these he ordered to surprise the fort, and turn out the Bannadala, not doubting his great credit with Xilimixa would bear him out in it. The three captains so well performed Nicote's orders that they gained the name of founders of the Portuguese dominion in the kingdom; and Rebeyro was like to carry the whole fame of this action, some affirming he was the real author of it." Bocarro tells a similar story, but at much greater length (*Decada*, 13, pp. 128-131).

Guerreiro makes no mention of the part played in these transactions by Salvador Rebeyro; yet it was mainly to his courage and resource that the Portuguese owed the preservation of the Syriam fort. During de Brito's absence at Goa in 1603, Rebeyro, who was left in command, was for eight months closely besieged by the Arakanese under the leadership of Bannadala, and it was with the utmost difficulty that he was able to hold out until de Brito returned with reinforcements at the end of the year. The defence of the fortress was very gallantly conducted; but Rebeyro's services seem to have met with little recognition. According to Portuguese records, when Philip de Brito returned to Syriam, Rebeyro resigned to him the crown with which the inhabitants of Pegu had invested him, and returned to Portugal, "where he is supposed to have passed the remainder of his days at his native village in the province of Minho; but his body lies in the chapter-house of a small Franciscan convent near Alemquer, some 30 miles from Lisbon, where an inscription records his name and history. Portuguese writers call him the Marcus Aurelius of the Decadence of India, and more than one poet has sung his praises" (*Report on the Portuguese Records relating to the East Indies*, by F. C. Danvers, pp. 20-21).

[3] These were the Fathers Andrew Boves, Andre de Nabais, Blasius Nunez and Natal Salerno (see note 10, p. 255). The two former returned to India, and the two latter went to Syriam.

[4] Evidently a mistake for Chatigam.

[5] The first attempt to establish Portuguese authority in the island of Sandip was made in 1602 by an adventurer named Dominico Cavalho, who had taken service with Chand Rai of Siripur, to whom nominally the island belonged. Cavalho was expelled the following year by the King of Arakan, who held the island until it was taken from him by the Mogul general Fateh Khan in 1607. In 1609, Sebastian Gonçalves, the foremost of the Portuguese pirates, recaptured Sandip, which he contrived to hold for about eight years, when it was again taken by the King of Arakan.

At the end of the year 1602, when the King of Arakan was making his preparations for the capture of Sandip, the Portuguese *bandel*, or settlement, at Chatigam was plundered, and many of the inhabitants were seized and imprisoned, amongst them the Fathers Francisco Fernandez and Andre Boves. The former, who was an old man, and in feeble health, died in consequence of the ill-usage to which he was subjected. These events are described in detail in Part II of Guerreiro's *Relations*, fols. 41a-44b. An English translation of this chapter by the Rev. H. Hosten, S.J., was published in the *Catholic Herald of India* (November 11th, 1908).

[6] The term *catur* was applied by early Portuguese navigators to certain light rowing vessels used on the west coast of India, generally for warlike purposes. The word is probably to be derived from the Arabic *katireh*, "a small craft," and may possibly be the parent of our

English word 'cutter' (see *Hobson-Jobson*, p. 165). For *jalea*, see note 2, p. 271.

[7] Cape Negrais forms the southern limit of Arakan. The actual 'point,' on rounding which the Bassein River is entered, is known as Pagoda Point. By the *barre*, or harbour, of Negrais, so frequently

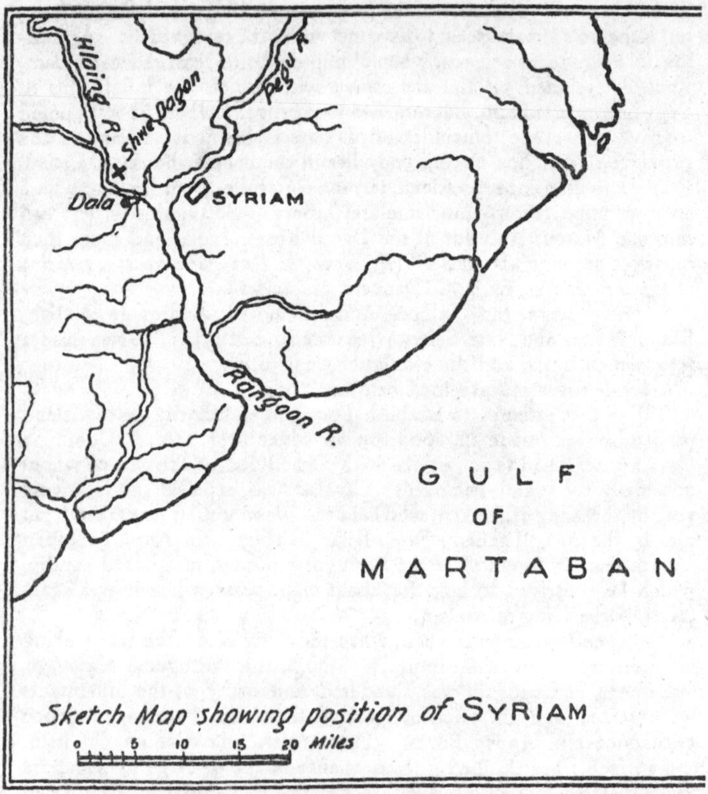

MAP IV

mentioned in Portuguese works, is meant the estuary of the Bassein River. The port of Bassein, formerly known as Cosmin (see *Hobson-Jobson*, p. 259) is situated some 70 miles up the river. As to the origin of the name 'Negrais,' Yule states that it is "a Portuguese corruption probably of the Arab or Malay form of the native name which the

Burmese express as *Naga-rit*, 'Dragon's whirlpool.' The set of the tides here is very apt to carry vessels ashore, and the locality is famous for wrecks" (*ibid.*, p. 622).

[8] The port of Syriam is 24 miles from the sea. It is situated on the left bank of the Pegu River and about 3 miles above its junction with what is now called the Rangoon River, which forms the eastern arm of the Irrawaddy delta. Owing to the strength of the currents, and to the presence of numerous and constantly shifting shoals, the navigation of the Rangoon River is very intricate. Today, every ship proceeding to Rangoon takes a pilot before entering the river, outside the mouth of which a brig, with a staff of pilots on board, is permanently anchored.

[9] According to Bocarro, the Archbishop of Goa, then acting as Governor, sent de Brito definite instructions that the Prince was to be set at liberty without ransom: "que tornasse o principe de Arracão a seu pae, sem por isso lhe pedir cousa alguma." Thereupon, de Brito, not to be balked of his plunder, substituted the word indemnity for ransom, and demanded the payment of two hundred thousand *tangas* to cover the damage his ships had sustained in the recent naval encounters. After endless haggling, the King suffered himself to be mulcted of one hundred thousand *tangas* (about £4,400), bitterly protesting that it was nothing more nor less than a ransom that he was being forced to pay. When this sum had been handed over, de Brito placed the Prince in a royal *jalea*, and sent him home, personally conducting him as far as the island of Cheduba, which was one of his fishing-grounds. As he sailed away from the island, he gave his released captive a parting salute. But, unfortunately, a pellet from one of the guns struck the helmsman of the *jalea*, who fell dead beside his lord. This circumstance, says Bocarro, aroused the suspicions of the Prince to such an extent that, from that moment, he never ceased contriving means for the destruction of de Brito and his fortress (see *Decada* 13, p. 144).

According to Archbishop Menezes (*vide* note 5, p. 270) the sum paid by the King of Arakan was 30,000 *pardaos*, or 150,000 *tangas*, one *pardao* being equal to five *tangas*. At the end of the sixteenth century a *pardao* was worth from 4s. 2d. to 4s. 6d. A *tanga* at the same period was equal to 60½ *reis*, or about 10½d. (see *Hobson-Jobson* under *Pardao*).

NOTES TO CHAPTER V

In which a Treaty is Made and Broken

[1] From Part IV of the *Relations*, fols. 103a-104b.

[2] To the Portuguese all the rivers and streams in Bengala were 'gangas.' "Gangas chamão os rios de que toda Bengala esta cortada" (*Relations*, V, fol. 95): "A terra he muito fresca, & nas partes que confinão com o mar esta repartida em muitas ilhas que se nauegão por rios que chamão gangas, as quaes se tem por certo serem braços do rio Ganges" (Pimenta's letter of 26th November, 1599). The Portuguese apparently became so used to the term in Bengala that they applied it, as here, to rivers having no connection with the Ganges. Thus they called the River Subarnarekha, which divided Orissa from Bengala, the Ganga, and it is so named on Levanha's map of the kingdom of Bengala. In Sanskrit the word *ganga* may denote either the River Ganges, or a river in general; but this, as is evident from Pimenta's letter, does not account for the use which the Portuguese made of the word. Mgr. Dalgado, in his *Glossario*, quotes the following from the *Conquista de Ceylão*, p. 31: "Esta palaura ganga em toda esta India he generica, e significa rio de agoa doçe, porque he tão celebre o rio Ganges, que parece, que tomarão daqui occassião para aplicarem a todos os outros seu nome, posto que tenhão outros particularas."

[3] Luang Praban, at this time one of the most important of the Lao states, is situated to the north-east of Chiengmai, on the Mekong River. It was known to the Siamese as Lan-chan, signifying, according to Yule (*Hobson-Jobson*, p. 503), "a million of elephants." Fitch called it 'Lange-jannes.' Other variations to be met with are 'Lan John,' 'Landjam,' 'Langiens,' etc.

[4] Up to this point Guerreiro has used as his authority a letter, dated October 17th, 1608, from de Brito to the King of Portugal, giving an account of the defeat of the Arakanese fleet and the capture of the Prince, and containing a further report on the advantages likely to accrue from the possession of Syriam. The King was evidently much impressed by de Brito's report, and especially by his proposals for compelling all merchant vessels to trade only at the port of Syriam. On the 4th January, 1608, His Majesty sent a long dispatch to the Viceroy at Goa (*Documentos Remettidos da India*, I, pp. 173-178) reproducing the substance of de Brito's letter, and directing that, in view of the commercial value of the fortress, and the facilities it afforded for communicating with the ports of the South, as well as on account of its position at the mouth of the Pegu River, all measures necessary for its

NOTES TO CHAPTER V

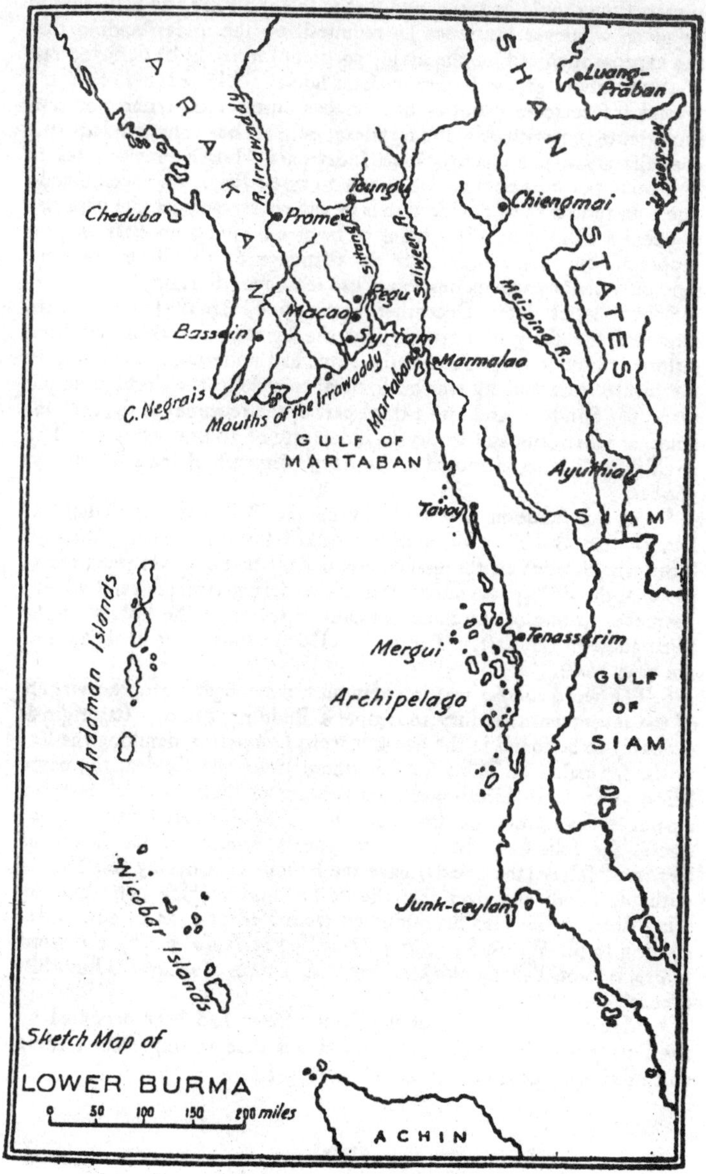

MAP V—LOWER BURMA

preservation should be taken, and that to this end Philip de Brito should be given whatever assistance he required, on the understanding that the expense involved, or the major portion of it, could be defrayed out of the revenues of the Syriam custom-house. "E porque, conforme a estas informações e outras que ha per outras vias, tenho por mui importante conservar-se a dita fortaleza, assi pela boa commodidade que com elle se alança na navigação da India para Malaca e mais partes do Sul, como por ficar em hua das boccas do rio de Pegu, vos encommendo que com tudo o calor devido trateis de sua conservação, e que para isso se deem a Filippe de Brito todos os favores e ajudas necessarios, pressuppondo que dos rendimentos da alfandega da dita fortaleza saira toda ou a maior parte da despeza n'isso se houver de fazer."

[5] In a letter dated December 20th, 1606, Archbishop Menezes informed the King of Portugal that the Prince of Arakan had been restored to his father, and that the latter had undertaken to abstain in the future from making war on Syriam, to cede to the Portuguese the island of 'Sundiva' and also a third part of the revenues of the custom-house at Chatigam, and to pay an indemnity of 30,000 *pardaos*. The Archbishop's letter is quoted in the King's dispatch of the 4th January, 1608.

[6] On this occasion it was chiefly on the Portuguese settlement at Dianga that the King of Arakan wreaked his vengeance. Amongst those who escaped in the galliot was Sebastian Gonçalves (see note 5, p. 265), the Portuguese adventurer whose daring escapades and villainies make up one of the most romantic chapters in the history of the Portuguese in the East. The raid on Dianga took place at the end of the year 1606.

[7] The word *talapoi* was in common use amongst European writers of the seventeenth century to denote a Buddhist priest. Its origin is probably to be found in the Sanskrit word *tala-pattra*, denoting the leaf of the fan-palm, or Talipot, of Southern India and Ceylon, the name being given to Buddhist priests on account of their habit of carrying a palm-leaf as a protection from the sun. Yule (*Hobson-Jobson*, p. 892) quotes the following from Robert Knox's *Relation of the Island of Ceylon*: "They (the priests) have the honour of carrying the Talipot with the broad end over their heads foremost; which none but the King does." See also his quotation from Pallegoix on p. 890. According to Sir W. Foster (*Early Travellers in India*, p. 36), the word *talapoi* is "the Talaing *tala poe*, 'my lord,' a form of address to Buddhist monks."

[8] Macao, at the mouth of the Canton River, had been occupied by the Portuguese since 1557, and was at this time an important trading and missionary centre.

NOTES TO CHAPTER VI

The Battle of Negrais

[1] This and the following chapter belong to Part V of the *Relations*, fols. 72a-79a.

[2] The Portuguese word is *galeota*, from which came 'gallivat' and also, probably, our English 'jolly-boat' (see *Hobson-Jobson*, p. 361). The name was applied to craft of various sizes; but was always used to denote a smaller vessel than a galley. Bluteau, in his *Vocabulario Portuguez Latino, etc.*, defines *galeota* as "a small galley with one mast, and with fifteen or twenty benches a side, and one oar to each bench." According to Orme, a 'gallivat' was a large rowing-boat built like a grab (a kind of Arab galley) but of smaller size, the largest rarely exceeding 70 tons; "they have 40 or 50 stout oars and may be rowed four miles an hour" (*Hist. Military Transactions*, I, 409). The origin of the word is obscure. Yule favours the suggestion of Friedrich Diez (*Etym. Worterb.*, 198-199), that it is to be derived "from the Greek γαλεὸς, a shark, or from γαλεώτης, a sword-fish—the latter very suggestive of a galley with its aggressive beak."

The word *jalea* appears to be another member of the numerous 'galley' family. Bocarro defines it as a vessel "that is used for fighting and trading at once." The word generally denoted a small craft; but there does not seem to have been any particular type of vessel to which it was applied. Very often there seems to be no distinction drawn between a *galeota* and a *jalea*.

[3] All that the Portuguese dictionaries have to say about the words *camelet* and *espera* is that they are the names of "pieces of ordnance formerly used." According to Pagés' *Diccionario de la Lingua Castellana*, a *camello* (of which *camelet* is the diminutive) was a short, heavy, and not very effective gun, used mainly for siege purposes, and firing a ball weighing sixteen pounds. An *espera* was a smaller gun firing a ball of thirteen pounds. Pagés quotes the following from B. L. de Argensola: "A otro dia se trujo á ella la artilleria que eran cuatro piezes, dos esperas, que echaban trece libras de bala y dos camellos de á diez y seis."

[4] A pavise is a shield covering the whole body. "*Pavezes de navio* are what our seamen call the 'fights,' being waste cloths which hang round about a ship to hinder the men from being seen in fight" (Lacerda, *Diccionario*). *Xareta* was the name given to the wire network used to prevent ships from being boarded by the enemy.

[5] The small dependent state of 'Chocoria' [Chokaroa], whose

Chief is dignified by Guerreiro with the title 'King,' lay to the south of Mrauku, the Arakanese capital, and to the east of Akyab.

[6] A sanguicel was a small and very light vessel mainly used for pursuit. It derived its name from Sanguicer [Sangameshwar ?], a port of Canara where many vessels of this type were built. Yule (*Hobson-Jobson*, p. 171) quotes Albuquerque, "Here was Nuno Vaz in a ship, the St. John, which was built in Camguicar," and adds, "there are many other passages in the same writer which make it practically certain that Sanguicels were the vessels built at Sanguicer."

[7] Both Faria y Sousa and Bocarro state that Paulo do Rego himself blew up his ship, to avoid falling into the hands of the enemy. The latter writer says : "E vendo Paulo do Rego sua perdição certa, estando ja atracado de grande quantidade de embarcações, não conhecendo mem vendo outro modo para os poder destruir e livrar se assim, por se não gloriarem os inimigos de o levarem ou vivo, ou morto, deu fogo á sua galeota, com que voou feita em pedaços, e todos quantos com elle vinham" (*Decada*, p. 145).

NOTES TO CHAPTER VII

The Siege of Syriam

[1] Bocarro gives a very different account of the last phase of the siege of Syriam. The King of Arakan, he says, having decided to make a grand combined attack on the fortress, sent a messenger to the King of Tangu to acquaint him with his plans. "The King of Tangu, learning what the King of Arakan had decided to do, and fearing that the 'Mogos' would leave him to conduct the siege by himself, determined to out-play them. Accordingly, he sent back word that he was fully prepared; and that if His Majesty would let him know the day and hour when he intended to begin the siege, he too would attack at the same time. But that night, at the beginning of the first watch, he silently struck his camp, and without a word as to his intentions, marched with all speed back to his country. In the morning there was not a soul to be seen in the place which the army of Tangu had occupied. As soon as they became aware of this the Pegus, with shouts of joy, sallied forth to seize upon any arms or supplies which the troops of the King of Tangu, to avoid impeding their movements, might have left behind them. On finding that the King of Tangu had given up the siege of the fortress by land, Philippe de Brito ordered his soldiers and captains to march out with banners, and drums and fifes, and the firing of guns, as though they had put the King of Tangu to flight. The King of Arracao, observing this unexpected movement of the Pegus along the bank of the river, and that others were launching ships as though they meant to come out and fight, and seeing no trace anywhere of either the King of Tangu or his camp, became even more scared than the latter had been; and imagining that all that Philippe de Brito had warned him of was about to be fulfilled, he signalled to his ships to weigh anchor, and sailed speedily away" (*Decada* 13, 147-8).

Faria y Sousa is less explicit; but he too attributes the sudden raising of the siege to dissensions in the enemy's camp. "The siege," he says, "continued so long, until the besieged were ready to surrender, when on a sudden upon some suspicion the King of Tangu quits the field by night, and he of Arracam found it to no purpose to lie longer upon the sea" (*Asia Portuguesa*, III, 159).

How the siege actually ended must remain a matter of conjecture. Faria y Sousa and Bocarro are, however, a strong combination; and their testimony, such as it is, must be held to outweigh that of Guerreiro, whose account is very probably based, like his references to the fate of Hawkins and the crew of the *Ascension* (*vide* note 20, p. 114), and his first account of the battle of Negrais (p. 222), on rumours which found their way to Goa, and thence to Europe, before the arrival of anything in the way of an official report.

[2] After his escape from Dianga (note 6, p. 270), Gonçalves lived by piracy, and became the recognised leader of the Portuguese 'sea-wolves' who infested the Bay of Bengal. For a time he cultivated the friendship of the Raja of Bacala, and made that place his port of refuge. His depredations made him the terror of the Bay, and the King of Arakan had good reason to be alarmed at his growing power. His descent on Dianga took place early in the year 1608; and another year had barely elapsed before he had expelled Fateh Khan from Sundiva and established himself in that island (note 5, p. 265). An account of his subsequent career can be read in Sir Arthur Phayre's *History of Burma*, pp. 174-177.

[3] Here again Guerreiro seems to have been misled by letters based on mere rumour. The dispatch at this time of an armada against Arakan is not mentioned by either Faria y Sousa or Bocarro, nor can I find any reference to it elsewhere.

NOTES TO CHAPTER VIII

The Fortress Captured

[1] As I have already stated, this account of the capture of the Syriam fortress is taken from the *Decada* of Bocarro (*Monumentos Ineditos*, Vol. VI, pp. 149-158). Without a plan of the Syriam fort (which I have not been able to procure) it is impossible to follow Bocarro's detailed, and very confused account of the actual siege operations. I have therefore presented this portion of his narrative in a condensed form. The victory mentioned in the first line refers to the defeat of the combined forces of the Kings of Arakan and Tangu described by Guerreiro in the last chapter.

[2] *Aliya* is the Singhalese name for an elephant. The Ceylon species is as a general rule tuskless; and this may possibly have led to the Portuguese application of the term *aliya* to the female Indian elephant.

[3] Lacerda's *Diccionario* defines a *berço* as "an ancient short piece of artillery," and a *roqueira* as "a sort of cannon which is loaded with stones instead of bullets."

[4] Marmulão [Moulmein] is situated on the southern side of the estuary of the Salween River, opposite to Martaban, which is on the northern side of the estuary. According to Yule (*Hobson-Jobson*, p. 591), the original Talaing name was *Mut-mwoa-lem*, which the Burmese corrupted into *Mau-la-yaing*, "whence the foreign (probably Malay) form *Maulmein*."

[5] De Brito's treaty of friendship with the King of Tangu had been made under direct orders from the Viceroy, Lorenço de Tavora. In reply to a letter from the King of Portugal, in which reference is made to the kingdom of Tangu, Tavora stated that de Brito had sent some Portuguese to assist the King of Tangu against his enemies, and that the King had shown himself very grateful for the same. "I myself," he added, "on being informed of these things sent an ambassador to Tangu with a present to the King of a horse, a suit of armour, some wine and other things, and urging him to take up his residence in some city nearer to Syriam where help could be sent to him more readily, and from whence he could, if hard pressed, seek refuge for himself and his treasures (which I am told are immense) in our fortress. I have also ordered Philip de Brito to maintain friendly correspondence with him, which I have every hope will result in great advantage to your Majesty" (*Monumentos Ineditos*, VII, p. 352). The Viceroy does not tell us how his friendly overtures were regarded. The King of

Tangu no doubt accepted the present, but declined the invitation to walk into de Brito's parlour. As the event showed, he might just as well have accepted both. The sack of Pegu was a scandalous breach of faith on de Brito's part. "Let us keep in mind," says Faria y Sousa, "these his unjust proceedings, and in its place we shall see them rewarded as they deserve. . . . Indeed it is to be admired, a Christian government should support such unchristian proceedings" (*Asia Portuguesa*, III, 140).

[6] 'Martabans' or Pegu jars have been famous in the East from very early times. They are mentioned by Ibn Batuta, Correa, Barbosa, and many other writers. Barbosa, in his description of the city of Martaban says: "At this town are made many great porcelain jars very big, strong and fair to see; there are some of them which will hold a pipe of water. They are glazed in black and greatly esteemed and highly prized among the Moors, who take them from this place with great store of benzoin in loaves" (*Barbosa*, II, p. 158).

[7] The Portuguese dictionaries define *carapuça* as a conical cap, usually of some blue or reddish material. Can the soldiers in question have been Kizilbashes, who were distinguished by their red caps, and many of whom were to be found in the Mogul armies?

[8] An 'ola,' or 'ollah,' generally denotes a letter written on a palm-leaf. The leaf used is that of the Palmyra tree, which is specially prepared for the purpose, and of which the Tamil name is *olai*.

[9] 'Canarins' was the name given by the Portuguese to the *Konkani* people of the territory of Goa (see *Hobson-Jobson*, pp. 152-4).

[10] Faria y Sousa states that de Brito was impaled alive, and lingered in agony for two days.

[11] Mr. J. P. Hardiman has sent me an interesting confirmation of Bocarro's statement: "In 1897, in the Sagaing district," he writes, "I was shown some Burmese who were said to be descendants of prisoners captured long ago, and who still profess the Roman Catholic religion." He has also drawn my attention to the following passage in the *Gazetteer of Upper Burma* (Vol. II, p. 46): "The Roman Catholic Mission in Myinmu has at present two stations, at Nabet and Chaungu. They do not do much proselytizing. They look after the native Christians, descendants of the Portuguese and others carried off as prisoners on the capture of Syriam by Maha Dhamma Yaza in 1613 A.D., and again on its sack by Alaung-paya in 1756 A.D."

N.B.—Some additional notes on this chapter will be found in the Appendix.

APPENDIX

Some Additional Notes

Page 62, *line* 15. The word 'darure' is for the Persian ***darvesh***, denoting a religious devotee, or *fakir*, the latter being the term more generally used in India. The 'feats' ascribed to these devotees are without number. In the *Qanoon-i-Islam* (Herklots), p. 297, we read: "They are so totally absorbed in religious reverie, that they do not discern between things lawful and unlawful, and regard no sect or religion. Sometimes they go about in a state of nudity, and lie down wherever it may chance to be, regardless of every kind of dirt or filth. Some among these become such powerful workers of miracles, that whenever they choose, they can instantly effect what they please; and what is strange, though some of them lie in one spot for months and years together, and there obey every call of nature, there is not the least offensive smell about them. They are, moreover, neither afraid of fire nor of water; for when they please, they stand on hot embers, or sit in a large frying-pan, or a boiling *caldron*, for hours together: and they dive and remain under water for two or three hours."

Page 195, *line* 10. After the break up of the Roman Empire, the name *Rum*, the Arabic form of 'Roma,' was given to the Seljukian kingdom in Asia Minor, and later to the Ottoman Empire (see *Hobson-Jobson*, p. 767). Hence the word 'Rume' or *Rumi* was used to designate a Turk, whether Asiatic or European. By certain writers, however, including Guerreiro, the name was restricted to the Turks of Europe.

Page 231, *line* 1. 'Magua' was the name, presumably, of one of the King of Arakan's allies.

Page 242, *line* 30. According to Sr. de Lima Felner, the editor of the *Decada*, the name Banhadela should be spelt Banhadala. Though Bocarro does not actually say so, this king of Martaban appears to be none other than the Arakanese Commander whom Philip de Brito, some six years previously, expelled from Syriam. That a dependant should reappear as a king, and sworn enemies as sworn friends, is all in keeping with the times. It is stated in the *Decada*, that, after being driven out of Syriam, the Banha fortified himself in the neighbouring 'island of Dala,' and that, on being again defeated by the Portuguese, he withdrew to Prome. Of his subsequent adventures we know nothing until we meet with him again in Martaban.

APPENDIX

Page 246, *line* 1. That the fortress was so inadequately manned at this juncture has been attributed to the machinations of de Brito's wife. How far this is true it is difficult to say. The circumstance is not mentioned in the *Decada*. Bocarro, however, must have heard the story, but apparently he attached no importance to it. In a footnote on page 159 of the *Decada*, Sr. de Lima Felner states the case against Dona Luiza as follows: " It is said that one of the chief causes which contributed to the loss of the fortress of Seriam, or Seriang, was the wanton conduct of Dona Luiza de Saldanha, wife of Philippe de Brito de Nicote. She was, as we have seen, the daughter of Manuel de Saldanha, brother of the Viceroy, Aires de Saldanha. Her mother, according to Faria y Sousa, was a native of the island of Java. She was brought up in luxury at Goa, where she was born, and was of handsome appearance, and vain of her looks. She married Nicote, the son of a French father, who had raised himself from the meanest degree to the position of a king, to whom she proved unfaithful, committing adultery with a Portuguese Captain. The soldiers of the fortress openly protested against this scandal; and the foolish woman, to diminish the number of her accusers, prevailed upon her husband to reduce the garrison of the fortress, which, she said, was larger than he required, and very costly. Nicote took her fatal advice. He denuded the fortress of its defenders, and paved the way for its conquest by the King of Ava. The King caused de Brito to be impaled, and though suffering this cruel punishment, he remained alive for two days. His wife the King ordered to be washed in the river, intending to take her as his concubine; and when, with unlooked-for courage, she refused to gratify his desires, he gave orders that her legs were to be flayed (or, according to others, that one of her legs was to be pierced through), and reduced her to the condition of a slave. These particulars, which are not given by Bocarro, can be read in Faria y Sousa's *Asia Portuguesa*, tom. iii., part iii., cap. ii., and in the *Journal* of Peter William Floris, from which an extract will be found in tom. v. of Prevost's *Histoire Génèrale des Voyages*, pages 322 and 323."

Page 246, *line* 10. Mr. J. P. Hardiman suggests that the word ' biay ' is the Burmese *paya*, used to denote any object of worship, and that ' degû ' is for *tigon* or *takun*, a word which, according to Professor Forchhammer, came into use in the sixteenth century to denote a pagoda or stupa.

INDEX

INDEX

INDEX

INDEX

INDEX

INDEX

INDEX

INDEX